D0879799

LIFEBLOOD

Lifeblood

OIL, FREEDOM, AND THE FORCES OF CAPITAL

Matthew T. Huber

A Quadrant Book

University of Minnesota Press
Minneapolis
London

Quadrant, a joint initiative of the University of Minnesota Press and the Institute for Advanced Study at the University of Minnesota, provides support for interdisciplinary scholarship within a new, more collaborative model of research and publication.

http://quadrant.umn.edu.

QUADRANT

Sponsored by the Quadrant Environment, Culture, and Sustainability group (advisory board: Bruce Braun, Christine Marran, Stuart McLean, and Dan Philippon) and by the Institute on the Environment at the University of Minnesota.

Quadrant is generously funded by the Andrew W. Mellon Foundation.

Portions of this book have appeared previously in "Refined Politics: Petroleum Products, Neoliberalism, and the Ecology of Entrepreneurial Life," *Journal of American Studies* 45, no. 2 (2012): 295–312; "Oil, Life, and the Fetishism of Geopolitics," *Capitalism, Nature, Socialism* 22, no. 3 (2011): 32–48; and in "Enforcing Scarcity: Oil, Violence, and the Making of the Market," *Annals of the Association of American Geographers* 101, no. 4 (2011): 816–26.

Copyright 2013 by the Regents of the University of Minnesota

All rights reserved. No part of this publication may be reproduced, stored in a retrieval system, or transmitted, in any form or by any means, electronic, mechanical, photocopying, recording, or otherwise, without the prior written permission of the publisher.

Published by the University of Minnesota Press
111 Third Avenue South, Suite 290
Minneapolis, MN 55401-2520
http://www.upress.umn.edu

Library of Congress Cataloging-in-Publication Data
Huber, Matthew T.
    Lifeblood : oil, freedom, and the forces of capital / Matthew T. Huber.
(A Quadrant book)
    Includes bibliographical references and index.
    ISBN 978-0-8166-7785-6 (pb : alk. paper)
    1. Petroleum industry and trade—United States. 2. Energy policy—United States.
3. Capitalism—United States. 4. Free enterprise—United States. I. Title.
    HD9565.H83 2013
    338.2'72820973—dc23
                                                    2013010519

Printed on acid-free paper

The University of Minnesota is an equal-opportunity educator and employer.

CONTENTS

Introduction: Oil, Life, Politics   vii

1 The Power of Oil?
   Energy, Machines, and the Forces of Capital   1

2 Refueling Capitalism: Depression, Oil,
   and the Making of "the American Way of Life"   27

3 Fractionated Lives: Refineries and the
   Ecology of Entrepreneurial Life   61

4 Shocked! "Energy Crisis," Neoliberalism,
   and the Construction of an Apolitical Economy   97

5 Pain at the Pump: Gas Prices, Life,
   and Death under Neoliberalism   129

   Conclusion: Energizing Freedom   155

   Acknowledgments   171

   Notes   175

   Bibliography   217

   Index   247

Oil, Life, Politics

In the summer of 2008, the global price of oil skyrocketed to $147 per barrel, and in the United States, gasoline prices reached a historic peak of $4.11 per gallon. President George W. Bush was acting very much like an "addict" leader of the country he accused of being "addicted to oil" in 2006.[1] Bush made two visits to Saudi Arabia within five months to plead with the kingdom to open up its valves to lower oil prices.[2] Later in the summer, claiming to speak for "American families,"[3] Bush attempted to lift a twenty-seven-year-old ban on offshore drilling on most of the eastern and western coasts of the United States.[4] In May, presidential candidates John McCain and Hilary Clinton found common ground in a proposal to offer a federal "gasoline tax holiday" for the summer driving season.[5] Both struck populist tones as Clinton spoke out for "hard pressed Americans who are trying to pay their gas bills at the gas station" and McCain said he just wanted "to give low-income Americans . . . a little relief." Although the proposal would serve to lower prices and guarantee more oil consumption, Clinton bizarrely claimed that opposing the policy would "stand with the big oil companies."[6] Perhaps the high point in McCain's otherwise floundering campaign was his mobilization of popular energy through pro-oil development slogans such as "Drill, Baby, Drill" and Newt Gingrich's illogical rallying cry, "Drill here, drill now, pay less" (published as a book).[7] Later in the summer, McCain held a rally of motorbike enthusiasts in South Dakota ridiculing then Democratic nominee Barack Obama's call for energy conservation measures such as basic tire inflation. He declared, "My opponent doesn't want to drill . . . he wants you to inflate your tires," as the crowd roared in laughter.[8]

With less than 5 percent of the global population, the United States is by far the largest global consumer of oil, using 19.1 million barrels per day—around 22 percent of total consumption (see Table 1). Despite popular fears of skyrocketing demand from emerging economies, it is worth pointing out that the United States still consumes more than the so-called BRIC (Brazil, Russia, India, and China) countries *combined*. Thus the gas tax holiday stood in stark contrast to opposite policy analysis that suggests the need to increase the already miniscule gasoline taxes in the United States in line with European levels in order to curb driving and oil consumption.[9] Yet such an increase is viewed as politically impossible.[10] As evidence of this political impossibility Barack Obama's campaign also placed the *lowering* of gas prices as the ultimate priority: "We do need to bring down gas prices, and as President, I will."[11] He also focused on the populist suffering of the American working class: "I hear from families every single day who are feeling the crushing burden of higher gas prices."[12] Sensing the political risk of opposing domestic drilling, in early August 2008, Obama reversed his early opposition and announced openness to some forms offshore drilling.[13] The concession was followed by President Obama's real proposal for the expansion of offshore drilling three weeks before the biggest maritime oil spill in U.S. history in the Gulf of Mexico in April of 2010.

Table 1. Top Ten Oil World Consumers, 2010

Country	Petroleum consumption (million barrels per day)	Percentage of world total
1. United States	19.1	22 percent
2. China	9.4	11 percent
3. Japan	4.4	5 percent
4. India	3.1	4 percent
5. Russia	3	4 percent
6. Saudi Arabia	2.7	3 percent
7. Brazil	2.6	3 percent
8. Germany	2.5	2.9 percent
9. South Korea	2.2	2.5 percent
10. Canada	2.2	2.5 percent
Total world consumption	**87.02**	**100 percent**

Source: Energy Information Administration, 2011.

After the release of Al Gore's *An Inconvenient Truth* in 2006 and the 2007 Intergovernmental Panel on Climate Change report, it seemed that real change of the U.S. energy system was not only necessary but actually possible. Yet the summer of 2008 revealed that hope of such change was false and that, more accurately, the winning campaign would be the one that promised more oil at cheaper prices. The 2012 campaign promised more of the same with a 2011–12 gasoline price surge constructed as danger for Obama's reelection bid.[14] The popularity of "Drill, Baby, Drill" sentiments and public outrage over high gas prices reveal the bewildering paralysis of energy politics in the United States. Since at least the 1970s, there has been a substantial consensus that levels of U.S. oil consumption forebode deepening ecological, geopolitical, and social crises. Yet no political coalition has been able to actually tackle this problem. While many on the environmentalist left are comfortable attributing this impasse to a conspiracy between the oil industry and the U.S. state, the uncomfortable fact, underscored by populist rhetoric, is that policies meant to curb oil consumption—such as gasoline taxes and fuel efficiency standards—are unpopular to a U.S. electorate for whom cheap gasoline has become a basic aspect of everyday survival in an era of eroding economic security. It seems that no amount of wars or oil spills—not even the prospect of the extinction of our species—is enough to push U.S. politics away from this kind of energy populism based on cheap-fossil-fueled livelihoods. It certainly does appear that the United States is indeed as a society addicted to oil. Yet the "addiction" metaphor presumes that oil is an overarching, uncontrollable force hovering over society. The question posed by this book is how this came to be.

Problematizing U.S. Oil Addiction

It has become "common sense" that the level of U.S. oil consumption is a massive yet intractable problem. It is important to be precise about the specific consumptive practices that rely on oil. In popular discourse oil is too often conflated with energy in general, but oil is mainly a source of energy as *liquid fuel* for the transportation sector—gasoline for automobiles, diesel fuel for trucks, jet fuel for airplanes, and heavy fuel oils for ocean tankers, railroads, and other kinds of mobile machinery.[15] Overall, 71 percent of U.S. petroleum consumption goes toward transportation, and 93 percent of all energy consumed in transportation comes from petroleum. The bulk of the rest of oil is used in the industrial production of a whole host of products from chemicals to plastics.[16] Ever since the oil shock of the 1970s, virtually none of the oil consumed in the United States is used to generate electricity, which is, of course, a major and quite different aspect of everyday energy consumption, from using televisions and lights to recharging batteries for iPods and cell phones (and increasingly automobile batteries now and in the future). Oil is primarily about powering a certain kind of mobility characterized by an individuated command over space, or what Raymond Williams called "mobile privatization."[17] Thus, when it comes to "oil addiction," most agree the problem is rooted in the particular form of auto-centric suburban development prevalent in the United States.[18]

We are well aware of the problems of "oil addiction." Ecologically, the combustion of petroleum in the United States is the leading emitter of carbon dioxide (43 percent of the total), and the extraction, transportation, and refining of petroleum produces ecological degradation all along the commodity chain.[19] Ever since the oil embargo in the 1970s, U.S. oil consumption also produces geopolitical discourses of anxiety over dependence upon foreign sources of oil from racialized zones of the Middle East implicated with authoritarianism, terrorism, and greed.[20] The sociospatial patterns of suburban life made possible by automobility and massive oil consumption create crisis narratives of declining social solidarity and community and the individualization of American culture.[21] Moreover, this geography of dependence is framed as utterly doomed because of the imminent arrival of "peak oil" and geological scarcity that will yield explosive price increases and usher in a *Mad Max*–style dystopia structured by scarcity and conflict.[22]

The "addiction" metaphor frames oil as an uncontrollable thing trapped in the American bloodstream—pernicious, yet practically unavoidable. A 2011 *National Public Radio* story featured citizens trying to "quit" oil, but they soon were overwhelmed by the inundation of petroleum products within common everyday practices: "Even those who carry on the most ascetic, pared-down existence depend on petroleum in some form or other."[23] Of course, there is the automobile, but plastics, food, and *any commodity* that is transported by truck is also tied to the use of oil. Clearly, the unavoidability of oil is central to the addiction narrative, which positions oil as an overarching force hovering over the public.

More than anything else, the discourse of addiction *naturalizes* petroleum consumption as an unavoidable aspect of life that cannot be changed through politics or culture. The very idea of addiction presupposes a *physicality* that supposedly escapes psychology, culture, and politics. Thus the "prescription" for ending this material addiction requires a form of technocratic behavioralism—policy mechanisms that influence behavioral change (e.g., traffic congestion pricing), subsidies that encourage alternative energy technological innovation (e.g., federal loans for electric vehicles), and market mechanisms that put a price on ecological destruction (e.g., a tax on carbon). Moreover, the problem of "oil addiction" is too often imagined as a *purely* material problem composed of the sheer amount of demand, the absolute space between home and work, the convenience of plastics, and the energetics of fossilized food production. In this book, however, I argue that the problem of oil addiction is about not only our material relation with energy resources but also how energized practices shape particular forms of thinking and feeling about politics. If the textbook definition of energy is the ability to do work, I pose a different question: can energy do political work? What if the most problematic relation to oil is the way it powers forms of social life that allow individuals to imagine themselves as severed from society and public life? Oil is a powerful force not only because of the material geographies of mobility it makes possible but also because its combustion often accompanies deeply felt visions of freedom and individualism. It turns out these ideals are much harder to shake than the built environment of petroleum-fired suburbanization. This is not an "idealist" proposition of the need to think about culture and politics *against* materialism but rather a perspective on materiality that is always already cultural and political.[24]

Those who emphasize the political and historical roots of our oil predicament often focus on large powerful forces shaping the social use of energy. Many scholars have told the history of "oil addiction" as simply the product of a class alliance of oil, automobile, and real-estate capitalists who conspired to destroy public transit and lock in internal combustion–fired automobility and suburbanization.[25] In this story, oil consumers are featured as "dupes" in the master plans of profiteering capitalists. In a broader sense, the story of oil is almost always told from the perspective of "big" forces—geopolitical strategy, oil kingdoms, titans of oil finance, and global oil capital.[26] The struggle for the oil 'prize' is a "great game" between powerful actors with the globe as their stage.[27] Yet the problem with these big stories of oil is they ignore the fact that oil is also incredibly *ordinary* because it is embedded in everyday patterns of life. In the realm of petroleum and everyday life, others have importantly focused on the more pernicious forms of injustice along the petroleum commodity chain—from the destruction of livelihoods in the Niger Delta to the segregation and violence imposed on the oil workers in Saudi Arabia[28]— but this injustice is reproduced through the other, ordinary ways in which oil consumption becomes naturalized in the United States and elsewhere. Approaching oil from the perspective of everyday life leads to much different understandings of oil politics: less big, geopolitical, and strategic and more banal, taken for granted, and "commonsense."

This approach focused on everyday practices of consumption is anchored through a focus on a quite ordinary idea—that of "life." The centrality of oil is not simply the product of self-interested capitalists seeking a market but also a product of wider struggles over the sociospatial stuff of everyday life—housing, transportation, and urban spatial form. Timothy Mitchell's important new work instructs us to "follow the . . . oil itself," but in order to understand the complex relations between oil and ideas of "the American way of life" we must also follow social relations, politics, and struggles over how life is lived that stretch far beyond the wells, pipelines, and refineries immediately stained with oil's toxic residues.[29] In the chapters that follow, I will trace the history of how oil became constitutive of a specific cultural politics of life in the United States. Indeed, as a recent Gulf Oil campaign suggests (Figure 1), oil is now *equated* with life itself, a life that *necessitates* a form of spatial practice "one mile at a time." Although the easy shorthand—"the American way of life"—best approximates this cultural politics, this phrase is all too often vague and all encompassing. My aim is to untangle the specific political logics underlying this vision of life and suggest that this broader politics has as much to do with the persistence of our "oil addiction" than anything else.

FIGURE I. "*LIFE* . . . ONE MILE AT A TIME."
Gulf Oil's ad campaign "*Life* . . . One Mile at a Time" was developed in the mid-2000s and persists today. It not only equates life with oil but also invokes a specific geography of mileage. Photograph by Michael Wall.

Oil and the Meaning of Life

In the aftermath of September 11, 2001, and specifically the revelation that fifteen of the nineteen hijackers came from oil-rich U.S. ally Saudi Arabia, U.S. oil consumption habits were increasingly framed as having specific linkages to emerging discourses of "terrorism."[30] Such a linkage obviously created much anxiety after a decade framed by low gas prices and the rising popularity of sport-utility vehicles (SUVs).[31] A November 2001 *New York Times* article titled "Made in America, and Never Mind the Gas Mileage" raised the question of a possible hypocrisy within a culture that both bought SUVs "like crazy," in the words of one car salesperson, and equated big American-made cars with a certain level of patriotism.[32] The reporter spoke with one woman loading groceries into her Chevy Tahoe; she said: "I don't think it's unpatriotic to use so much gas. . . . It's very patriotic. It's our way of life. . . . Why should we cut back? . . . We're an affluent society. Should I hate my neighbor because she has a better house, a better car, more money?"[33] It is easy to caricature such views as evidence of American profligacy, excess, and arrogance. Indeed, according to certain perspectives aligned with the consumer-as-dupe outlook, American culture is easily ridiculed as wasteful and blithely unaware of the profound relations of destruction bound up within each tank of gas. Take peak oil icon James Howard Kunstler, who is well known for his infantilization of U.S. culture and "the American way of life": "We've become a nation of overfed clowns and crybabies, afraid of the truth, indifferent to the common good, hardly even a common culture, selfish, belligerent, narcissistic whiners seeking every means possible to live outside a reality-based community."[34] In essence, according to Kunstler, we are a zombie nation of cultural dupes too self-absorbed to wake up and face the "real world" of impending energy constraints.[35]

Yet such easy caricatures belie the complex subjectivities and cultural politics that underlie such an equation of "using so much gas" with "our way of life." The concept of "way of life" or *livelihood* is commonly mobilized as a claim to justify access to resources.[36] Whether articulated by indigenous groups or shared ideals of national ways of living, these claims create moral economies around resource practices. Again, as political ecologists have so often shown, what is most important is not purely the material relation to those resources but the cultural and political depth of such livelihood claims.[37] Thus it is essential to dig deep into this *moral economy* of "the American way of life." It is not simply a cultural form of entitlement to the resource-intensive geographies but rather a vision of life itself as "made" within a field of competitive market subjects. The woman quoted crucially asks, "Should I hate my neighbor because she has a better house, a better car, more money?" This question fundamentally interrogates the assertion that the money and material commodities accorded to individuals are not deserved. Rather, it suggests that this particular way of life is structured by a social field wherein wealth and material goods *justifiably flow* into privatized hands that "worked hard" to achieve a particular material standard of life.

Following Michel Foucault's recently translated lectures on neoliberalism, I call this imaginary "entrepreneurial life."[38] I argue that this vision of life came to be equated with what is known as "the American way of life" based on privatized social reproduction, single-family housing, and automobility. This vision of "entrepreneurial life" has deep roots in American culture and politics. From Jeffersonian agrarianism to Emersonian self-reliance, from Horatio Alger tales of rags to riches to the Protestant work ethic, American politics has always been shaped by an ideology of self-made lives.[39] Yet I propose that prior to World War II, it was rather difficult to translate this vision of life into a popular mass appeal—the lives of the majority of workers in the United States were too structured by material deprivation and either an urban proletarian or rural smallholder sense of injustice. In the U.S. context, the absolute despotism of machine production and the deprivation of working life reached its ideological and economic limits with the Great Depression of the 1930s. To create a populist politics of entrepreneurial life—a view that one could actually shape a life as one's own—it took, in a word, *energy*—political and biophysical. It is well known that during the New Deal, mass political movements among workers and consumers pushed the state to profoundly restructure capitalist social relations around high wages (for some) and the Keynesian Welfare State.[40] Out of the crisis emerged social struggles and political projects reconfiguring the geographies of social reproduction—what Cindi Katz calls "the messy, fleshy stuff of everyday life"[41]—for a specific stratum of workers in the United States: a postwar social construction of life as composed of homes, cars, and yards.

It took biophysical energy as well—access to the prodigious powers of fossil fuel was further generalized to the public in the form of internal combustion engine–powered cars and a whole host of household appliances.[42] Therefore, rooted in the *material transformation* of social reproduction centered upon the spatiality of single-family home ownership and automobility, oil helps power what others have called "the real subsumption of life under capital," where subjectivity itself mirrors the entrepreneurial logics of capital.[43] This transformation gave millions of Americans the wages, the public infrastructure, and the financial institutions to mobilize a whole host of energy-intensive machines in everyday life that surrounded what was once called the "electric-oil-auto complex."[44] Energy powered the privatization of social space. By extending the productive forces of capital—large-scale industry powered by fossil fuel—to the reproductive forces of everyday life, a specific stratum of American workers could now live, think, and feel an individuated sense of *power* over the geographies of everyday practices. Life appeared to some as a coherent space of privatized freedom—the house, the car, the family, the yard—that was entirely produced by and reducible to one's own life choices and entrepreneurial efforts. This way of life became synonymous with capital—an entrepreneurial life of choice and freedom to *make* a life for oneself.

Understanding the meaning of life cannot become a transhistorical, speculative exercise but rather must make clear the historical specificity of *capitalist* life. Too often injustice and environmental destruction is blamed on the noun *capitalism*. Yet, as Marx instructs, "capital is not a thing but a social relation."[45] Capitalism should not be an explanatory concept; capital's reproduction must be the object of explanation. "Life" under capitalism is only made possible through working for a wage (working under the command of capital) and thereby gaining access to the commodified means of subsistence. The precarious dependence of life upon capital must continually be produced and reproduced through what might be called the cultural politics of capital: the lived practices and meanings that naturalize capitalist forms of power and hegemony. For my purposes, the distinction between production (work) and reproduction (life) is critical.[46] The centrality of oil to a particular construction of "the American way of life" is itself a specifically capitalist construction of "life" opposed to "work." As Marx put it, "life for [the worker] begins where this [work] activity ceases."[47] As I will discuss at length, fossil-fuel-powered machinery is critical to the construction of a specifically capitalist form of despotism over "work"—or the labor process. On the other hand, oil specifically has become important in efforts to compensate for that despotism through the construction of a "way of life" aligned with the logics of capital—freedom, property, and entrepreneurialism.

Toward a Historical Ecology of Neoliberalism

In this book, I argue that oil's relation to "the American way of life" is central to the rise of neoliberal hegemony in the United States. In so doing, I aim to intervene in debates on neoliberalism in two ways. First, I follow recent historical research examining how the rise of conservatism in the United States was based on the mobilization of suburban populist anger over high taxes and government efforts at wealth redistribution.[48] While most of these studies have focused on the particular cultural and political discourses emanating from suburban geographies, I focus on the material and ecological relationships that make those geographies possible in the first place.[49] Oil is but one of many of a whole host of material- and energy-intensive products that came to saturate suburban life in the post–World War II period. I'm specifically interested in the ways in which the incredible reservoir of "work" provided by fossil energy has provided the ecological foundation for a peculiarly privatized sociospatial existence. Rather than simply lament the ecological "footprint" of these practices, I seek to understand the ways in which their very materiality actively shapes political structures of feeling, reinforcing what Evan McKenzie calls "an ideology of hostile privatism."[50] It is the entrenchment of oil within these cherished ideas of property, freedom, family, and home that makes its deleterious ecological consequences that much harder to reverse. Indeed, while there has been considerable work on the neoliberalization of "the environment" or "nature" as a contained field of governance over naturalized realms of water, forests, wetlands, and fisheries,[51] we need to further understand neoliberalism itself—its ideologies, its core practices and policy prescriptions—as fundamentally shaped by the societal relation to resources, energy, and waste. In short, we need to move from understanding the politics of ecology and toward the ecology of politics.[52]

Second, I aim to complicate the standard *periodization* of neoliberalism as emerging out of the crisis of the 1970s and reigning until the present.[53] Although there are tremendous accounts of the *intellectual* prehistory of neoliberalism in the post–World War II period—from Mont Pèlerin to Milton Friedman's steady work in the 1950s—the popular roots of neoliberal hegemony were also *laid* in the postwar era through the steady expansion of suburban geographies in the Sunbelt and throughout the United States.[54] My contention is that the postwar period must be viewed as neoliberalism's *incubation period* wherein popular resentment of government, taxes, and Keynesianism festered and built itself until the political moment of opportunity in the 1970s emerged—a moment structured in no small part by concerns over "oil shocks." In fact, the historical roots of neoliberalism stretch back to the contradictions of the New Deal project itself (if not much earlier). Although New Deal liberalism was based around collective narratives of public solidarity and the beneficial role of state intervention, it created the conditions for a privatized geography of suburbanization. Despite the substantive gains achieved by a specific white male breadwinning factory worker, what has been called the "golden age" of capitalism or the "capital–labor accord" was structured by profound exclusions based on race, gender, and ideas of citizenship.[55] It was precisely those divisions that were mobilized by the forces on the right in the 1960s and 1970s to construct efforts to extend civil and economic rights to African Americans, migrant farm workers, and women as forms of "unfair" redistribution of wealth from working-class white males to an "undeserving" underclass.[56] Thus the rise of neoliberal hegemony can be seen as a rather predictable consequence of the limitations of the ultimately liberal–reformist nature of the New Deal project to *restore capital* rather than as a fundamental challenge to its core precepts.[57] Specifically, the "capital–labor accord" maintained what Marx calls "the despotism of capital" in the realm of social life called "work" or "production" and fundamentally reproduced a class of workers who depended upon commodity relations and wages (however "high") to survive in the realm of "life."

Ecology and the Forces of Capital

As a natural resource and key element in contemporary discussions of climate change, a political economic perspective on energy must also speak to what Margaret Fitzsimmons famously referred to as "the matter of nature."[58] The theoretical analysis of the ecology of capital has been primarily concerned with the ways in which capitalism is inherently destructive of a domain called "nature." Many ecological Marxists argue that ecological degradation—the pollution of water or the spewing of greenhouse gases into the atmosphere and consequent climate effects—is not a form of market or regulatory failure but rather an internal product of specifically capitalist forms of competition and accumulation. James O'Connor argues that capitalist competition drives individual capitalists to systematically externalize costs onto the environment and society.[59] Thus the "second contradiction of capitalism" is its inherent tendency to degrade the *conditions* of production, which include the *ecological systems* such as water systems, soil fertility, and the climate. John Bellamy Foster and others have also charged a social realm called capitalism with inducing a "metabolic" rift with natural patterns of ecological circulation from soil nutrient recycling to the overloading of the biosphere with greenhouse gases.[60] Overall, these perspectives tend to construct a curious and undialectical dualism between capitalism and nature—as if nature is solely the depository of capitalist waste and destruction.[61] This not only ignores the many theoretical debates over the impossibility of pure distinctions between nature and society, but also assumes there is a realm called "capitalism" that is purely social.[62] Thus theories of the capitalist destruction of an externalized nature fail to consider how ecological relationships with resources, wastes, and ecosystems already constitute the social and material geographies of capitalism itself. Focusing only on the moments where socialized capital confronts an externalized nature only skims the surface of the deeper metabolic relation between nature and society. While we cannot downplay the spectacular history of capitalist degradation of an externalized and imagined nature, an effective ecological critique of capital must also seek to understand the ecology internal to capital itself. By focusing on fossil fuel, we can begin to construct an ecology of capital where nature is not only seen as something "produced" by capitalism or as an external, uncommodified "condition" of production but is constitutive of and internal to the productive forces and social relations of capital.[63]

More empirically, there is a rich tradition of political ecology and resource geography that seeks to uncover place-based engagements between society and nature.[64] Yet these studies as a whole also assume that the real societal relation to nature is visible on the ground in specific sites of "nature-based" engagement (mines, forests, agricultural fields, and even urban parks and water systems) or the expulsion of waste into nature as "sink" or "environment." This allows one to assume that the societal relation to nature begins and ends in these naturalized spaces.[65] I contend that we must seek to also confront *denaturalized* geographies of nature–society relations—geographies constructed as highly unnatural and dominated by large-scale technologies and the built environments of intensive material and energy consumption and waste production. Indeed, it is these industrial spaces of massive energy and material throughput that are most responsible not only for global environmental concerns like climate change but also for more local concerns with air and water pollution. As this book will show, understanding the geographies of petro-capitalism requires understanding not only the politics of extraction or refinery pollution (although this is critical—see chapters 2 and 3) but also the socioecological relations of gasoline stations, single-family homes, automobility, and the dominance of petrochemicals and plastics in everyday life.

Materiality and the Plan of This Work

This book centers upon oil and the role of energy in shaping a particular regime of mass consumption.[66] But consumption, or consumerism, is often spoken of in the very abstract terms of the market itself—as an undifferentiated "mass" of goods and commodities that serve to reproduce a standard of living. Ben Fine's "vertical" approach to the "world of consumption" insists that each particular commodity—as a specific use value—is contained within its own "system of provision": "Each commodity or commodity group is best understood in terms of a unity of economic and social processes which vary significantly from one commodity to another, each creating and reflecting upon what will be referred to as its own system of provision."[67] While this approach is often used to focus on cultural and economic processes underlying consumption, each commodity is also situated in a specific *ecology* of provision.[68]

Oil is too often constructed as a fetishized *object* of geopolitical conflict, state formation, corporate profits, or profligate consumption habits and not as an active material force in itself. The system of petroleum provision is structured by the specific materiality of the processes of extraction, distribution, refining, and consumption. Indeed, understanding the ecology of the forces of capital means a deeper understanding of the materiality of oil: how the biophysical attributes of oil itself—its dense energy, its liquid propensity to flow, its chemical composition—actively shape not only "the politics of oil" but also *politics* more broadly. This book is structured chronologically, but also materially—each chapter focuses on a specific aspect of the materiality of oil and how it shapes its "system of provision." Chapter 1 provides a theoretical introduction. Chapters 2 through 5 examine particular moments of crisis and stability in the long-term development of petro-capitalism in the United States (e.g., 1930s, 1945–73, 1970s, and 2000s). In chapter 1, I offer a theoretical critique of what I call the "fetishism of oil" that is reproduced in much of the critical political economy literature. I propose a broader historical–materialist perspective, taking into account the role of energy (and fossil fuel specifically) in the production and reproduction of life under capitalism. In sections on production and reproduction respectively, I argue that fossil fuel in general, and oil in particular, needs to be theorized as a specifically material aspect of the alienated—seemingly autonomous—power of capital over living labor. Specifically, I situate oil as a central energy resource shaping the forces of social reproduction, or what I call the real subsumption of life under capital. Under this form of subsumption, life *appears as capital,* or what Foucault's calls the "the enterprise form" so central to neoliberal subjectivities.

In chapter 2, I argue that the social struggle to produce the conditions for an oil-fired and commodified "American way of life" were complicated by problems of oil overproduction rooted the contradiction between a U.S. legal regime of private property and the materiality of petroleum as a *subterranean resource*. During the 1930s, this property regime led to massive overproduction, glut, collapsing prices, and eventually a political regime dedicated to curtailing how oil reached the U.S. market. This created what was called the prorationing system that set "allowable" production quotas for thousands of wells across the United States. My goal is to situate these struggles over oil with the larger reconstruction of capitalist life surrounding New Deal reforms in housing, labor, and infrastructure policy.

Mitchell instructs that we need to "follow the carbon," but, in the case of petroleum-based life, it is perhaps more important to follow the *hydrocarbons*.[69] In chapter 3, it is oil's status as a complex chemical assemblage of hydrocarbons that allows the oil industry not only to extricate thousands (millions?) of petroleum-based products from a given barrel of oil but also to craft narratives emphasizing the unavoidability of oil through the saturation of chemicals, plastics, medicine, food, and gasoline in everyday life. The torrent of petroleum products produced through the refining process not only came to symbolize a specific set of cultural practices encircling "the good life" but also increasingly supplemented a vision of entrepreneurial life as an atomized project made possible through a specific set of material products in the postwar period.

Perhaps the most important material feature of oil in shaping larger visions of scarcity and geopolitics is its exhaustibility and the uneven geography of reserves. In chapter 4, I discuss how the peaking of U.S. oil production combined with the concentration of massive and highly productive (low-cost) fields in the Middle East shaped the geopolitical anxieties of the "oil shocks." Although these concerns of scarcity and geopolitics proliferated throughout the public imagination, I argue that the popular interpretation of the "oil shocks" was that the crisis itself was not "real"—if by "real" we mean natural scarcity and a market response of high prices—but rather a *contrived* crisis engineered by anticompetitive forces intervening within what should be an apolitical and pure space of the market. Drawing from letters written to newspaper editors and the Nixon administration, I show how popular disdain for monopolistic oil companies, racialized oil sheiks, and government oil price controls all coalesced to reproduce an emerging neoliberal idolatry of a pure, free, and, most important, *competitive* market. For the decentralized suburban "Silent Majority" of Richard Nixon and Ronald Regan's America, fairness was only realizable through the expurgation of large, centralized and visible forces intervening in the market—of which oil cartels, unions, and governmental redistribution were all representative forms.

Finally, in chapter 5, it is the liquid nature of petroleum that represents the condition of possibility of the *liquid landscapes* of mass gasoline availability in pumping stations scattered throughout the urban, suburban, and rural geographies of American life. It is this *omnipresence* of gasoline and its price that structures what I call the pain at the pump discourse of the 2000s, which bemoans high gas prices as a pervasive form of everyday oppression under neoliberalism. I argue that populist anger at high gas prices was less about cultural entitlement and excess, and more about life (and death) under the neoliberalism characterized by falling wages, mounting debt, and increasing job insecurity. Although cheap energy and natural resources represented a short-term reprieve from these forces in the 1980s and 1990s, the rising cost of energy and food in the 2000s represented the last in a long line of threats to social reproduction for working people in the United States. Yet the popular resistance to high energy prices—often framed in neoliberal terms as "energy taxes"—has disturbing implications for an ecological and anti-imperial politics.

I conclude by interrogating the relationship between oil, energy, and a central idea of "entrepreneurial life"—freedom. Just like imaginaries of freedom beyond work implicit in the idea of "the American way of life," Karl Marx hoped for a society beyond capital based on a "realm of freedom" made possible through the capitalist development of the productive forces and quarantined in a space for individual creative development *apart* from material production. Yet for Marx, this vision of freedom was only emancipatory *for all* if was achieved through the democratic control over society's productive powers. The neoliberal concept of freedom certainly created expansive geographies of *privatized* social control over the home, the car, and the family (for some small sectors of the global working class), but even for the suburbanites of the United States, it ultimately ceded the world of work, production, and the market to the despotism of capital. The ecological and economic crisis before us lays bare the need to assert democratic social control over not only the production and distribution of energy resources but also economic life in general.

CHAPTER ONE

The Power of Oil?

Energy, Machines, and the Forces of Capital

Across the world, oil is invoked as a machine of destiny. Oil will make you rich, oil will make you poor, oil will bring war, oil will deliver peace, oil will define our world as much as the glaciers did in the Ice Age.

—Peter Maass, *Crude World*

The Fetishism of Oil and Its Secret

As the previous statement indicates, oil is seen as a powerful thing. Because of its extremely useful biophysical properties, oil is endowed with a kind of "magical" social, financial, and geopolitical power.[1] Those social actors who come to control oil are automatically accorded tremendous wealth and power. Historically, the discovery of oil promised instant generation of wealth and prosperity. "Big Oil" companies are imagined as wielding tremendous control to set prices, garner immense profits, and shape whole national energy and environmental policy programs.[2] As a former Shell executive put it, "oil breeds arrogance, because it's so powerful."[3] Where national governments hold subsurface mineral ownership rights (e.g., Venezuela and the Middle East), oil is mobilized as a unique commodity that will lay the basis for national prosperity and development.[4] Where individual landowners hold subsurface rights (e.g., the United States), oil discoveries create "booms" of investment and profits for oil developers and lucrative royalty payments for local landowners.[5] Recently, however, oil is being charged with a quite different kind of agency. Rather than wealth and money, oil is increasingly framed as a "curse" to both local extractive communities (contaminating water and destroying local livelihoods) and national political economies (engendering endemic corruption and narrow commodity-centric economic development).[6] Paradoxically, as Terry Lynn Karl put it, oil simultaneously invokes wealth and poverty, booms and busts, and freedom and authoritarianism.[7]

Oil and the international geographies of oil conflict also seem to represent the epitome of what John Agnew calls "the modern geopolitical imagination."[8] It is a "strategic" and fundamental resource fixed in few spaces that becomes an object of geopolitical competition for territorial control. A prime example is, of course, the role of the U.S. state and military in shaping the geopolitics of oil in the Middle East, of which the war in Iraq is the most recent example. Access to oil reserves and production in the Middle East is generally recognized at the core of U.S. foreign policy and "national security."[9] Examples abound: Franklin Delano Roosevelt's (FDR) meeting with King Ibn Saud of Saudi Arabia in 1945, Jimmy Carter's 1980 doctrine that any threat to Persian Gulf oil would be repelled with military force, and Dick Cheney's statement in 1999 that the Middle East "is still where the prize ultimately lies."[10] Any attempt by Middle Eastern countries to take non-U.S.-sanctioned control over oil reserves is seen as putting the United States in a vulnerable position. Dick Cheney admitted as much when Iraq invaded Kuwait in 1990 when he said, "[After the invasion] he [Saddam Hussein] was clearly in position to be able to dictate the future of worldwide energy policy, and that gave him a stranglehold on our economy and on that of most of the other nations of the world as well."[11]

Since control over oil is seen as so critical in the global geopolitical dramas of world domination, the prospect of oil scarcity is seen as an automatic trigger of "resource wars."[12] As Michael Klare asserts, "petroleum stands out from other materials—water, minerals, timber, and so on—because of its pivotal role in the global economy and its capacity to ignite large-scale combat."[13] Oil, by itself it seems, has the peculiar capacity to ignite war and geopolitical conflict. Out of these critiques emerges an oppositional logic animating the antiwar proclamation of "no blood for oil," which attempts to expose the triviality of violence and death in Iraq and elsewhere over a mere thing, oil.

Those focused on the geopolitics of oil—whether Dick Cheney or Michael Klare—rely on an undialectical conception of what David Harvey calls *absolute space*—"space [that] is understood as a preexisting, immovable, continuous, and unchanging framework."[14] From this perspective, oil is a strategic object amid the absolute spaces of national territories, pipelines, oceans, and military bases. Analysis takes on a spatial fetish fixated on the thing itself and conjuring centripetal spatial logics—where nation-states, foreign policy elites, military planners, and indeed some critical theorists—are fixated on the thing, the stuff in the ground, the prize, the oil! This undialectical geopolitical optic remains on the spatial surface of oil–society relations where analysis starts and ends at the site of extraction and the self-evidence of the thing, oil. Thus even dialecticians such as David Harvey describe the Middle East as the "global oil spigot"[15]—a centered absolute space on the map where control over the global economy is secured.

Oil appears to automatically generate wealth and conflict, because it is also seen as the singular commodity responsible for a particular standard of living. As a representative of the U.S. House of Representatives put it in 1941, "the progress of the people as a whole depends on upon this lifeblood of commerce and industry—petroleum."[16] As the societal "lifeblood," oil's finite quantities become an intense object of social concern and scientific contestation. Since at least the 1920s, petroleum geologists have warned of the imminent exhaustion of U.S. petroleum supplies.[17] The most recent incarnation is composed of those proclaiming the imminence of "peak oil" when global production reaches its peak then goes into decline, and modern society withers away.[18]

Unifying these discourses is a remarkable agency bestowed upon oil itself. How does it do it? My wager is that *it* doesn't do anything. Oil has no inherent power outside the social and political relations that produce it as such a "vital" resource. In fact, according oil such tremendous social and political power in itself is a prime example of what Karl Marx referred to as fetishism.[19] According to Marx, fetishism is rooted in circumstances where "certain social relations appear as the natural properties of things in society."[20] As capitalism is governed through abstract and impersonal relations of exchange, particular objects or things—the railroad, the Internet, a national territory—appear as "autonomous figures endowed with a life of their own."[21] When a particular object reaches the status of what Michael Taussig called "thinghood,"[22] it does not appear as it really is— the product of social relations—but rather "as objective characteristics of the products of labour themselves, the socio-natural properties of these things."[23] Thus the power of oil itself appears to be rooted in its "socio-natural properties"—its versatility, its abundance, its liquidity—rather than the particular historical geographies and social relations that harness these capacities in particular ways.

Marx's answer to fetishism was a dialectical materialist analysis that sought to go beneath the self-evident world of things and appearances.[24] Unlike positivist efforts to fix and isolate particular variables and casual mechanisms, a dialectical perspective refuses to accord any particular object or thing the force of independent causality (e.g., oil causes war). Rather than seeking fixed external relations among objective things, dialectics attempts to analytically come to grips with open systems constituted through internal relations and dynamically shifting processes. Therefore, the apparent power of "things" can only be understood as itself a product of generative relations and processes. Moreover, dialectics can be applied to the analysis of natural resources. As David Harvey put it long ago, "'resources' can be defined only in relationship to the mode of production which seeks to make use them and which simultaneously 'produces' them through both the physical and mental activity of the users. There is, therefore, no such thing as a resource in abstract or a resource which exists as a 'thing-in-itself.'"[25]

There is no such thing as a natural resource—no such *thing* as oil-in-itself. Oil is better understood as a social relation. This is not the same as saying that oil is a cultural construction or that nature is simply a cultural product of human discourse. Rather, it is a simple assertion that oil's biophysical capacities only come to be mobilized in specific historical circumstances and through particular social relations. Thus from a dialectical perspective that refuses nature–society binaries, oil is a more concretely a *socioecological* relation that requires taking seriously both the materiality of petroleum and the social projects that channel its biophysical capacities in particular ways.

How should one analytically approach these constitutive processes and relations? Discussions of commodity fetishism often hinge on questions of true or false. Often under the framework of "commodity chain analysis," the goal is to "unveil the real" social relations "behind" the commodity.[26] Thus in order to unearth the truth behind the false consciousness of oil we simply need to empirically trace the networks of oil rig operators, pipelines, refinery workers, tanker drivers, and gas station owners who were socially necessary in the production of petroleum products—the actual useful, refined products that emerge from crude oil. Uncovering the "hidden" material geographies of oil extraction, transportation, refining, and so forth is undeniably a worthy pursuit and one that has been performed in a variety of contexts.[27] It reflects the power of Marx's theory of value, which forces us to go back and examine the conditions under which commodities are produced. However, I wish to approach oil fetishism somewhat differently. Thingified discourses around oil as the cause of wealth, poverty, democracy, authoritarianism, war, and peace are not so much false as they are discursive expressions of particular social and ecological relations. Understanding the relations and processes that produce the *idea* of oil as a powerful thing is a different and perhaps less dogmatically materialistic exercise than simply tracing the geographies of oil's material production.

As Harvey has pointed out, a resource is only defined in relation to its users and the mode of production that seeks to make use of it. This requires approaching not only the material geographies of labor necessary in a commodity's production but also the social relations surrounding the use, or consumption, of the commodity itself. The use value of a commodity is not natural or fixed but rather only emerges out of particular historical geographies, lived practices, and meanings through which a commodity comes to be imagined as *useful*. With petroleum, it is common to point out that its material capacities were harnessed as useful in many different ways in different historical contexts (e.g., ship calking in the ancient Middle East, lamp oil in China, illumination in late nineteenth century).[28]

Going beyond the fetishism of oil holds promise for a different perspective on the relationship between oil and social power. For good reason, much of the critical literature on the political economy of oil is focused upon geopolitical conflict and imperialism.[29] Again, the power of oil as a thing—which power seeks to grab a hold of—is central to many left critiques of U.S. foreign policy. Apart from geopolitics, oil is also seen as generating a form of economic power marked by the monopolistic industrial organization of oil capital. Since the era of Rockefeller and Ida Tarbell's muckraking exposés, "Big Oil" has become an unquestioned actor in political discourse whose power over prices, the economy, and the political process are self-evident simply because they control and distribute so much oil (and the wealth it automatically generates).[30] Those states whose governments and national oil companies own or produce and distribute the oil are seen as a specific expression of oil-based state power known as the "petro-state." While the discourse of the "resource curse" ignores many cases where oil wealth is used for the benefit of the population (in contexts as varied as Venezuela and Norway), it also assumes that oil itself causes abuses of power like corruption, authoritarianism, and state violence.

In short, oil appears to generate monstrous forms of Power with a capital P. Yet this vision of oil and its endowed power neglects decades of debate within social theory over the nature of power itself. Whether stemming from a Gramscian perspective on hegemony or a Foucauldian focus on bodily discipline, critical social theorists have turned their attention to the micropolitics of everyday practice, or what Henry Lefebvre referred to as "the very soil on which the great architectures of politics and society rise up."[31] Power is not only amassed and centralized in corporations, states, and large organized social movements but is also reproduced through the contested field of everyday practices.[32] When considering the effort to understand the social relations that produce the *idea* of oil as a powerful thing-in-itself, it is equally clear that a critical analysis of petro-capitalism must not only fixate upon the corporate board rooms of "Big Oil," the "War Rooms" of the architects of empire, and the coffers of the moneyed petro-state but must travel further into the complex and ordinary patterns of everyday life. Moreover, once oil's centrality to everyday practices of thinking and feeling is taken into account, our explanations of why petro-capitalism persists become much less simplistic. Rather than a basic story of "Big Oil" rigging a market for profit, we must confront how oil hegemony also harnesses cherished ideals of freedom, security, national pride, and life itself.

This everyday approach to oil and power considers the wider geographies of social relations, lived practices, and meanings through which oil is objectified and fetishized as a vital and strategic "thing." Rather than assuming oil's centrality to U.S. capitalism and hegemony, it requires asking deeper questions about how this centrality was historically and geographically produced in the first place. This requires interrogating the multiple spaces through which particular forms of accumulation and subjectivities are tied to the refining, distribution, and consumption of petroleum products. My proposition is that the geopolitical fixation upon oil is but a moment in a larger historical relationship between fossil-fuel energy and capitalist social relations. How can we understand this broader relationship between energy and capitalism?

"An Earthly Basis for History"

Given my focus on the geography of natural resources, it is critical to understand that the materialist foundation of Marx and Engels's historical analysis is centered upon the societal relation to nature. In *The German Ideology*, they critique the German idealists for failing to establish "an earthly basis for history."[33] Such a basis emerges from a very simple foundation: "The first premise of all human history is, of course, the existence of living human individuals. Thus the first fact to be established is the physical organization of these individuals and their consequent relation to the rest of nature."[34]

In order for human history to unfold, groups of individuals (whether small-scale communities, nations, or the world) need to produce their means of subsistence in the form of food, clothing, shelter, and other socially mediated necessities. And the set of relations through which subsistence is *produced* is inextricably linked to particular forms of interchange with ecological systems and culturally defined resources. History and geography reveal considerable diversity in the different societal forms of nature–society interaction. Moreover, a particular mode of production is also "a definite form of activity of these individuals, a definite form of expressing their life, a definite *mode of life* on their part."[35] In other words, producing *life* is a process composed of activities and practices that are not simply material but cultural and political *expressions* of life itself.

In opposition to the vulgar economism sometimes ascribed to Marxian political economy, in 1884 Engels attempted to reframe historical analysis away from an economic "base" determining a political–ideological superstructure.[36] He wrote, "According to the materialist conception, the determining factor in history is, in the last resort, the production and reproduction of immediate life."[37] The focus on "immediate life" harkens back to *The German Ideology* forty years prior. Rather than a materialist focus on some level deemed "the economic," a focus on "the real life-process"[38] is a much more open avenue toward a wider political, cultural, and economic analysis of nature–society relations. With this broader focus the materialist framework enrolls a whole set of practices, cultural expectations, and everyday politics around the "life-process." Through a rescue of a historical–materialist focus on "life" we can further develop the already productive dialogues between Marxist critiques of capital and biopolitical critique of the embodied forms of power and subjection.[39] With the focus on "production and reproduction," we can also avoid a kind of productivism—a focus exclusively on the point of production (e.g., the factory floor) as the privileged site of materiality and politics. Rather, by including reproduction, Engels includes not only biological reproduction[40] but also the everyday processes of *social reproduction* so critical to the social relations of capitalism.

Energy, Space, and the Cultural Politics of Life

From a historical–geographical materialist perspective the task is to trace the role of oil in shaping "the production and reproduction of immediate life." From this perspective, it is even more absurd to focus exclusively on the site of oil extraction, because the biophysical capacities of oil are harnessed in the production and reproduction of life in many contexts that stretch far beyond oil's geological state. More to the point, despite also being a material feedstock for innumerable commodities, oil is overwhelmingly harnessed as a *source of energy*. Energy is *life itself*. Without solar energy bathing the world of plant life, life is impossible for plants and the animals that feed upon them.[41] From a human perspective, energy is the stuff of material life—the food, the fuel, the muscles, the winds, the water, the soot, the smog, and the fire.[42] From the calories expended by human hunters in the pursuit of wild game to the coal combusted in a steam engine, all production, *all life,* depends on access to and control over energy. Moreover, energy is constitutive of what Henri Lefebvre referred to as the social production of space.[43] Specifically, not only is energy the object of geopolitical conflict and state territoriality, but the consumption of energy in particular ways makes specific spatialities possible—the trade winds of mercantile exchange, the steam powered railroads and ships of global market integration in the nineteenth century, the natural gas heating the space of a home, and the gasoline powering individuals through dispersed suburban geographies.

Yet energy's role in the production and reproduction of immediate life—and the production of space—is not *purely* material or mechanistic. It also incorporates the ways in which energized practices make possible ways of living, thinking, and feeling. Material practice is best understood in relation to wider cultural forms of power and domination.[44] Italian Marxist Antonio Gramsci's theory of hegemony provides a productive framework toward understanding the discursive–material facets of social power.[45] Paying as much attention to consent as coercion, Gramsci's theory of hegemony requires considering the ways in which ethics, morality, and education become embedded in material practices and commonsense ways of thinking.

Gramsci's focus on common sense and consent as embedded in ordinary life is crucial to my focus on energy and space. As Raymond Williams makes clear, hegemony is best theorized as a *lived process*: "[Hegemony] is a whole body of practices and expectations, over the whole of living: our senses and assignments of energy, our shaping perceptions of ourselves and our world. . . . A lived hegemony is always a process."[46] On the one hand, the geographies of life—"the whole of living"—itself must be materially produced out of particular relations with energy: relations with food, heating fuel, transportation fuel, and so on. On the other hand, these historically sedimented geographies themselves produce and are produced by a particular cultural politics of "life." The cultural politics of life focuses on how wider narratives make normative claims about particular modes of living as a universal model that everyone ought to aspire to. The materiality and cultural politics of life always invokes historically specific geographies—forms of spatial practice entangled with particular normative visions of what constitutes "the good life." Although specific forms of life are constructed as natural and normal, the construction of an ideal life necessarily posits that it is exclusionary and not universally available. Thus through a focus on everyday practice we can unite both the materiality of life and the cultural politics of life as simultaneously reproduced through the rhythms of daily practice.

It is not as important to expand on such transhistorical generalities about humanity's need for energy at all places and in all moments. Rather than tracing universal thermodynamic laws of energy, the challenge is to understand what is historically and geographically *specific* about energy relations and the capitalist mode of production; or, put more broadly, the capitalist mode of *life*, which is a mode of living ensconced in what Moishe Postone refers to as forms of "abstract domination" rooted in the commodification of labor power and the dependence on generalized relations of commodity exchange.[47]

Fossil Fuels, the Productive Forces, and the Time–Space Compression

The historical specificity of a capitalist energy regime is necessarily related to the use of fossil fuel. Fossil fuels are first and foremost about sociotechnical relations of the power to transform nature, or what Marx referred to as the productive forces. As many have pointed out,[48] the rise of fossil-fuel-powered industry represents an important historical break from solar-powered societies primarily driven by human and animal *muscles* (and, to a lesser extent, wind and water power) toward social formations drawing from immense reservoirs of *nonliving* fossilized energy to power machines.

Through this shift from living to nonliving productive forces, fossil fuel powers an epochal break in both the temporalities and spatialities of material life. On the temporal level, fossil fuels (coal, oil, and natural gas) are themselves the biotic *concentration of time*—the product of millions of years of concentrated solar energy, or what Jeffrey Dukes refers to as "buried sunshine."[49] This temporal concentration of past life produces an enormously dense energy source compared with other short-lived "fuels" such as wood, peat, or other biomass.[50] This very dense source of nonliving—nonmuscular—power allows for the temporal *acceleration* of the pace and productivity of production. As Altvater points out, fossil-fueled automatic machinery need not break its frantic pace in line with the biological rhythms of seasonal or bodily change.[51] The pace and throughput of production can be constant and relentless, allowing for a vast expansion in the material bulk of commodities.

On the other hand, as is becoming increasingly evident, the gases emitted from the combustion of this concentrated life produces a temporal *acceleration* of wider atmospheric processes, or what Clark and York call a "biospheric rift" characterized by the climate system's inability to absorb those gases.[52] As Chakrabarty discusses, the politics of climate change is first and foremost over conceptions of "natural" versus "anthropogenic" time.[53] Ironically, as capitalism accumulates thanks to geological accumulations of biological time, climate time is accelerated in the short term. Today urban–industrial society is increasingly framed as a geological force in the history of the planet itself, ending the Holocene and ushering in the Anthropocene era of human-driven climate change and mass extinction.[54]

Time is dialectically related to space. The fossilization of time produces a massive shift in the spatialities of social life, or what Marx referred to as "the annihilation of space by time."[55] First, fossil fuels are fixed in specific places as *subterranean* resources. This sounds obvious enough, but the implications are wide ranging. The reliance upon subterranean fuel represents a shift from what economic historian E. A. Wrigley calls the "organic" economy wherein the bulk of energy, food, and fiber are derived from land-intensive (i.e., space-intensive) resources (e.g., cotton, wheat, livestock) toward a "mineral-based energy economy . . . freed from dependence on the land for raw materials."[56] As industry moved from timber and natural fibers to iron ore, aluminum, and coal energy, the relief of what has been called "the land constraint" was remarkable.[57] Prior to the industrial fossil era, production powered by muscular power could only subsist energetically through the production of food and fuel that could only be derived from expansive spaces of land. For example, the muscles of horses helped immensely to supplement human farm labor, but consider the vast acreage it took to grow oats and hay for those animals.[58] Moreover, fuel for space heating, cooking, or metallurgy had to be obtained (and often still is) through the expansive geographies of woodlands and forests. In particular, the smelting of iron ore (and metallurgy in general) took thousands of acres of forests to turn wood into charcoal.[59] It is simply inconceivable to imagine the world of steel and metals without access to non-land-based fuel. The use and combustion of subterranean fuel not only freed up land in the sense of powering land-based production (i.e., tractors do not need land to feed them like mules do) but also limited pressure on the terrestrial landscapes of forests.[60]

Fossil-fuel energy also powers nearly all forms of transportation and commodity circulation over space. From coal-powered steam locomotives to petroleum-fueled container ships, fossil-fuel-powered mobility ruptures biological limits on human and animal muscular capacities to traverse space. In the nineteenth century, the spatial extension of commodity circulation itself—particularly through steamships—began to stitch together worldwide networks of competition and create truly *global* markets for a whole host of commodities such as wheat, gold, and eventually oil.[61] Thus as Altvater points out, fossil fuel is constitutive of what David Harvey calls the "time-space compression" characteristic of recent waves of globalization, but it is also characteristic of modern global capitalism more generally.[62] Fossilized time–space compression represents the conditions of possibility for the very ideas of global markets, global civil society, and global states.

Given the importance of this energy shift to the spatiotemporalities of industrial capitalism, various perspectives have integrated energy into economic and historical analysis. Several historians have realized "energy regimes" to be an explanatory factor in the historical development of industrial capitalism and even world domination.[63] For instance, as Burke recently put it, "seen in the light of energy conversions, human history assumes a rather different, indeed remarkable shape." He suggests a project "to rethink modernity in terms of bioenergetics."[64] Ecological economics situates the laws of thermodynamics as the biophysical basis of all economic activity.[65] Specifically, they have focused on the second law stating that entropy, or the incapacity of an energy system to do work, tends to increase over time. As the combustion of fossil fuels yields greater and greater entropy dissipation, the second law of thermodynamics should predict that human societies will inevitably come up against profound and, perhaps, unsolvable energy constraints.[66] The *exhaustibility* of fossil fuels is projected as a fixed thermodynamic barrier to the sustainability of the time–space rhythms of globalized capitalism.

The strength of these perspectives is their recognition, unlike many Marxist perspectives, of energy as a basic ecological foundation of the core *productive forces* of society. Indeed, Martinez-Alier suggests that this is the missing link between ecological economics and Marxism— "The ecological view of the conditions of human existence *could* have been easily connected with Marxism through an adequate definition of the productive forces and productive powers."[67] The problem with these perspectives—like many cases of oil discussed in the introduction— is that energy is *fetishized* as a thing-in-itself with singular independent casual powers over the economy, history, and power.[68] From this perspective, it is not social relations—it is not politics—that shape history and society but rather energy flows. Through transhistorical thermodynamic laws, energy becomes devoid of its political, social, and cultural content.

Despite accusations that Marx is a technological determinist,[69] according the productive forces such independent power over society is hugely problematic from a dialectical perspective.[70] As Derek Sayer puts it, "things . . . are not, in or of themselves, productive forces."[71] Focusing on the primacy of the things we call productive forces—energy, machines, computers—sidesteps a more difficult and properly dialectical question, asked by philosopher Jason Read: "How to think [about productive] forces and technology as [social] relations and how to think [about] social relations as [productive] forces?"[72] From Marx's perspective, the forces of capitalist production were nothing more than the socialized productive powers of human labor embedded in not only things like machines but also knowledge, science, and other cultural practices. As we will see later, it is historically specific to capitalism for social change to *appear* as the product of fetishized things—machines, technology, oil—rather than social labor. These "things" then appear to have an alien power over society itself. While we understand very well the role of fossil fuel as a powerful thing, we need a better understanding of how the fossil-fueled productive forces are embedded in the social relations of production, reproduction, and what I've called the cultural politics of capital.

The Forces of Capital I: Production, Dead Ecologies, and the Real Subsumption of Labor

In the "hidden abode" of capitalist production,[73] the shift from the reliance on human and animal muscle power toward the inanimate powers of dense fossilized forms of energy needs to be understood in social and political terms. This shift was materialized through the development of large-scale machine production in factories powered by coal-fired steam engines. Marx asserts that large-scale machinery was "the material foundation of capitalist production" and that the "technical foundation of the factory system [was] the substitution of machines for muscular power."[74] With the development of large-scale machinery, the forces of production were no longer driven by the skills and hands of human power but rather an automatic mechanism fueled by inanimate energy: "A system of machinery . . . constitutes itself as a vast automaton as soon as it is driven by a self-acting prime mover."[75] This is not simply a historical relic of the industrial revolution but is rather an ongoing process toward more and more automation of productive processes formerly driven by muscular or other forms of living human power. From something as banal as automatic car windows to the vast sociotechnical networks of computing power now reshaping the geographies of information, since the nineteenth century society has been constantly undergoing a process of mechanization and automation.[76]

Yet if an automatic form of production does not rely on human or animal muscle power, it must obtain energy from somewhere. Indeed, much of the early industrial revolution in Britain and the United States was powered through *water power* and the location of factories on powerful river systems.[77] Yet as capitalism became increasingly reliant upon steam power, the concentrated and ultimately mobile power of fossilized coal proved more *geographically* versatile.[78] With coal-fired steam engines, capital could move beyond the restricted geographies of river systems—which were not only located in fixed spaces but also froze during the winter—and gain the power of spatial concentration in urban industrial districts. Thus fossil fuel—first coal—allowed for a rupture of the biological constraints of material production presented by both living muscles and living landscapes. Insofar as automatic large-scale machinery was not powered by muscles, it appeared as a force of nature—a force beyond human control. Large-scale industry, or what Marx sometimes called the "gigantic natural forces,"[79] only became both gigantic and natural through the accumulated eons of past life embedded in "buried sunshine."[80] Thus in the production process, the dead labor of machinery becomes ultimately dependent on the *dead ecologies* of fossilized energy.[81] Most often, it is only through the assemblage of dead ecology and dead labor that automatic machinery is brought to life. Indeed, much of the current (and past) warnings of oil or coal depletion are rooted in fears of dead labor *lying idle*—cars that cannot move, machines that cannot produce. As globalized capitalist society has become more and more dependent on the sociotechnical assemblages of machines and fossil energy, the fear of fossil-fuel depletion is at core a fear of a return to huddled masses of muscles representing the productive forces of society. Of course, upon the material foundation laid by fossil capitalism other forms of energy have emerged, such as nuclear energy and industrial hydropower—and indeed the great hope of alternative energies such as solar and wind—but approximately 81 percent of global energy consumption is still derived from fossil fuels as of 2010.[82]

Machines are not simply technological but also political tools.[83] Under capital the machine is "not only an automaton but an autocrat"[84] and becomes the material and technical basis of the despotism of the workplace. The specifically *capitalist* application of machinery is aimed toward not only efficiency and productivity but a technical basis for the domination of living labor power. Unlike handicrafts (and what Marx calls "manufacture"), where production depended upon the skills and muscles of living labor, large-scale machinery allowed for complete control of capital over the pace and organization of the productive process: "Since handicraft skill is the foundation of manufacture, and since the mechanism of manufacture as a whole possesses no objective framework which would be independent of the workers themselves, capital is constantly compelled to wrestle with the insubordination of workers."[85]

This constitutes what Marx refers to as the transition from the "formal to the real subsumption of labor"[86] where production itself is no longer driven by worker knowledge or worker control but by the alien, and seemingly autonomous, direction of capital. The real subsumption of labor is not only a social relation (wage–labor) but a sociotechnical transformation of the labor process where "machinery, etc. becomes the real master of living labour."[87] Fully controlling the forces of production, capital obtains a full monopoly on not only the "means of production" (the machines, the factory space, the inputs) but also the knowledge implemented in production. Thus through the automation of production the dead labor ecologies of machines, technologies, and knowledge confront living labor as an external oppressive force.[88] Only in this historical context is it logical even to speak of the "means of production" concentrated in the hands of capital, because for the first time the productive powers of society were not concentrated in human muscles.

While machinery allows for an often brutal domination of living labor in the production process, it also helps produce a wider cultural politics of capital, or the practices and meanings through which capitalist power is naturalized. The concrete political result of this is that the productive power of society—both in the material results of production and the scientific innovation that underpins it—appears as the product of capital. "[The] accumulation of knowledge and of skill, of the general productive forces of the social brain . . . appears as an attribute of capital."[89] The cultural politics of capital in large part depends on the idea that machines and technology are forces improved solely through the entrepreneurial forces of capital. With machinery reliant upon nonliving forms of energy, dead ecologies form a material basis for this cultural politics. Through the forces of fossil-fuel power, automatic machinery is posited as an external force separate from the vast majority of living workers. Thus only through dead ecology can dead labor *appear* as devoid of labor (as human muscles) and, thus, as purely capitalistic.

Yet very few forms of automatic large-scale machinery require no living labor whatsoever. Ironically, the dead labor of capital can only reproduce itself through living labor—"dead labor . . . vampire-like, lives only by sucking living labour, and lives the more, the more labour it sucks."[90] The demands for living labor from large-scale industrial production are subject to the extreme vicissitudes of accumulation and crisis: "Large-scale industry, by its very nature, necessitates variation of labour, fluidity of functions, and mobility of the worker in all directions."[91] Thus capital accumulation is ultimately dependent upon the *flexible and versatile* commodification of living labor power. Even if one brackets the controversies over whether or not living labor power is the source of all surplus value (and value), capital—materialized through dead labor and machinery—can only be brought to life through the "form-giving fire" of living workers.[92] I would argue that the bulk of Marx's aim in *Capital* is to particularize the commodification of labor power as a social relation adequate only to extremely specific historical-geographical circumstances and power relations. Indeed, in eras where human muscle power represented a major productive force of society (e.g., the American antebellum South, Egyptian civilization), slavery—the direct ownership of human beings—was the particular accumulation strategy of those seeking to consolidate domination over the means of production: land and labor.[93] The wage–labor relationship is historically novel because the human's "capacity for work" becomes commodified (not the human beings themselves). The social relations of capitalist production differ from earlier epochs in the sense that capital depends on a "versatile" labor force, capable of fluid movement from one sphere of production to another, while in earlier historical eras, it was control over human power itself that allowed for the reproduction of power relations. In order for capital to adapt to the conditions of market exchange and competition, which entail a relentless quest for labor-saving devices, it is imperative for capital to be free to modify, at will, the quantity invested in what Marx calls *variable* capital—or the value portion spent on labor power for production.

As Kenneth Pomeranz notes, "no matter how far back we may push for the origins of capitalism, *industrial* capitalism, in which the large-scale use of inanimate energy sources allowed an escape from the common constraints of the preindustrial world, emerges only in the 1800s."[94] Of course, wage labor predates industrialization, but the emergence of large-scale (fossil-based) production allowed for the *extension* of the wage–labor relationship on an expanded scale. Thus it is large-scale automatic machinery that hastens the ongoing transition from the formal to the real subsumption of labor to capital.[95] The role of fossil fuel in establishing what Marx calls the specifically capitalist mode of production allows us to understand what is not only historically but ecologically specific to capitalist social relations.

Through commodification, labor power becomes disposable to the requirements of the valorization of capital, and those requirements become more and more fickle. As production is more and more driven by nonhuman, nonliving forces of fossil-fueled machines, living humans become more and more disposable, interchangeable and, thus, exploitable. Capital's "autocratic power" is only reproduced through a class of workers "freed" from any means whatsoever of producing their own livelihood; workers who must sell their labor power to capital in exchange for a wage in order to survive. Thus the "primitive accumulation" of capital ultimately depends on the radical separation of a class of workers from the means of production and subsistence. The history of capitalism can be seen as a constant class struggle to reproduce the conditions of this radical separation of people from their own means of subsistence. Thus class struggle is not simply over workplace conditions—wages, safety regulations, and so on—but more broadly over the social reproduction of life itself outside the workplace, the geographies through which living workers obtain the socially mediated necessities of life. Indeed, it is historically specific to capitalism to construct such binaries between work and life and, more geographically, between work and home.[96]

The Forces of Capital II: Reproduction, Oil, and the Real Subsumption of Life

The waged and unwaged workers in capitalist society are both faced with a constant tension between production, or the realm of "work," and reproduction, or the realm considered "life." For the particular commodity of labor power, reproduction constitutes all the social practices necessary to bring the worker back to work on an everyday basis. It is a presupposition of the wage relation that the individual worker must take control of his or her own social reproduction through both commodified and uncommodified necessities of life. As Marx put it, "the capitalist may safely leave this to the worker's drive for self-preservation and propagation."[97] Part of the necessary means of life is obtained through wages and commodity relations, but many are not; feminist Marxists have long emphasized all the forms of productive, yet unpaid and uncommodified, *work* necessary for the reproduction of labor power, including cooking, cleaning, washing, traveling, shopping, and planning[98]. The realm of "life" takes a tremendous amount of work.

If the nineteenth century represents an industrial revolution of the productive forces of capitalist production, the twentieth century can be framed as an industrial revolution of the reproductive forces of everyday life for certain sectors of the industrial capitalist economies. Marx and Engels were famous for detailing the absolute deprivation and poverty of proletariat life under nineteenth-century capitalism.[99] After working in factories where their bodies were subjected to the despotism of capitalist machine production, workers returned to overcrowded housing characterized by unsanitary conditions, lack of adequate food and water, and exploitative landlords. In fact, the "immiseration" of proletariat life became a key aspect of Marx's critique of capital and a rallying cry of socialist (and other forms of) struggle throughout the nineteenth and early twentieth centuries. Propertyless and in a state of misery and deprivation, "the proletarians have nothing to lose but their chains. They have a world to win."[100]

In the face of the despotism of capitalist production and the obvious deprivation of proletariat life, bourgeois notions of freedom, property, and the enterprise of the marketplace obviously did not hold much popular resonance. Intensifying crises in the early twentieth century threw the economic and ideological survival of capitalist social relations into question. With its most perfect sociospatial expression found in the United States, the resurrection of capital in the twentieth century was achieved through a material and technical transformation of the geographies of everyday life and social reproduction for a specific stratum of workers. Given that capitalist production depends on the control over the labor process and access to a pool of workers who only survive through waged commodity relations, it is possible to restructure the conditions of reproduction—workers' actual lives outside the workplace—without fundamentally alerting those basic preconditions of capitalist production. First of all, this new way of life centered upon something Marx theorized the proletariat as without— property, or specifically a single-family home on a parcel of land. Second, it required the spatial decentralization of property into low-density suburban settlements characterized by an abundance of privatized spaces for privatized families.[101] Third, in order to traverse such vast spaces, it required more general access to the new privatized and commodified form of transport known as automobility.[102] As I detail in chapter 2, this particular spatiality of single-family homes, cars, yards, and highways came to be constructed as a specifically "American way of life." Although the suburban lifestyle was very popular among the bourgeois and upper classes throughout the nineteenth and early twentieth centuries,[103] it became a generalized social phenomenon among mainly middle- to upper-income white male workers and their families after World War II.[104] Of course, not everyone was included in this postwar reconfiguration of the geographies of social reproduction. Capital accumulation is not only reproduced through the uneven relations between labor and capital but also thrives on exclusionary distinctions based on race, gender, and notions of citizenship that divide (rather than unite) the working class between higher and lower strata. In the U.S. experience, the consumer society was a racialized and gendered society of white privilege and patriarchy. While this landscape of mass consumption is often cast as a functional response to the needs of "accumulation" and the lack of "effective demand,"[105] it was also a key response to a serious legitimation crisis of capitalist social relations in the 1930s. In response to the political outrages of proletariat life, this geography of reproduction—of life itself—was increasingly couched as a life of freedom, property, and enterprise in the context of a renewed and prosperous competitive market society. The realm of work, or production, was not included in this imaginary of freedom and property. Work remained only a means to an end—a means to produce a life for oneself expressed as a home, a car, and a family.

Following others,[106] I call this process the transition from the formal to real subsumption of life under capital. The subsumption of everyday life under capital is formalized through the wage relation and dependence on commodity relations but is only made "real" through a *material* transformation. While the subsumption of the labor process is materialized through the introduction of automatic machinery into factory production, the latter is also characterized by the increasing centrality of automatic machinery in everyday life. The internal combustion engine is the most salient and culturally powerful example. While in earlier industrial eras, workers walked to work or used public transit,[107] the automobile represented an individualized purchase—an apparent material expression of one's own work and earnings—that greatly extended the spaces of mobility between home and work and leisure places. Moreover, the home—increasingly a standalone single-family home in a suburban neighborhood—suddenly had to be equipped with a particular set of machines (e.g., washing machines, dishwashers) that automated reproductive labor.

Just like the real subsumption of the labor process is based on automatic machinery and access to nonliving fossil-fuel energy, the real subsumption of life to capital is actively powered not through muscles through but fossil-fuel combustion. In the following chapters, I only focus on petroleum as a constitutive energetic force underpinning this entire geography of social reproduction.[108] This energy must be understood in ecological terms: as highly concentrated dense fossil energy that is the product of millions of years of solar energy. Not only was petroleum more energy dense than coal—roughly 50 percent higher[109]—but it was much easier and cheaper to transport due to its liquidity and propensity to *flow* through networks of pipelines, refineries, and marketing outlets.[110] As I discuss in chapter 5, petroleum's propensity to flow cheaply allowed for a more generalized dispersal of petroleum products to the point where its properties were increasingly harnessed in private, individuated forms. Most notable among a whole host of petroleum products (see chapter 3), gasoline became harnessed to produce a specifically *privatized* mode of spatial mobility. It becomes the central fuel propelling the dispersal of individual atomized subjects throughout the sprawling sites of social reproduction between home, work, school, and shopping center. Moreover, besides the gasoline-fired automobile, the electrified home is linked to a vast electricity grid that is also overwhelmingly powered through access to fossil fuel, although nuclear and hydropower are also major components of the electricity mix.[111]

Just as in production, the cultural politics of capital also shifts in the transition from the formal to the real subsumption of life. In the realm of production, machines and technologies appear, in themselves, as the singular product of capitalist innovation externalized from living labor. Within the realm of reproduction, real subsumption is achieved when *living labor appears as capital itself.* In other words, one's own life—expressed through a home, a car, and a family—is seen as an individualized product of hard work, investment, competitive tenacity, and entrepreneurial "life choices." Although the machines of reproduction are clearly not powered by the individual, the individual believes it is his or her own work and earnings that set these machines into motion. The glow of a flat screen television and the acceleration of the automobile are the products of work and the expression of life.

Neoliberalism and the Cultural Politics of Entrepreneurial Life

This particular cultural politics of capital can be understood in the specific historical–geographical context of the politics of American capitalism. I will argue throughout this book that the real subsumption of life itself is key to understanding the recent political hegemony of neoliberalism in the late twentieth and early twenty-first centuries. As postwar accumulation was materialized through the construction of vast sprawling suburban housing tracts, liberal Keynesian ideas of government intervention and the social safety net were slowly transformed into more and more privatist forms of politics, or what McKenzie calls an "ideology of hostile privatism."[112] As stated in the introduction,[113] the political victories of the right in the United States—and with it the neoliberalization of American capitalism—depended on the mobilization of a petite bourgeois strata of mostly white suburban homeowners increasingly distrustful of government handouts, high taxes, and the redistribution of wealth. This disdain for the public sector is rooted in what Thomas Edsall and Mary Edsall call "conservative egalitarianism," which posits that everyone has an equal opportunity to work hard and succeed in life and, moreover, that life success is itself purely a product of entrepreneurial life choices.[114] Thus from this perspective, government programs were seen as "unfair" handouts to individuals who simply had not worked hard enough.

The Gramscian perspective on hegemony mapped out previously—grounded in lived practice—is quite useful for understanding suburban homeowners as a specific "historical bloc" essential to political victories of neoliberalism in the United States, securing popular consent to neoliberal logics and common sense. Yet such a broad hegemonic perspective is less useful for understanding the complex micropolitics of neoliberal subjectivity. As many others have realized, Gramsci's understandings of hegemony can be usefully combined with Foucault's writings to understand the specific embodied practices through which individual subjects actively perform and thereby produce wider social and hegemonic projects.[115]

The real subsumption of life and the cultural politics of life as capital are enriched through a reading of Michel Foucault's 1978–79 lectures on neoliberalism recently translated into English as *The Birth of Biopolitics*.[116] These lectures, given during the infancy of neoliberal hegemony, hold tremendous insight into the micropolitics of neoliberal subjectivity. According to Foucault, what distinguishes neoliberalism from classical liberalism is the former's concentration on mechanisms of competition and the latter's focus on market exchange. Constituting the *neo* of *neoliberalism,* a society regulated through competition requires the generalization of the enterprise form: "I think the multiplication of the enterprise form within the social body is what is at stake in neoliberal policy."[117] According to Foucault's account of German strands of neoliberal thought in the postwar period—or "ordoliberalism"—the materialization of this enterprise form is assured through private property: "First, to enable as far as possible everyone to have access to private property."[118] Putting *property* at the center of social reproduction is central to the multiplication of entrepreneurial subjectivities. "What is private property if not an enterprise? What is the house if not an enterprise?"[119] Indeed, the private homeowners run their houses like businesses. So-called responsible homeowners are supposed to construct a family budget tracking spending against revenue, make investments with savings and pensions, and maintain a healthy long-term relation with credit markets. In this context, "the individual's life itself—with his [*sic*] relationships to his private property, for example, with his family, his household, insurance, and retirement—must make him into a sort of permanent and multiple enterprise."[120]

In opposition to more common critiques of neoliberalism focused on consumer choice and the realm of exchange,[121] Foucault's critical insight is his focus on neoliberal subjects as *producers* of their own lives: "The stake in all neoliberal analyses is the replacement every time of *homo economicus* as partner of exchange with a *homo economicus* as entrepreneur of himself [*sic*], being for himself his own capital, being for himself his own producer, being for himself the source of his own earnings."[122]

Thus the construction of a propertied mass of homeowners—an ownership society, as George W. Bush called it[123]—creates a situation where your *very life* is seen as a product of your entrepreneurial choices. Your entrepreneurial capacities all combine to make a life—to *make* a living—for yourself. As is becoming more and more common, and as seen in Figure 2, this logic is expressed as "You are the C.E.O. of your life."[124] In this particular imagery, "life" is not only expressed through the pillars of social reproduction—the mother and child—but is actively managed through a series of "investments," such as the mutual funds offered in this particular advertisement. The overall product of a "successful" life is expressed through the material requisites of oil-based privatism—a home, a car, a family.

Again, this cultural politics of life differs markedly from Marx's—and most orthodox Marxist—vision of *proletariat* life. For Marx, the

FIGURE 2. "YOU ARE THE C.E.O. OF YOUR LIFE. . . . THINK ABOUT IT. YOUR LIFE IS A BUSINESS. IT MAKES SENSE THAT YOU'RE THE ONE IN CHARGE." Discover's campaign circulated during the 1990s, a decade of intoxicating financial triumphalism. Its stereotypical imagery of social reproduction (mother and child) is critical to the politics of life against work.

proletariat was defined by his or her propertylessness. The question for a propertyless proletariat is, "How will I live?" The answer was of course to desperately sell one's labor power in exchange for a wage that usually provided the bare minimum of subsistence (and often not because of the very disposability of wage labor). On the other hand, the question for the propertied mass of workers in the United States is not "How will I live?" but "What will I make of my life?" Of course, this question is undergirded by the very idea of making something of oneself that assumes that one's life itself is purely a product of atomized choices and individualized efforts. It is only in particular historical circumstances that such a question takes on such popular significance.

Perry Anderson suggested that the key to "consent" under capitalism is the "fundamental form of belief by the masses that *they exercise an ultimate self-determination within the existing social order.*"[125] The logic of neoliberal hegemony—and its material and cultural basis in a propertied mass of suburban white male middle- to upper-income homeowners—is more understandable (although no less defensible) through the lens of this cultural politics of entrepreneurial life. Again, government welfare was seen as skewing the competitive landscape and unjustly rewarding uncompetitive bodies that were marked for not making the right choices "in life." Worse still, government was itself seen as a public taking of private, hard-earned money (taxes) that was, again, the product of one's own individual entrepreneurial capacities. The language of entrepreneurial life also found considerable parlance within the often religious language of "family values" and the centering of life around the home and family as a privileged site for cultural cultivation and refinement against a hostile and degraded external culture. Contrary to some arguments,[126] family values centered on the home are not uneconomic or purely "cultural" values but are absolutely fused with economic concerns with one's own entrepreneurial capacities to make a living, keep a job, pay bills, act responsibly, and so on.

While this entrepreneurial subjectivity employs neoliberal ideas of "freedom" and "choice" in the realm of social reproduction, the realm of production remains under the despotic control of capital. Thus the key to neoliberal hegemony is the quarantining of politics and agency, in the realm of "life"—home, family, and consumption. This does not challenge the first precondition of capitalism—the autocratic control of capital over the productive process engineered and mobilized with only one goal in mind, the self-expansion of value "accumulation for the sake of accumulation; production for the sake of production."[127] As the other precondition of capital is the radical separation of living labor from its own means of subsistence, the real subsumption of life under capital only deepens to workers' entanglement in commodity relations as a basis for survival. As Michel Aglietta points out, postwar American capitalism is characterized by "the *domination of commodity relations over noncommodity relations.*"[128] Indeed, the extension of home and automobile ownership also extends the mass of living labor into the circuits of credit, debt, and financial markets. The cultural politics of entrepreneurial life is only made common sense through access to credit and the accumulation of debt, where one's own working life is forever entangled in a constant process of paying down debt. Such a life conforms to the logic of what Foucault calls "a grid of economic intelligibility"[129] but what more concretely can be described as the abstract relations of money, interest, commodities, and value.

This particular cultural politics of entrepreneurial life is not possible—is not made common sense—without the *material transformation* of the everyday life centered upon reproductive geographies of single-family home ownership, automobility, and voracious energy consumption. The dense, versatile fuel of petroleum fuels a particular lived geography—a "structure of feeling"[130]—that allows for an appearance of atomized command over the spaces of mobility, home, and even the body itself. With all the "work" (or energy) accomplished through the combustion of taken for granted hydrocarbons, individuals could more and more imagine themselves as masters of their own lives severed from ties to society and public forms of collective life. Once oil became more and more entrenched within the reproductive forces of everyday life, those *forces* informed a politics of "hostile privatism" where individual homeowners imagined themselves as autonomous, hardworking subjects whose very freedom was threatened by the ever-extending tentacles of "Big Government."

While a Gramscian perspective usually posits "a dual perspective . . . reduced to two fundamental levels . . . the levels of force and consent," petroleum can be seen as a constitutive element of the *forces* of consent.[131] From Foucault's perspective, the privatized geographies produced through oil consumption undergird a particular form of biopolitics that segments each individual body—each individual life—as a product of entrepreneurial efforts. Figures 3 and 4 more explicitly connect gasoline-powered automobility with a kind of atomized, entrepreneurial command over one's own life. Figure 3 presents the character of the "everyday conqueror" who is "comfortably in command." Armed with an SUV and plenty of fuel, he takes firm control over his schedule, which includes all the demands of life and work under capitalist social relations. This ad

FIGURE 3. "THE EVERYDAY CONQUEROR . . . COMFORTABLY IN COMMAND."
GMC's ad campaign, which also included a female version, epitomized the mid-1990s celebration of the SUV as *the* answer to the frantic lifestyles of social reproduction under neoliberalism.

Work hard all your life and where does it get you? Park Avenue.

It rewards you with increased power from its new 205-horsepower 3800 Series II V6 engine. Dual air bags. Available heated front seats and dual ComforTemp climate control. Plus the security of anti-lock brakes and available traction control. You've worked hard to get where you are. Park Avenue will work beautifully to get you where you're going. To learn more, call 1-800-4A-BUICK.

BUICK
The New Symbol For Quality In America.

FIGURE 4. "WORK HARD ALL YOUR LIFE AND WHERE DOES IT GET YOU?" A single question in a mid-1990s Buick ad campaign draws together the relations between power, space, and automobility in ideas of "entrepreneurial life."

underscores the ways in which everyday command over space both mimics and sanctions wider global geographies of imperial command over petroleum reserves. Figure 4 presents the entrepreneurial logic of hard work and a just reward—specifically a luxurious mode of automobility. This particular car offers a reward of a variety of techniques for optimized control, comfort, and above all *power*—a V6 engine that promises the *muscle* equivalent to two hundred fifty horses reminding us of the energetic constraints of preindustrial transportation. It is gasoline that forms a material basis for this form of power to appear (and only appear) as the purely the autonomous product of individual effort.

Conclusion

Through the lens of fetishism, oil is envisioned as a vital and strategic "thing" through which imperial relations are solidified (petro)states are formed, and local livelihoods are violently destabilized. Thus the site of extraction becomes the territorial center through which conflicting social forces congregate and struggle over the oil "prize" unfolds. Oil is not a thing-in-itself. Contrary to fetishistic discourses of "oil states," "oil wars," and "oil addictions," a dialectical approach must seek to understand oil as a socioecological relation. I have proposed a much broader historical–geographical materialist perspective that situates oil in particular, and energy more broadly, within the "production and reproduction of life." Thus political resistance to the geopolitical games of imperial control over oil reserves must cast their critical sights toward not only the U.S. military state but also the geographies of social reproduction that situate oil as a necessary element of "life." The cries of "no blood for oil" assume oil is a trivial "thing," but a more effective antipetroleum politics must struggle against the more banal forms through which oil-based life gets naturalized as common sense.

Yet it is not oil that caused the proliferation of entrepreneurial subjectivities. It is much more critical to understand the wider social struggles over "life" itself that created the social conditions for particular patterns of living to become generalized. Specific regimes of energy consumption are better understood as products of these struggles. Energy is not simply a single policy issue that is contained through particular struggles over oil imports, electric efficiency, or methods of oil extraction. It is not simply a technical problem or a problem of market failures. Regimes of energy consumption are the product of struggles over the production and reproduction of life itself. Often, struggles that are named as struggles over labor, housing, mobility, and culture, are simultaneously struggles over how energy is put to use. Thus the forms of life organized under capitalist social relations must be the objects of political concern in efforts to reform energy–society relations. In the United States, the last time the sociospatial organization of life—and energy consumption—was profoundly reorganized was during the 1930s.

CHAPTER TWO

Refueling Capitalism

Depression, Oil, and the Making
of "the American Way of Life"

In 1922, the chief executive of General Motors Alfred Sloan created a front company called National City Lines. In the recessionary early 1920s, Sloan feared the consumer market for automobiles was saturated and wanted to promote the transformation of urban public transit systems away from electric streetcars to diesel-fired internal combustion buses. In the mid-1930s, National City Lines was transformed into a holding company that included various corporate pillars of what might be called the auto–petroleum industrial complex—Firestone Tires, Phillips Petroleum, and Standard Oil of California.[1] Between the mid-1930s and late 1940s, National City Lines bought out the supply contracts for dozens of urban public transit systems throughout the United States, including those in Los Angeles, St. Louis, Detroit, and Phoenix. The conglomerate swiftly destroyed the infrastructure of those systems, ripping up rail lines, disposing of streetcars into dumps, and in the case of Los Angeles, dumping some of the cars into the Santa Monica Bay.[2] They replaced the streetcars with General Motors manufactured buses that relied on products sold by the other companies. In 1949, those companies were convicted in federal court of violating antitrust laws by forcing American cities to purchase buses. But the damage had been done. By 1949, suburbanization was in full swing, automobility was taking hold, and the possibility of mass electric-powered transit systems in the United States was slowly fading away.

What has been variously referred to as the "General Motors conspiracy" or the "Great Streetcar scandal" stands in as the stock historical explanation for "oil addiction" in the United States. For those on the left, it is a compelling story of corporate greed and manipulation of an unsuspecting consumer public. While not contesting this story, it is nevertheless incomplete; it is too simple, too easy. As critics of the General Motors conspiracy theory like point out, public transit ridership in the United States peaked in 1923 well before National City Lines's destruction of public transit systems.[3] Automobility, and the consumption of oil to fuel it, is much more social than a corporate plot. The social capacity to consume the mass quantities of oil cannot be explained within the confines of a single industry or set of industries manipulating the market. The mass consumption of oil only emerges out of a wider social context through which massive amounts of workers can actually afford single-family homes, automobiles, and the multitude of other petroleum-derived products that saturate everyday life. In other words, we need to see the mass consumption of oil as emerging not only out of narrow elite conspiracies but out of a wider cultural politics of, literally, the meaning of "life," how life should be lived, and what constitutes "the good life." Figure 5, an ad campaign from 1917, reveals that this wider cultural politics of the good life in the United States was well under way before Mr. Sloan concocted his great conspiracy.

FIGURE 5. "THIS IS THE LIFE. . . . THIS IS NOT."
From the beginning of the automobile age, car companies attempted to contrast the privatism of cars as superior to the crowdedness and unreliability of public transportation. This ad appeared in *Ladies Home Journal* in 1917.

Struggles over the production and reproduction of life under capitalist social relations constitute what Marx referred to as the "value of labor power." The "value of labor power" contains "a historical and moral element" situated around cultural "habits and expectations with which the class of free workers has been formed."[4] The value of labor power does not simply tend toward subsistence wages but rather is constituted through social struggles over historically and geographically specific notions of a "standard of living" (and the wages that would provide such a standard). In this chapter, I argue that the Great Depression and the New Deal response of the 1930s constituted a massive reconfiguration of the value of labor power—and the cultural politics of life. This reconfiguration was itself produced out of social struggles between labor, capital, and the state over wages, housing, living conditions, and public provision of services and basic infrastructure. Out of these struggles emerged a particular vision of a specifically "American way of life" of freedom and prosperity only materialized through massive levels of home and automobile ownership.

I want to examine the New Deal project to refashion "the American way of life" as not only a social, cultural, and economic project but a material and ecological one as well. Indeed, the materialist conception of history laid out in chapter 1 demands that any notion of a particular "standard of living" connotes often invisible relations with material commodities, natural resources, energies, and wastes. The politics and struggles that produced the New Deal ushered in a dramatic material transformation of the "standard" of life and living for millions of workers in the United States. If not always explicitly, this transformation centered on the mass consumption of cheap energy. Indeed, Roosevelt himself recognized and promoted the provision of cheap energy as central to what he often referred to as "the abundant life." His views on electricity at the time are suggestive of his larger perspective on energy: "We are going to see . . . electricity made so cheap that [it] will become a standard article of use, not only for agriculture and manufacturing but also for every home within reach of an electric light line . . . the experience of those sections of the world that have cheap power proves that the cheaper the power the more of it is used."[5]

The idea that using more power might have wider socioecological consequences simply was not considered in this modernist "machine age" characterized by the celebration of technology seen in projects like the Hoover Dam and the Tennessee Valley Authority. Therefore, although the New Deal is often heralded as a transformative period in terms of social policy (labor rights, housing, social security, etc.), it was also a transformative period of energy policy. As one commentator at the time put it, FDR's project was to "adapt capitalism and democratic liberalism to a new social order made inevitable by the dissemination of cheap, liquid energy collectively applied."[6] By creating the institutional and material conditions for a particular "way of life," ways of consuming energy became locked into entrenched geographies of social development that we still live with today.

Yet "cheap energy" was not simply waiting to be consumed by masses of worker–consumers. The other goal of this chapter is to illustrate how broader struggles over the production of "a way of life" in the 1930s were contingent on concomitant struggles with the materiality of petroleum itself. Just as mass unemployment illustrated a dramatic breakdown in labor markets on a national scale, collapse also lurked for the oil industry. While we often think of oil crises in terms of scarcity, the problem of the 1930s (and indeed even parts of the 1980s and 1990s) was *the abundance of oil* on the market—that is, overproduction, glut, and prices falling below the standards needed for profitable accumulation in the oil sector.[7] This overproduction had a lot to do with the tensions between the subterranean geologies of petroleum and the capitalist system of private property rights that chaotically attempted to delimit access to it. The politics of oil overproduction paralleled the wider politics of the Depression era in that it called into question the viability of the capitalist mode of commodity production for profit. Yet these struggles over oil production can only be understood in the context of the wider New Deal efforts to provide the basis for a new "way of life" underwritten by oil consumption. It is this broader story to which I turn now.

Fordism and Industrial Despotism

In chapter 1, I discussed the constitutive role of nonliving energy in the capitalist use of machinery in the domination of living labor power. Automatic machinery in the hands of capital powered not by living muscles but through dead ecologies allows for a despotic control over the labor process wherein the worker can only act as a mere "appendage of the machine."[8] In the context of the United States, this form of industrial despotism reached its pinnacle in the first three decades of the twentieth century. Encapsulating what some call the "second industrial revolution," this period witnessed a transition away from the heavy machinery of the early nineteenth century (e.g., steam engines powered by coal) toward compact electric motors and assembly line production.[9] The key to this transition was the widespread availability of electricity for industrial production at the end of the nineteenth century. Smil reports that between 1899 and 1929 the capacities of industrial electric motors skyrocketed from 5 percent to 80 percent of all installed mechanical power: "Highly efficient electric motors—combined with precise, flexible, and individual power control in a better working environment—brought much higher labor productivities."[10]

Thus, if the coal-fired steam engine represented the first shift in the dominating of living labor by automatic machines, electrified industrialism perfected this form of domination, making it much more efficient and productive. Typified by the assembly line of Henry Ford's automobile factories, this mode of industrial production began to be referred to as "Fordism." Writing from an Italian prison in the early 1930s, Antonio Gramsci recognized the rationalization of the labor process under Fordism required a new form of "psycho-physical adaptation to the new industrial structure . . . developing in the worker the highest degree of automatic and mechanical attitudes, breaking up the old psycho-physical nexus of qualified professional work, which demands a certain active participation of intelligence, fantasy, and initiative on the part of the worker."[11]

These views on the scientific management of labor were popularized by Frederick Taylor, who famously claimed "it would be possible to train an intelligent gorilla" to do the type of work methods expected of the new industrial despotism.[12] Taylor believed that scientific production required depriving workers of control over the pace and motion of their work, which is better determined "in accordance with the laws of science."[13] While using stopwatches and experimental methods to determine the precise speed and motions of work necessary for maximum productivity was relatively easy, the real challenge for scientific management was to produce "a complete change in the mental attitude of the working men."[14] Thus adapting to the demands of mechanized production required not only new work methods but new subjectivities.

From a political perspective, what Gramsci recognized was that the project to create "a new type of worker and . . . man" in the United States concentrated as much if not more on controlling worker bodies outside the workplace in the realm of social reproduction.[15] He discusses the contrived attempts by capitalists to morally police worker's sexual habits, alcohol consumption, and wage expenditures. Although Gramsci wouldn't live to see it fully,[16] he understood that this project could not be achieved by the policing of individual capitalists. It required a much broader social project to create "a specific mode of living and of thinking and feeling life" that would represent "a new culture" and a "new way of life" along the lines of an "Americanized system of living."[17] In the United States, it took the calamity of the Great Depression to provide the conjunctural political conditions for such a project to be undertaken. What Gramsci didn't emphasize, but what Roosevelt and the New Dealers clearly recognized, was creating a "new way of life" was not just about producing new ideologies or subjectivities; it was more importantly about a *material* transformation in the basic infrastructures of everyday existence.

Bare Life in the Great Depression[18]

The Great Depression in the United States produced conditions where the reproduction of life under capitalism was thrown into question. Millions of workers who lived only so far as they found employment were unable to toil for capital even if they so desired. From the Hooverville slum dwellers to the dust-bowl strewn migrants, huge numbers of living bodies experienced massive displacement through unemployment, eviction, and foreclosures. A New Deal worker surveying the mood among the unemployed reported widespread "fear . . . cracking nerves; and an overpowering terror of the future."[19] In 1937, Franklin Delano Roosevelt (FDR) famously stated, "I see one-third of a nation ill-housed, ill-clad, ill-nourished."[20] The image of the bread line underscored desperation for the basics of food and subsistence. One doctor in Chicago reported, "People starved on the street and on streetcars. . . . Every day, somebody would faint on a streetcar. . . . People were flopping on the streets from hunger."[21] In a societal context where mobility and the frontier were central, the Depression evoked a landscape of hopeless transiency, of forced mobility with no certain destination. Housing was often precarious and temporary, as one man recounted to Studs Terkel: "Here were all these people living in old rusted-out car bodies. I mean that was their home. . . . People living in whatever they could junk together."[22] While the hardest hit were the unskilled wage workers and agricultural workers, the Depression had a dramatic impact on the middle class, instilling a "fear of falling" into conditions of poverty and despair that were all around evident.[23]

While the statistics do a kind of epistemic violence to the real conditions of human suffering, they bear repeating. Between 1929 and 1933, gross domestic product plunged 46 percent; industrial production, 33 percent; and national income, 42 percent.[24] Of course, the most widely cited statistic is that of fifteen million unemployed in 1933: 25 percent of the working population as a whole but 37 percent of nonfarm workers.[25] As much as these figures indicated economic breakdowns of monetary

systems and labor markets, the crisis also represented an ideological chal-
lenge to the legitimacy of capitalism itself. Senator Robert Wagner (New
York)—famous for championing landmark labor legislation—remarked,
"We are in a life and death struggle with the forces of social and economic
dissolution."[26] Many left-leaning writers and artists excitedly believed
"they were witnessing the imminent demise of capitalism."[27] In 1934, a
New York Times editorial summed up the mood with the title "Capitalism
Is Doomed, Dying or Dead."[28] In New York City in the same year 3,000
people attended a debate "on whether communism or fascism is preferable in the United States as the new social order to supplant capitalism."[29]

Thus the New Deal was not only a project for economic recovery
but also a wider cultural political project to restore faith in capitalism.
The political terrain of this new faith in capitalism centered upon the
category of "life." In his 1932 campaign, Roosevelt claimed that "every
man has a right to life; and this means that he has also a right to make
a comfortable living."[30] By the mid-1930s, with the specters of fascism
and communism lurking, politics began to center on a notion of a specifically "American way of life." Although the notion of "the American
way" proliferated beforehand, the 1930s saw the first widespread use
of the postfix "way of life" evoking a particular set of lived practices
and conceptions of freedom.[31] In FDR's fiery antibusiness 1936 nomi-
nation speech, he spoke of a project "to restore to the people a wider
freedom . . . an American way of life." He explained that a cadre of
"economic royalists" had created a form of "despotism" and "industrial
dictatorship" that went against any concept of a life of freedom. "Liberty requires opportunity to make a living . . . a living which gives a man
not only enough to live by, but something to live for . . . For too many of
us life was no longer free; liberty no longer real."[32] The New Deal was
a dramatic effort to create the material conditions for the emergence of
a specifically "American way of life" that could be held up against the
examples of communism and fascism.

The Great Depression did indeed illustrate the profound emptiness of
capitalist slogans of freedom and property in the face of industrial despotism and material deprivation. What changed with the crisis of the 1930s
was an idea that it was not only up to individuals and philanthropic corporate paternalists to provide a decent living for workers; it was also up
to the state.[33] It was not only the enlightened "brain trust" of the New
Deal that realized this but concrete labor struggles that forced the state to
take responsibility for issues such as union rights and social welfare. Out
of these struggles emerged three key material foundations to such a life:
wages, housing, and infrastructure. Without this material foundation, the

massive levels of oil consumption that emerged in the postwar period and, indeed, still afflict us today would not have been possible.

Waging Freedom

Well before the Great Depression many capitalists realized that it might be necessary to pay their workers higher wages not only to provide demand for their products but, perhaps more important, to *retain* a work force that would be more willing to subject itself to harsh factory work. The most celebrated of these capitalists is, of course, Henry Ford, who in 1914 attracted a mass of workers by offering five dollars for an eight-hour workday. Ford was forced into this concession: "So great was labor's distaste for the new machine system that toward the close of 1913 every time the company wanted to add 100 men to its factory personnel, it was necessary to hire 963."[34] Ford later called the measure "one of the finest cost-cutting moves we ever made."[35] But Ford was not alone. Especially during the 1920s, several corporations instituted paternalistic programs to improve workers' lives, including wage increases, benefit plans, and educational programs.[36]

Could capital be trusted to improve the life of the worker? As Marx put it, "capital . . . takes no account of the health and the length of life of the worker, unless society forces it to do so."[37] Through systematic wage cuts (even by Ford!) and massive unemployment, the Depression underscored that the well-being of workers could not be left to the benevolent paternalism of capital. Just after his inauguration in 1933, FDR bowed to the pressure of labor unrest by inserting some prolabor provisions (section 7a) into the National Industrial Recovery Act (NIRA) of 1933 promising workers the right to join unions and bargain collectively with employers. Yet shortly thereafter, it appeared as if these provisions were not being enforced as capital either set up faux "company unions" or refused compliance on the basis of a widespread belief that the measures were unconstitutional. The response from workers was dramatic. As labor historian Irving Bernstein put it, "in 1934 labor erupted. There were 1856 work stoppages involving 1,470,000 workers, by far the highest count . . . in many years."[38] In Toledo, where unemployment was at an amazing 80 percent,[39] autoworkers organized a strike of auto parts factories that were vital in the overall supply chain of the greater auto manufacturing belt in the upper Midwest. In Minneapolis, the teamsters' union brought "all trucking inside the city to a standstill."[40] In San Francisco, longshoremen revolted against low wages and abysmal working conditions in the ports and organized a four-day general strike with the teamsters and other small businesses that literally shut down the city. Another factor strengthening the power of the striking workers was the movement of the "unemployed councils" demanding social assistance ("relief") in the face of the destitute conditions of life wrought by the Depression.[41]

All these actions were met with bloody state violence and deadly sacrifices by workers, but the strikes strengthened a general sense among New Dealers that some major labor reforms were needed. On March 1, 1934, Senator Robert Wagner had already introduced a bill to more effectively deploy the power of the federal government in the form of a National Labor Relations Board that would arbitrate conflicts between employers and workers. The tumultuous labor struggles of the summer of 1934 convinced many others that this legislation was a necessary corrective to the NIRA.[42] By May 1935, FDR finally voiced support for the labor legislation just before the NIRA was deemed unconstitutional by the Supreme Court. In the vacuum, the Wagner Act was passed by both houses of Congress and signed into law by FDR on July 3, 1935. Calling it an act of "common justice," FDR couched the legislation in decidedly market-friendly terms: "By assuring the employees the right of collective bargaining it fosters the development of the employment contract on a sound and equitable basis . . . it seeks, for every worker within its scope, the freedom of choice and action which is justly his."[43] Yet, in the wake of the NIRA decision, once again capital assumed the law to be unconstitutional. It took two more years of labor strife, including the 1936–37 epic sit-down strike of auto workers in Flint, Michigan, before the legislation was declared constitutional by the Supreme Court on April 12, 1937.[44]

At this point, with fascism intensifying in Europe, the significance of the labor legislation took on a wider scope. After the Supreme Court decision, Wagner flatly claimed the legislation a victory for democracy and what he specifically called "the American way of life." Order in industrial life could only be brought about through two paths—authoritarian rule or "creating a partnership between labor and industry. . . . Fascism begins in industry, not in government . . . but let men know that they are free in their daily lives, and they will never bow to tyranny in any quarter of their national life."[45] The key to the Wagner Act was the mobilization of the power of the state to actually enforce the rights of labor to collectively bargain, organize, and not be fired for joining a union. By 1945, the National Labor Relations Board had already handled 74,000 cases involving unfair labor practices and 24,000 elections of union leaders.[46] As Piven and Cloward put it, "it was the Wagner Act and federal support of unionization that was most important in shaping the workers' political future."[47] Indeed, as it turned out, this state power was probably socially necessary to prevent the kind of labor strife, strikes, and work stoppages so vexing to the pace of the capitalist machine lines and their profits: "The old system of paternalism had broken down and . . . something was needed to take its place if production and profits were to be maximized."[48] The use of state power to back unions actually did much to bring industrial peace, or what many have called the "great compromise" between capital and labor.[49]

As regulationist Michel Aglietta emphasizes, the key to this labor legislation was providing labor with the capacity to collectively bargain for wages conducive to the development of a "social consumption norm."[50] The Wagner Act represents the institutional basis for mass consumption levels aligned with the productivity of the mass production "machine age." The Depression created a political consensus that capital would not allow this on its own. The Wagner Act was justified in exactly these terms, as a number of labor, consumer, and social policy thinkers had identified the lack of consumer "purchasing power" as the root cause of the Depression.[51] FDR claimed, "During the process of over-speculation and overproduction—in the twenties—millions of people had been put to work but the products of their hands had exceeded the purchasing power of their pocketbooks."[52] Wagner argued that "a failure to maintain a balance between wages and industrial returns will be attended by the same fatal consequences of the past."[53] Thus, insofar as under capitalist social relations life is only mediated by the wage relation and the commodified means of subsistence, the Wagner Act attempted to construct the social basis for an "American way of life" based on higher wages and increased purchasing power for a specific stratum of workers. Within this specific construction of "life," consumption outside the workplace (i.e., social reproduction) began to take on increased social, cultural, and indeed ecological significance as the critical medium through which "freedom" in daily life was imagined and performed. Thus producing the institutional conditions for high wages is a critical aspect of the material transformation of everyday life, or what I called in chapter 1 the real subsumption of life under capital.

Of course, the Wagner Act was legislation for the white, middle-class, male breadwinning worker. Perhaps because of Roosevelt and the Democratic Party's tenuous coalition with racist Southern Democrats, Wagner completely ignored the National Association for the Advancement of Colored People and other civil rights groups concerns over long-standing forms of racial exclusion within the U.S. labor movement.[54] Moreover, agricultural workers—perhaps the most devastated social group of the Depression—were excluded entirely from the labor law, "simply because of the power of the farm bloc in Congress."[55] In the wake of labor's victories, Mike Davis estimated that while the postwar economy raised perhaps one-quarter of the American population (mainly white, semiskilled workers) to "middle class" levels of home and auto ownership in the 1950s, "another quarter to one-third of the population . . . including most Blacks and all agricultural laborers, remained outside the boom, constituting the 'other America' which rebelled in the 1960s."[56] Thus, from the outset, the construction of "the American way of life" was based on a certain set of exclusions that tangled up the categories of race, class, and gender. The stark hypocrisy of a law purporting to enact "common justice" is revealed in Margaret Bourke-White's iconic photo of African Americans lining up for food assistance after a devastating flood in Louisville in 1937 in the shadow of the wholesome white family living "the American way" based on mobility (see Figure 6).

FIGURE 6. "WORLD'S HIGHEST STANDARD OF LIVING: THERE'S NO WAY LIKE THE AMERICAN WAY."
The construction of the "American way of life" during the 1930s was premised on exclusion. Photograph *Louisville Flood Victims* by Margaret Bourke-White, The Masters Collection, Time and Life Pictures/Getty Images.

A Nation of Homeowners

The value of labor power is constituted through a historically specific cultural politics of life—and the wages needed to make such a life possible. But the cultural and politics stuff go well beyond the abstract medium of money wages. Life is imagined through a bundle of commodities, or use values, that are constructed as necessary to a particular standard of living. During the 1930s and into the postwar period, perhaps no use value was more important to the construction of the "American way of life" than the home—specifically, a private, detached, single-family house in a suburban location.

According to John Archer, during the nineteenth century the bourgeois ideal of the "detached single-family home . . . became recognized as instrumental to the moral and political welfare of the nation."[57] Of course, this ideal was only financially available for small numbers of elites and only geographically available to those situated near the streetcars linking suburbs to cities.[58] As alternatives to capitalism emerged in the interwar period, many believed that the key to salvaging capitalism was to give the propertyless proletariat access to property. In the 1950s, William Levitt famously stated that "no man who owns his own house and lot can be a communist . . . he has too much to do."[59] Yet it was during the 1920s, in the wake of the communist revolution in Russia, that political leaders began to position home ownership as the bedrock of a society based on free enterprise and competition. Herbert Hoover warned of the "unrest that inevitably results from inhibition of the primal instinct in us all for home ownership."[60] He argued that "maintaining a high percentage of individual home owners" creates a social mass of people who "have an interest in the advancement of a social system that permits the individual to store the fruits of their labor."[61] Calvin Coolidge called for a national ambition to create "a nation of homeowners." By generalizing property ownership to the masses, home ownership would engender "a feeling of proprietorship and ownership" able to satisfy "the longing which exists in every human breast to say, 'This is mine.'"[62] A wider movement to promote home ownership, "Better Homes for America," had the slogan "As is the home, so is the community and the nation."[63]

Elite sensibilities that mass home ownership was the key to social and economic stability did not ensure such a society was possible in the social context of 1920s capitalism. As the previous section indicates, such a society requires a sufficient purchasing power from workers with wages high enough to afford homes and mortgage payments. Even more important, however, was producing the financial conditions through which banks and other credit institutions would be comfortable giving out long-term mortgages to middle-income workers. It took the crisis of the Great Depression and the balance of social forces wrapped up in New Deal reform to produce the institutional conditions for the mass availability of home mortgages.

Prior to the 1930s, those who wanted to purchase a home were forced to pay risk-averse banks 50 percent of the value of the home, or take out a second mortgage at high interest rates of 20 percent or more that had to be paid in five years or less.[64] Shortly after his inauguration Roosevelt announced mortgage legislation as "the declaration of a national policy. . . . [T]he broad interests of the nation require that special safeguards should be thrown around home ownership as a guarantee of social and economic stability."[65] What New Deal programs like the Federal Housing Administration (FHA) and Home Owners Loan Corporation did was to provide banks with a pool of state-backed capital and insurance to create mortgages that lasted thirty years at interest rates no higher than 5 percent. The extension of credit into the housing market was modeled after its success in other consumer durable industries in the 1920s, most notably the automobile market. The "American dream" of a house and car was made possible through credit.

Although Frederick Jackson Turner claimed the American frontier was closed at the close of the nineteenth century, the frontier mythology of the self-reliant individual landowner persists today. If the real subsumption of life under capital is a material transformation, the home—or individual landed property—represents the *anchor* of that material transformation. The New Deal, and later the GI "homes for vets" bill, inaugurated a second frontier expansion of American history marked by the movement of white, middle-class families outward from densely populated cities into the suburbs. The ideal of an atomized slice of property materialized as the detached, single-family home in the suburbs represented the ideological foundation of this wider social project. Informing much of this ideology was, of course, the political vision of the dense, urban city as a site of filth, vice, and social decay.[66] Roosevelt suggested that the automobile made it "possible for those of us who live in cities to get out into the country, whole families at a time."[67] One of FDR's brain trust members, Rexford Tugwell, explained the ultimately failed "greenbelt" program: "My idea is to go just outside centers of population, pick up cheap land, build a whole community and entire people into it. Then go back into the cities and tear down whole slums and make parks out of them."[68]

Once again, the apparently democratic vision of an "American way of life" based on property and home ownership was itself erected on the basis of exclusion. By the 1960s, less than 3 percent of FHA loans were made for housing in the inner cities—the rest, in the suburbs.[69] The Home Owners Loan Corporation was notorious for only providing financing for single-race (usually white) neighborhoods. As suburbanization was geographically expressed as "white flight," race became infused in the very circuits of real estate capital.[70] Suburban white homeowners viewed the entrance of nonwhite residents as a threat to property values. Indeed, within the logic of entrepreneurial life, property values became the central object of a localist defensive politics of policing neighborhoods in the interests of the private accumulation of real estate wealth.[71] In the 1940s, the National Association of Real Estate Board's code of ethics stated, "A realtor should never be instrumental in introducing into a neighborhood a character of occupancy, members of any race or nationality, or any individual whose presence will clearly be detrimental to property values in the neighborhood."[72] Yet the basis of home property values itself relied upon a wider social infrastructure than the individual homeowner could provide.

"Over Space, Man Has Begun to Win Victory"

The notion of a "way of life" implies a set of practices situated within a particular geography. In capitalism, without much historical precedent, the geography of everyday life is structured by a spatial separation between home and work.[73] Given that the New Deal promise of home ownership celebrated a particular form of low-density suburban residential development, the infrastructures required to link the masses of worker–consumers through the dispersed sites of social reproduction were immense.

Again the role of the state in providing investment where capital would not was critical. In 1916, the first federal road act distributed funds to the states for highway construction.[74] Yet it was during the 1930s that the federal government set the precedent of financing highway construction as a crucial infrastructural precondition of the auto–home complex. The New Deal provided four billion dollars in federal funds between 1932 and 1942.[75] The Works Progress Administration (WPA) employed an average of 2.3 million people per year building 600,000 miles of roads and 75,266 bridges, in addition to airports, libraries, sewage treatment plants, and other foundations of an increasingly sprawled metropolis in the United States.[76] This all set the precedent for what Flink describes as "the most ambitious public works program initiated in our history"—the Federal Aid Highway Act of 1956, which funded the construction of the nation's interstate highway system.[77] Insofar as these roads were constructed with public money to ensure both private mobility and *guaranteed profits* for interested industries, he also describes the program as "an indirect subsidization of the automobile and oil industries."[78]

This massive state commitment to the public infrastructure of automobility and massive petroleum consumption did not come automatically and without pressure from interested parties. Perhaps the most spectacular instance of corporate promotion of a state-subsidized auto-centric vision of the future was the General Motors "Futurama" exhibit at the 1939 World's Fair in New York City. The exhibit invited spectators into a moving tram viewing a landscape below: "The World of Tomorrow, 1960," a massive diorama of highways, industrial plants, farms, and suburban settlements. Specifically, the exhibit celebrated a modernist dream of technological efficiency achieved through vast, interconnected highway systems. In a supplementary film released in 1940, *To New Horizons*, the narrator heralded "a growing appreciation of the wisdom of applying the road tax monies to the road building program for which they were designed."[79] He spoke of spectacular highway intersections and efficient one-way motorways "with seven lanes accommodating traffic at designated speeds of 50, 75 and 100 miles per hour . . . engineered for easy grades and for speed with safety."[80] The film celebrated the new landscape brought by government money as perfecting "the American scheme of living whereby individual effort, the freedom to think, and the will to do, have given birth to a generation of men who always want new fields for greater accomplishment." Vividly, General Motors promoted a particular sociotechnical infrastructure for a new *geography* of everyday life, a new and unprecedented command over space itself: "Over space, man has begun to win victory . . . space for living, space for working, space for [play] . . . all available for more people than ever before."[81] Only through state financing was such a conquest possible. The New Deal provided the much-needed investment in the infrastructures of everyday life, and those infrastructure have constrained and conditioned how life has been imagined ever since.

The New Deal ushered in a dramatic material transformation of everyday life for millions of workers in the United States. This material transformation—what I call the real subsumption of life under capital—was expressed through a particular suburban landscape: a geography of mass consumption. The point of detailing the dramatic reconfiguration of social reproduction through struggles over wages, housing, and infrastructure is to argue that our present "oil addiction" must be understood in this historical and social context. Indeed, the petroleum industry understood very well that demand for its products was predicated on a wider social context of demand for housing and automobiles.

Shortly after World War II, Conoco reported to its shareholders that "the major contributing factor to the high level of business activity of the country was the continued high demand for housing and automobiles, two industries which vitally affect the consumption of petroleum products."[82] What is now viewed as an "addiction" was then viewed as the "lifeblood" of a newly emerging "way of life" that was seen as the key to rescuing capitalism and democracy from the specters of fascism, communism, and war. As Roosevelt claimed, "the nation is dependent upon its petroleum resources, in peace and in war, in its comforts and in its necessities."[83]

Many political economists have emphasized how suburbanization itself represented the solution to the entrenched problems of "effective demand" and excess capacity witnessed in the 1920s and 1930s.[84] But this explanation need not be so Keynesian in its materialistic focus on "the economy" in the aggregate.[85] Whether or not mass consumption fueled accumulation,[86] the geography of suburbanization strengthened the cultural politics of capital at a moment when it was presumed to be "doomed, dying or dead." As I will explore in the next chapter, life in the suburban landscape was reproduced through a privatized command over space that led many to imagine themselves as entrepreneurs of their own lives. While the original frontier period in American history idealized the self-reliant homesteader producing his own subsistence, the suburban frontier represented a form of independence subsumed within the logics of capital circulation. Through this logic the stuff of life became more embedded than ever before in the world of money—wages, mortgages, car payments, grocery bills. Individuals came to view their parcel of land as a value and investment, and the daily commute became contingent on all the commodified things that make automobility possible (insurance, oil changes, tires, gasoline). Space itself was commodified, and mobility through space became contingent on one's individual buying power. As capital, jobs, and a tax base fled the central cities of the United States, whole populations were left without the buying power to achieve this automobility and thus were forced to rely on unreliable and inadequate forms of public transit.[87]

The great "class compromise" of labor peace for high wages was only made possible through an enormous ecological compromise. The very notion of "mass" consumption presupposes a mass of materials, energies, and wastes channeled into the geographies of social reproduction and the cultural politics of "the American way of life." Petroleum represents but one of the many resources that became absolutely indispensable to the social reproduction of life for more and more workers throughout the postwar period. Although it took high wages and credit for masses of workers to afford automobiles, it took the ecology of "buried sunshine"—in the case of petroleum, millennia of concentrated phytoplankton[88]—to power this dispersed geography of atomized, auto-bound subjects. With oil, and specifically the gasoline-fired internal combustion engine, a daily commute that was once powered by human and animal muscles (walking and horses) or public transit was transformed into an automated, privatized burst through vast spaces.

Yet the production and provision of oil and gasoline is not automatic. It is not simply waiting to be easily extracted and distributed to consumers. Contemporaneous with these struggles over "the American way of life" in the 1930s were struggles over the production of oil in the United States. In the 1930s, the United States was (and would be for the next three decades) the largest producer of petroleum in the world. When Roosevelt took office in 1933 the domestic industry was on the brink of bankruptcy with a glutted market and prices collapsing. And the culprits for this overproduction were the very pillars of the cultural politics of capital—competition and private property. Just as questions of whether or not capital could provide a decent life for workers were being asked, many wondered whether or not the capitalist system of competition and private property could provision the "vital" oil needed for such a life.

Drowning in Oil

During the 1930s, although scarcity was *experienced* by the masses of unemployed and uprooted migrants, the problem in natural resource markets and in the economy as a whole was one of abundance, glut, excess capacity, and lack of demand. The following passage comes from the final pages of a novel titled *Hot Oil* published in 1935. The fate of its main character stands in for the state of the oil market as a whole:

> Now the black flood covers the pipe entrance. Cowering back, the man retreats to the far wall. His desperate screams echo emptily. Outside surely someone will hear him. Someone will come to shut off the oil to release him from his tragic trap. But the black tide rises relentlessly. It reaches his ankles. He slides, slips, falls, his face momentarily submerged, his mouth, eyes, ears choked with oil. . . . "Stop it! For God's sake, *stop the oil!*" Climbing, he batters the bolted door with the fury of moral terror. Below, the black sea mounts swirling, bubbling, frothing to fine spume where the stream enters. The oil is racing now, sucked from the hill-top tank, charging down the buried pipeline. There is no one to hear the beat of his fists, curses, sobbed prayers and screams as he clings in the dark, waist-deep. . . . The

frayed rope is parting, the desperate finger slipping. The black tide
rises . . . breast-high . . . chin-high.[89]

In the same year as the Wagner Act and the Social Security Act, the
imagery of a man drowning in pool of unstoppable oil was a metaphor
for a national market glutted seemingly with no mechanism to stop the
production of oil. In the context of overproduction and market collapse,
the period between 1930 and 1935 witnessed a complex struggle between
multiple and conflicting forces within the oil industry and the state over
the oil market. Although the actual mechanisms of achieving the goal
were unclear, the desired outcome of these struggles was understood by
all involved: constrain production in line with consumer demand. The
project to constrain production—which, in effect, produced the scarcity
necessary for prices to function and profits to be made—required the formation of an "institutional fix" for the U.S. oil market.[90] Before detailing
the complex politics of this "institutional fix" however, I must first provide some background on property rights and the legal geography of U.S.
oil production that caused the market dysfunctions in the first place.

The Rule of Capture and the Irrationality of Private Property Rights

For most of the nineteenth and early twentieth centuries, the U.S. system of oil production was constantly threatened by overproduction. As
Mills writes, "economic disaster stalked the industry with the discovery
of each new field."[91] While much debate around oil nowadays is focused
on its scarcity or the looming "peak" of global production, it is crucial
to recognize that for most of oil's political and economic history—and
as recently as 1986 and 1999, and even the fall of 2008—the largest enemy has been glut.[92] The tendencies toward overproduction were
rooted in the unique system of oil property rights in the United States.
In most of the rest of the world, subterranean oil deposits are *de facto*
the property of the state (and usually a centralized national state). In
the middle of the twentieth century, this meant that multinational oil
companies would be granted concessions from a central government
to extract oil so long as taxes and royalties were paid to the "landlord
state."[93] In the United States, the situation was completely different
as ownership rights to subsurface petroleum resources were delegated
to private property owners on nonpublic lands. This created a situation through which petroleum producers and their associated "land
men" were forced to negotiate with a variegated geography of private

property owners, often small-scale farmers, or other landowners to set the terms of a particular "lease."[94]

Thus the geography of private property created a landscape of multiple producers that often had shared property rights to a *single* oil deposit stretching across property lines. The multiplicity of producers did not in itself guarantee overproduction, but a legal decision in 1889 by the Pennsylvania Supreme Court (130 Pa. 235, 18 Atl. 724 [1889]) did. The court ruling became known in the oil industry as (perhaps the curse of) "the rule of capture." The court stated:

> Water and oil . . . as still more strongly gas, may be classified by themselves, if the analogy be not too fanciful, as minerals *ferae naturae* [Latin for "wild animals"]. In common with animals, and unlike other minerals, they have the power and tendency to escape without the volition of the owner. Their "fugitive and wandering within the limits of a particular tract is uncertain." They belong to the owners of the land and are part of oil and are subject to his control; but when they escape, and go into other land, or come under another's control, the title of the former owner is gone. Possession of the land therefore, is not necessarily possession of the gas. If an adjoining, or even a distant, owner drills his own land, and taps your gas, so that it comes into his well and under his control, it is no longer yours, but his.[95]

Classifying petroleum resources as akin to "wild game" in its "fugitive" ability to flow under the surface of the earth was problematic for two reasons. First, oil deposits—though varying in size and scale—never corresponded to the neat, parcelized geography of private property tracts. Thus private property owners—sometimes hundreds of them—believe they had reasonable "property rights" to an oil pool beneath the surface. Because of the "rule of capture" the only rational response to this situation was to pump as much oil, as quickly as possible, in fear that if you held back your neighbor would suck the oil from underneath your property.[96] Thus an oil discovery almost automatically created a chaotic rush to produce as much oil as possible from each individual tract or "lease." This created perhaps *the* emblematic image of the landscape of U.S. petroleum production—the "forest of derricks," each producing against the other in a mad, competitive race to maximize wealth from a limited resource (see Figure 7). As one small producer recounted, "boy, when you get in there with a good rig, with probably 30 or 40 rigs right around you, and everyone trying to beat the other one, it's fascinating."[97] The competitive "race" mentality of oil production often had disastrous consequences from the standpoint of petroleum geologists. Since the rush to produce was so great, producers

FIGURE 7. *FOREST OF DERRICKS.*
The landscape of multiple derricks producing side by side was iconic
throughout the early history of American oil production. A quite illogical
way to organize oil extraction, it was the result of the legal regime of private
property rights and the "rule of capture." Photograph courtesy of the Texas
Energy Museum, Beaumont, Texas.

could deplete the gas or water pressure needed to push the oil above the
surface and sometimes leave thousands of barrels of trapped petroleum
underneath the surface. Beyond the geological considerations of waste,
overproduction produced substantial market volatility and the constant
threat of collapsing prices.

The phenomenon of overproduction raises the question of production
over what. In conservation debates, the real problem was production over
"market demand," or what was often referred to as "reasonable market
demand."[98] If production were restrained in line with demand, not only
would prices be stable, but oil would not be wasted in storage. Because of
its liquid and volatile properties, oil is most stable *flowing*. As petroleum
economist Edith Penrose describes it, "oil is a dirty liquid, and in some
of its forms it is volatile and dangerous. It is best managed if allowed to

flow continuously from the well, through pipelines, into tankers if necessary, and through refineries, unseen and untouched. Storage is expensive and dangerous."[99]

For economic and physical reasons, it was increasingly seen as necessary to constrain production in line with "market demand." Of course, the demand for petroleum was constructed as the unquestioned lifeblood of the newly emerging "American way of life." Thus, though it may seem odd from our current anxiety regarding overconsumption, the conservation debates of the time were almost completely focused upon wasteful methods of *production*. If production methods could be reformed so as to not destroy well pressure, or leave gallons of oil flowing through local waterways, and constrained so as not to exceed "market demand," conservation was achieved. The idea that consumption or demand might become a "conservation" problem was simply not a consideration in a modernist age wherein highways, electricity, and automobiles were equated with progress and the technological sublime.[100]

How could production be controlled? From the rational perspective of many petroleum engineers and geologists, the obvious solution to this contradiction between private property and geology was to rescale the control over petroleum production in harmony with the natural shape of the geological pool. This was central to the "unitization" movement that believed all oil pools should be rationally managed as a single unit to prevent the exhaustion of underground pressure and allow for the maximum possible recovery of petroleum.[101] But "private property" was embedded in the long-standing social geographies of small-scale homesteader land ownership buoyed by the hope of oil wealth. On the other side was the person who could develop this oil—the iconic "independent oil wildcatter" who, out of sheer determination and entrepreneurial tenacity, discovers and develops his own oil. As Texas oil regulator E. O. Thompson put it starkly, "I am of the opinion that unitization means the extermination of the little man."[102] Within each natural "unit" of an oil pool existed countless "little men"—both "little" landowners with oil underneath and "little" independent producers.[103] The idea of centralized, collective management of oil pools as a natural unit was, in Erich Zimmermann's words, a "drastic and large scale departure from the basic principles of maximum freedom for individuals."[104] Indeed, the cultural power of that image— "the little man" and its associated imagery of American petite bourgeois entrepreneurialism and laissez faire competition[105]—proved to be much more important than any geography handed down by geology. The question was how scarcity could be produced without violating the ideological core of American capitalism. This question was not fully confronted until the problems of overproduction took on national scope in the context of the Great Depression of the 1930s.

The Black Giant

As endemic as overproduction was, its market effects remained regional until the late 1920s and early 1930s.[106] In October 1930, an independent wildcatter named Columbus "Dad" Joiner discovered the single largest lower-forty-eight oil field in the history of the United States—the Black Giant, or the great "East Texas Oil Field."[107] It was forty-two miles long and four to eight miles wide, containing thousands of private property tracts.[108] Just in time for the slackening of Depression-era demand for petroleum products, production from the East Texas Field soared. By June 1931, 700 wells were drilled and the field was producing 350,000 barrels per day, or nearly 15 percent of total domestic consumption.[109] At the same time, the price of oil plummeted—$0.15 oil hit the national market. In some parts of Texas, oil was selling for as little as $0.02 per barrel in an industry that considered $1.00 oil a bare minimum of profitability.[110] The discovery of the East Texas field—and consequent glut of fresh or "flush"[111] production—threatened to render unprofitable not only the capital-intensive and highly integrated major producers but also the thousands of small independent producers whose rigs and wells were suddenly unviable. With the oil market in such disarray, it was clear that some mechanisms had to be put into place to control production—especially in East Texas.

By August of 1931 production was at one million barrels per day, and prices were still well under the acceptable threshold of $1 per barrel.[112] In the nearby oil state of Oklahoma, Governor William Murray was forced to declare "martial law" and close 3,016 wells in the state. He vowed not to allow production until the price reached $1. The governor of Texas—former oil executive Ross Sterling—was reluctant at first to go to such lengths. However, word started to circulate from East Texas that a coalition of landowners and fifteen hundred oil producers were organizing to violently dynamite drilling rigs, pipelines, and other property associated with producers of what was called "hot oil" (illicit oil produced and transported in excess of the Texas Railroad Commission [TRC] laws). The major company, Humble Oil and Refining, Co. (later bought by Exxon), hired armed security guards to protect its property.[113]

Fearing the prospect of violent revolt, on August 17, 1931, Sterling declared that "there exists an organized and entrenched group of crude petroleum and natural gas producers in said East Texas oil field . . . who are in a state of insurrection against the conservation laws of the State."[114] Martial law was declared in the East Texas fields, and four thousand troops were sent to enforce the field's "allowable" level of production as dictated by the state's conservation authority, the TRC.[115] According to historical accounts, initially the "troops encountered no resistance . . . [and] . . . compliance was prompt and universal." By the end of August, prices started to rebound toward $0.70 per barrel.[116]

Calling the situation an "insurrection" was a stretch. The revolt was not seen as an action of organized armed groups against the state but rather a multiplicity of individuals, usually "independent" oil producers, armed with nothing more than a drilling rig and a derrick. In this situation, the *insurgent was oil itself*. As Nordhauser remarked, the "insurrection was suppressed by turning a set of valves."[117] Insofar as the state military apparatus is seen as necessary only in exceptional times of violent revolt or war, the violent imposition of martial law was quite remarkably over something economic—overproduction. Of course, the flood of East Texas oil was a direct product of the heralded capitalist forces of competition and private property. The irrationality of multiple private proprietors over a single geological pool created a situation where competition produced waste and economic ruin. The very geography of production made it impossible for oil to be produced as a commodity. Precisely because oil was not scarce, such overproduction frustrated the ability of the price mechanism to stabilize at a high enough level to support profitable accumulation. If anything, prices were profoundly volatile, characterized by violent booms and busts. Scarcity, and the effective commodification of oil resources, had to be *enforced* militarily.

By late in the fall of 1931, prices rebounded to over $1 per barrel. For the most part Sterling and Murray were credited with saving the industry by using their executive power to produce the scarcity necessary for oil industry profitability. Yet in early 1932, martial law was declared unconstitutional by the federal courts when independent refiners (upset over militarily raising the price of their principal input, crude oil) sued the state of Texas, calling martial law "an arbitrary and tyrannical taking of property."[118] Sterling claimed the martial law was necessary in terms of the "law of self-defense as applied to nation or state."[119] It was difficult for Sterling to convince the courts that the mere production of oil constituted an "insurrection," threatening the state itself. But after his failure to get reelected in 1932, Sterling was more candid about the real purpose of martial law: "I have no apology for martial law in East Texas. . . . It saved the state $6 million in taxes and it saved the people of Texas

$40 million in the value of their products."[120] In other words, violence was necessary to save the capitalist system of value production upon which Texas's power and wealth depended.

Calling for an Oil Dictator

The oil crisis of the 1930s paralleled conditions in most other industries at the time—overcapacity and catastrophic deflation. During the Depression, modern capitalism was often seen as inherently prone toward instability and ruinous competition. As Brinkley points out, many economists and policy makers viewed competition "as an obstacle to economic stability." Brinkley quotes New Deal brain truster Rexford Tugwell claiming, "Unrestricted individual competition is the death, not the life of trade."[121] Thus, during the early 1930s, the challenge for the state was to construct institutions that did not go so far as socializing the means of production but to create a regulatory environment that paradoxically stunted the ruinous competitive forces of capital while still allowing for the *appearance* of a freely competitive capitalist marketplace.

At stake in the collapse of the oil market was a contradiction between the spatial fixity of oil resources in specific geographies of state regulation and local property rights, on the one hand, and the emerging view of petroleum as a critical *national* resource that was central to defense and a way of life on the other. National narratives constructed local resource practices (such as in Texas) as a haphazard and wasteful squandering of national resources. On the other hand, any effort to consolidate *national* federal control over an industry was seen by many around the oil industry as an unconstitutional violation of state's rights and private property. An op-ed accompanying the *Dallas Morning News* went as far as to suggest that "doubtless the states . . . have permitted oil to be wasted. But even the finest conservation plans are not worth the sacrifice of the rights of the states."[122]

The use of violence to produce the scarcity that eluded market competition illustrated just how dysfunctional the capitalist oil market had become. After martial law was declared unconstitutional and violence was no longer an option, the oil market quickly resumed its descent to prices well below the threshold of $1 per barrel. It was in this context that President FDR came into office along with his raucous secretary of interior, Harold Ickes. FDR placed Ickes in charge of dealing with the oil crisis, and Ickes quickly became convinced that a federal role was needed to stabilize the industry.

Much criticized for his scant knowledge of the oil industry at the time of the appointment, Ickes immediately began voicing his support for state planning as necessary to rescuing "the American way of life." Without government control, Ickes reasoned, the oil market left alone "would continue to throw oil and yet more oil upon an already glutted market."[123] It did not take long for Ickes to suggest to FDR in a memo dated May 1, 1933, that perhaps the situation called for dramatic action:

> The oil industry is in a more chaotic situation and is rapidly approaching a condition, according to many observers, of utter demoralization. . . . It is obvious that oil cannot continue to be sold at ten cents a barrel without grave results to the oil industry and to the general economic situation in the country. To meet this situation groups of oil interests, mainly major ones, have drafted and presented to me a bill which they hope will be enacted into law at this session of the Congress. This bill, declaring that an emergency exists, provides that the Secretary of Interior, for the period of two years, shall in effect be an oil dictator.[124]

Even in the context of increased New Deal intervention in the market, the use of the term *dictator* is striking.[125] Ickes makes clear that generalized economic recovery would not be possible *without* a healthy oil industry. Surprisingly, the notion of an "oil dictator" achieved substantial political support in an era of lost faith in the market mechanism, even in unexpected social and geographical contexts. Many within the oil industry were calling on Ickes directly to fix prices. In 1933, new Texas governor Miriam "Ma" Ferguson unambiguously supported the establishment of federal control legislation: "In this emergency I desire to approve your expressed policy to provide national control of the oil industry and I am in favor of any legislation that you approve."[126] One telegram from a producer in the East Texas town of Tyler stated unambiguously to FDR, "We want an [oil] dictator."[127]

The oil crisis produced internal struggles within the state and the oil industry itself. The core of the struggle was the status of oil as a commodity; or, rather, the very question of whether or not oil should be produced by private capitalists for profit. There were the antimonopolists composed mainly of small, low-cost producers and independent refiners who opposed any form of production control as a violation of the competitive law of supply and demand. There were high-cost producing independents represented by Wirt Franklin, the president of the Independent Petroleum Producers of America, who believed price fixing was necessary in order to avert the abandonment of the thousands of wells across the nation. There were major company officials, like Harry Sinclair, who believed price fixing was necessary to save the industry. There were other major company officials, like Walter Teagle of Standard Oil–NJ (Exxon), who found the notion of price fixing a dangerous precedent for an industry putatively founded upon free enterprise. When administrator of the National Recovery Association Hugh Johnson set out with industry to create a petroleum code as part of the NIRA, he found it impossible to reconcile these multiple and conflicting interests. When he proposed production controls without price fixing many interests threatened noncompliance; when he proposed fixing gasoline prices through a fixed ratio to crude, both sides were lukewarm.[128] Meanwhile, the crisis of the oil industry continued.

Ickes was the strongest voice for federal control of the industry. He believed that state government conservation commissions—such as the TRC—had proven incapable of controlling production. For whatever production they did constrain, an equal amount was produced and transported illicitly as "hot oil," or production in excess of state allowances. Yet, as he wrote in his diary, Ickes believed that actual fixing of prices would be a "radical departure for the Government."[129] In the summer of 1933, he settled on a federal role in setting quotas for each of the oil producing states, which, in effect, indirectly controlled prices by constraining production with projected demand.

Thus the political battle over 1933 and 1934 was fought not over whether or not production would be artificially controlled but *at what scale* control would be exercised. The politics of oil is structured through social struggles over multiple scales—the scale of the oil deposit itself, the scale of a property tract, the state (or provincial) scale, the national scale, and ultimately the global scale of the major companies and the global oil market. Ickes, who spoke of petroleum as "an irreplaceable national resource," believed it was in the interests of the nation as a whole for centralized federal control over oil to prevent waste.[130] Some, including Governor Miriam Ferguson, had come to believe federal control was necessary, but the spatial fixity of tremendous oil reserves within the state of Texas emerged as a barrier to an all-out oil dictatorship. Texas, at the state scale, was not only the epicenter of the crisis with East Texas still producing at high levels but also clearly the nation's most important producing state. Because the underlying exigency for oil regulation was founded upon the notion that oil was central to *national* economic recovery, any attempt to "stabilize" the national oil market hinged upon Texan cooperation and, more specifically, the state regulatory arm of conservation policy—the TRC. In August of 1933, E. O. Thompson, TRC commissioner—along with multiple Texas oil men—urged FDR to allow the federal government only to "recommend" production quotas to the states and have zero authority to fix prices. Realizing that scale of Texas was perhaps the key component to any successful legislation at the national scale, FDR quickly acquiesced.[131]

In May of 1934, Ickes voiced support for a newly drafted Thomas-Disney oil bill that would give the federal government control over oil quotas. He claimed, "Federal supervision . . . is absolutely necessary to reinforce State activities."[132] Once again Texan congressmen blocked the way. Senator Tom Connally and Congressman Tom Rayburn from Texas organized opposition to the bill, precluding its passage. The *Tyler Courier Times Telegraph* claimed, "Texas independents . . . have carried on the fight for states' rights and against the Thomas-Disney bill [which was seen as] a first step toward complete federal regimentation of the oil business."[133] The Texas independents, who themselves served as the image of the entrepreneurial "little man" of the industry, aligned with the popular belief in the sanctity of "state's rights," providing the conditions for alliances against all that was "big" and hovering over the oil industry. E. O. Thompson claimed the bill threatened "to change our system of government, and violates every principle of sovereignty of the states."[134] As Childs puts it, "Thompson personified himself and the commission as defenders against monopoly forces, whether major oil firms or federal bureaucrats, and as staunch enforcers of state law."[135] The spatial fixity of those oil pools within the territorial delimitations of Texas proved too powerful to allow a complete scalar reconfiguration of petroleum governance toward national federal control.

The last hope for federal control came in mid-November of 1934 when Ickes boldly stated that if Texas could not control its own production, "the Federal Government may consider that it is its duty to consider declaring the oil industry a public utility."[136] These remarks mobilized a variety of independent oil interests against federal control and Ickes's statement instantly became political fodder for countless telegrams and lobbying efforts against federal control. Ickes's dictatorial aspirations had been thwarted.

Even with the failure of federal control, the depressed state of the oil market made it clear that some sort of extralocal form of production constraint had to be devised. Those within the industry and the state sought some sort of institutional mixture between national, state, and local control— what Neil Smith called a "scalar fix."[137] This "scalar fix" would need to recognize private property and states' rights but still assure national-scale balance between supply and demand. One proposal was to create an "interstate" organization that could coordinate state conservation policies in line with the national market demand. Such an organization would provide the national-scale coordination everyone realized was desperately needed but leave control to the states. While the states would have the ultimate power to control production within their own territories (what was called "prorationing"), the federal government would retain power to regulate "hot oil" that flowed beyond state control and the Department of Interior's Bureau of Mines (BOM) would publish monthly projections of national consumer demand that would serve as "recommendations" for the Interstate Compact and the state conservation authorities.

In May of 1935, Roosevelt expressed his support for this particular compromise. He called for a system "whereby the States and the Federal government, each within its own sphere, can work together in a common purpose. The problem is one of National and State concern, and I feel its solution will be obtained more readily if it is considered in the spirit of mutual helpfulness."[138]

On August 27, 1935, acceding to FDR's support for the compact, Congress ratified the Interstate Oil Compact Commission (IOCC) for a period of two years until 1943, after which four-year intervals were instituted. It is still functioning today (albeit in much different circumstances).[139] The original signatories were New Mexico, Oklahoma, Texas, Colorado, and Illinois.[140]

The "scalar fix" of the IOCC worked remarkably well in bringing stability to the oil market. Figure 8 shows the relative stability achieved for nominal crude prices after 1935. While different states constrained production more than others—Illinois was known for its lack of discipline—Texas provided the role as the critical swing producer increasing or decreasing production in line with market conditions throughout the postwar period.[141] By maintaining high prices, these policies actually served to protect a multiplicity of high-cost independent producers from the perils of unrestrained competition. Indeed, much of the impulse for regulation was to save an already existing geography of small producers who were only a product of the irrational system of private property rights. As Libecap argues, "the underlying political concern was the devastation to local economies and the careers of politicians if thousands of small, high-cost oil firms, refineries, and well service and supply companies were to fail."[142] Given that the Texas railroad commissioner was an elected position, these political concerns were paramount. State conservation commissions often exempted high-cost "stripper" wells from any control whatsoever. Thus the prorationing system was a kind of state-based cartel—an arrangement that in fact inspired the Organization of Petroleum Exporting Countries (OPEC)[143]—promoting the existence of multiple producers that ended up standing in as evidence of a diverse

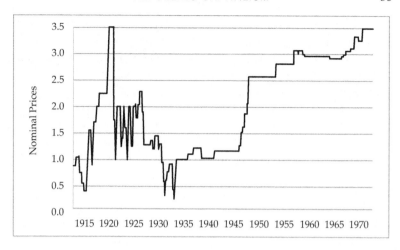

FIGURE 8. NOMINAL CRUDE OIL PRICES IN THE UNITED STATES, 1913–72 (DOLLARS PER BARREL).
Adapted from Libecap, "The Political Economy of Crude Oil Cartelization in the United States," 842.

market based on free competition and entrepreneurialism. But, as Lovejoy and Homan put it, "the whole system of conservation regulation is designed to prevent market competition."[144] The system only used active state management to produce the *appearance* of competition. In line with the "market" for labor, housing, and social infrastructure, the oil market was made to appear functional through the power of the state.

Central to this arrangement was the construction of oil market stability. The importance of oil price stability to ordinary consumer and investment planning should be understandable in our current period of tremendous oil price volatility.[145] Not only cheap but stable prices laid the foundation for the entrenchment of oil consumption during the postwar era. Indeed, the mechanisms put into place to protect high-cost independent producers ensured that oil prices were not nearly as cheap as they could have been—the result during the postwar era was *stable, cheap-enough oil*.

Projecting Demand, Fixing Supply

As mentioned, the entire edifice of this so-called conservation policy was constructed upon a given and unquestioned basis of "reasonable market demand." In the depths of the crisis, Ickes laid out the stakes in constructing "a system of stabilizing production to keep it balanced with our national consumer demand so as to protect adequately our stocks of crude petroleum, which are so essential to our modern civilization, national welfare and national defense."[146] Thus conservation policy in the United States was based around the "reasonability" of demand itself rooted in the value of labor power and the geographies of militarization. Indeed, in the wake of these policies, petroleum trade journals like *Esso Oilways* featured "educational" cartoons that *equated* petroleum consumption with a high "standard of living." One 1950 cartoon featuring the image of a horse and buggy (1900) contrasted with the automobile (1950) and asked, "Did you know that a nation's progress (and its standard of living) can be measured pretty well by its consumption of petroleum?"[147]

In order to inform conservation policy, demand had to be projected ahead of time. Just as petroleum consumption was becoming necessary for the reproduction of life it became necessary to construct statistical tools to measure that demand as an indicator of the "life" of the population. Constructing "reasonable market demand" depended upon newly emerging statistical tools that were increasingly being integrated into all forms of economic governance. Following Foucault's concepts of biopower and governmentality,[148] Timothy Mitchell points out it was through these forms of statistical aggregation that an object called "the economy"—and the associated "life" of its population—was discovered.[149]

Starting in 1936, BOM was charged with publishing monthly projections of petroleum demand on a national scale and also partitioning that demand among specific petroleum-producing states and refining districts. It estimated the total demand for motor gasoline by multiplying the average fuel use per vehicle by the total number of registered vehicles in operation, subtracting fuel imports and gasoline stocks. Similar data were produced with the number of oil-burning heating units in operation. The amount of crude needed for specific petroleum products was then estimated via a yield factor—for example, the average amount of crude it takes to yield a given amount of gasoline. The bulk of this data depended upon access to the individualized forms of data that attach specific bodies to particular cars (auto registrations) and homes (deeds, property taxes, etc.). Through this biopolitical imaginary the BOM could project what the average body, or family of bodies, consumes in motor fuel and heat in order to live in the increasingly sprawled suburban geographies of mid-twentieth-century America. Such estimates required taking into account the seasonal fluctuations that effect demand—from the summer "driving season" to winter demand for heating oil. All in all, these methods allowed each petroleum-producing state to know with considerable accuracy how much oil should be produced so as not to exceed market demand.[150]

The estimates, of course, depended upon a form of statistical calculation that individuated bodies and the technologies that supplemented their daily activities. The calculation of "demand" was couched explicitly in terms of the reproduction of the needs and improvement of the population as a whole. In hearings on the purpose and function of the BOM demand projections, one senator claimed, "I know the Senators on this committee have interpreted your figures on demand as the amount that would be required to sustain our economy and keep our people comfortable."[151] In the heading each month, the forecast only claimed— "It is an estimate of probable consumption based on actual industry conditions and policies in effect."[152] The BOM never purported to estimate demand at variable prices—that is, to project a neoclassical "demand curve." Rather, the going price and "actual industry conditions" were assumed *a priori*. In a certain sense, then, the BOM projected a *specific* demand at a specific price—a price high enough to keep "little oil" afloat in the domestic oil market and a price low enough to spur mass consumption of petroleum products. Still the BOM figures led to a *naturalization of demand levels* reflecting "actual industry conditions" as inherently reasonable. These figures then became the edifice upon which the whole regulatory machinery of conservation was erected. As is obvious today, what was once constructed as the lower limit of conservation policy—demand—actually ended up locking in mammoth patterns of oil consumption that have led to current geopolitical, ecological, and social concerns with the United States' "addiction" to oil. As I have stated, the idea that demand itself might represent a conservation problem simply never entered the minds of the relevant policy makers.[153] The regulatory machinery of constrained production for mass consumption worked well into the postwar period.

Conclusion

> The coalition worked. It did not produce socialism, but that wasn't Roosevelt's intention. He saved our society in a new bourgeois reform way. . . . Capitalism remains.[154]
>
> —Max Schactman, Socialist Organizer

It is painfully banal in contemporary times to claim petroleum is central to economic life.[155] This pronouncement—often proceeded with a statement such as "Like it or not"—stands in as the ultimate justification for the continuation of petroleum-based capitalism no matter what the social, geopolitical, and ecological costs. Without petroleum, life could not go on—or so the story goes. This is the central argument underlying the assumption that "decades" (always decades) stand between the present moment and an alternative energy future. But the idea that energy in general and oil specifically was foundational to a way of life did not emerge naturally. It was produced out of a wider set of struggles and crises of capitalism. New Deal policies did not declare a new national energy policy; rather, they proposed new imaginaries of living life in the context of a profound breakdown of social reproduction. These imaginaries encompassed a whole set of practices and geographies that locked in ways of consuming energy—energy that was assumed as available.

The forces behind the New Deal attempted to rescue capitalism through the construction of a new way of life based around high wages, home ownership, and auto-centric suburban geographies predicated upon the provision of cheap and abundant oil. Yet the material contradictions between the geology of petroleum and the geography of property relations did not cooperate with this larger vision. Just as the New Deal reforms proposed radical new interventions within labor markets, housing markets, and the provision of federal social services, they also reformed long-standing contradictions in the oil market. The result was a regularization of a system of constrained petroleum production for mass petroleum consumption where the domestic market was not "cleared" through the decentralized workings of the price mechanism but *literally fixed* to create fine-tuned stability between supply and demand. The key for oil producers and consumers was to erect forms of state intervention that provided stability without violating the ultimate principles of capitalist social life. For millions of oil-consuming workers, "the American way of life" was still a life utterly dependent upon commodity relations for survival. Moreover, through this particular vision of "life," freedom and prosperity emerged only in the realm of social reproduction—the house, the car, the family—and the realm of production was still, for the most part, controlled by the dictates of accumulation and profit (albeit along with concessions of higher wages and benefits). For oil producers, the complex system of oil constraint known as prorationing was done with the purported goal of conservation, but a real goal was propping up *profits* for high-cost independents. In this case, profits did not function in the competitive fashion of the neoliberal imagination where profits induce competition and shake out inefficient producers. Conversely profits were an *object of social regulation.*

The geographies of oil production and consumption were not particularly rational from an ecological perspective. A complex set of institutional mechanisms emerged to *balance both irrational geographies at once.* On the one hand, collective bargaining, housing policy, and state-led infrastructural development promoted uniquely wasteful patterns of mass oil (and other commodity) consumption. On the other hand, interstate cooperation and prorationing emerged to enforce scarcity in order to promote the survival of wasteful and uncompetitive production methods. Overall, the simultaneous balancing of these two irrational geographies required the ultimate "compromise"—cheap (enough) oil with prices high enough for the independents and low enough for consumers. By reproducing the central wage relationship of capitalist society and accumulation in the oil sector, this "compromise" did not ensure "conservation" as much as accumulation.

Of course, this system only worked so far as there were domestic petroleum reserves to fuel it. Given that the United States was the highest producer at the time, and given the Keynesian economic focus on national economic development, the New Deal set the stage for a postwar American capitalism based on petroleum autarchy, a nationally circumscribed petro-capitalism based on mass petroleum production for mass petroleum consumption. During the 1930s and 1940s, U.S. multinational oil companies expanded into the lucrative fields of the Middle East, but their concern was mainly to *control* the flow of that oil from becoming the next global "East Texas" to glut the market. Middle Eastern oil was only to be marketed to Europe and Japan, and in fact, the international oil market would be constructed in isolation from the particularities of the satiated U.S. domestic market. It was not until the 1970s that people started to think that there might be something wrong with petroleum itself—and something wrong with orienting the entire life of a nation around it. And it came as quite a shock. Before we get to that shock, however, it is important to examine the postwar period of naïve petro-capitalism and the centrality of petroleum products to its particular vision of life.

CHAPTER THREE

Fractionated Lives

*Refineries and the Ecology
of Entrepreneurial Life*

As discussed in the previous chapter, class struggle in the 1930s secured greater power for industrial unions in most manufacturing industries, and this included the petroleum industry. But as early as the late 1950s, petroleum capital was limiting this power in the stage of the petroleum commodity chain most prone to labor strife—refineries. While the last chapter discussed the crises in balancing the geographies of crude oil extraction with intensive oil consumption, crude oil itself is not the prized "use value" of modern capitalism.[1] Only through the refining process does crude oil become transformed into a variety of "petroleum products" that serve various uses in industrial and everyday economic life. Refineries, and their workers, are an often invisible but nevertheless central metabolic site within the overall socioecological relations between petroleum and capitalist society.

While always a capital-intensive portion of the process, refineries were traditionally run by a two-tiered labor force of white-collar engineers, chemists, and other administrative personnel and the more unionized production workers who supervised the gauges, pumps, furnaces, and other aspects of the refining process.[2] In the first decade after World War II, labor unions organized effectively to secure high and steadily increasing wages and benefit packages for production workers. The height of union power in the refinery sector culminated with the merger of the Oil Workers International Union and the United Gas, Coke and Chemical Workers to form the 183,000-member Oil, Chemical and Atomic Workers International Union in 1955.[3] As with most unions, the power of oil workers' unions derived from their capacity to strike. In the early 1950s, the Oil Workers International Union (among others) successfully shut down refineries all along the Gulf Coast in Texas, winning significant concessions from capital.[4]

A key tactic of class struggle from capital's perspective is to introduce machinery that not only is more efficient than living human power but, perhaps more important, can drive the productive process automatically in ways that obviate humans altogether. As I discussed in chapter 1, nonliving fossil energy is a key energetic or biophysical basis of automatic machinery and its capacities for making living human beings irrelevant to the labor process. By the late 1950s, refineries were becoming increasingly automated with the introduction of computer technologies that could monitor and control refining processes. In 1959, a celebratory piece in *Business Week* reasoned, "Whether or not computers result in a small net reduction in manpower is a minor consideration. Computers do a job faster and more dependably than human crews alone could ever hope to do."[5]

In his studies of automation in French refineries, French sociologist Serge Mallet theorized that the automation of production produced new opportunities for class struggle over technology and knowledge, but this was not the case in the United States.[6] With increasing automation of refining processes, strikes were less effective. In fact, the removal of labor through strikes allowed capital to make discoveries about the virtues of automation and the inconsequence of living labor power. In an article titled "Refinery Strikes Suggest Plants Can Be Run with Still Fewer Men," the industry-friendly *Oil and Gas Journal* boasted, "One of the ironies of the strikes has been the discovery by the companies that they could run the refineries with still fewer people without sacrificing safety or efficiency."[7] In 1961, after 3,700 striking workers walked out of a Gulf Oil Refinery in Port Arthur, Texas, the refinery was able to produce 130,000 barrels a day of petroleum products, or 65 percent of normal plant capacity, with only a mere six hundred nonunionized nonproduction workers.[8] The death knell for refinery workers came in August 1963, when the Oil, Chemical and Atomic Workers International Union "settled" with Shell Oil with a modest wage increase and an agreement that allowed Shell to fire 433 workers. With nearly 2,200 workers striking for a year, the refinery was still able to operate at nearly full capacity.[9] The *New York Times* reported that the strike "was a vivid example of the ineffectiveness of labor's traditional strike weapon in highly automated industries."[10] Since the core of the capital–labor "accord" of the postwar years was a commitment to job security and full employment,[11] the automation of refineries and elimination of what the industry called "manpower requirements" confounded the orientation of traditional labor organizing. Rather than wages and benefits, unions were forced to organize around the decidedly neoliberal concern with "job security" a couple decades before this phrase saturated labor politics from the 1980s onward.[12] In 1962, the *Wall Street*

Journal quoted a union official saying, "If a man doesn't have job security, then wage hikes, health insurance, pensions, and other benefits don't mean anything to him."[13] The automation debates of the postwar period foreshadowed the coming neoliberal assault on organized labor and state interventions in labor markets. Writing in 1963 for the American Enterprise Institute, University of Chicago economist Yale Brozen argued that labor's problems should not be blamed on automation but rather on "minimum wage rates set by laws, by government administrators, and by agreements between unions and employers." He continued: "Adaptation to automation would be easier if the wage structure were less rigid. It could take place, then, by the acceptance of lower wage jobs by some individuals as well as by attaining higher skill levels."[14] Of course, by the 1980s "some individuals" forced to accept lower wage jobs had exploded to include large sections of the U.S. economy.

The 1963 strike settlement marked the beginning of the end of working-class power in the refineries in the United States. Much like other industries, union membership in the petroleum refining industry began declining in the late 1970s and fell from 31.9 percent to 20.1 percent between 1983 and 2009.[15] The concentration of the refining and chemical industries along the Gulf Coast of Texas and Louisiana provides a fitting geographical region for witnessing the decline of working-class power. A classic Sunbelt city, Houston is perhaps the central site of the suburban populism, antiunionism, and oil politics that fueled the rightward shift in American politics away from the New Deal liberalism discussed in the previous chapter.[16] The postwar period witnessed tremendous growth of suburban areas around such Sunbelt cities as Charlotte, Atlanta, Houston, Los Angeles, and eventually Phoenix and Las Vegas.[17] This growth was driven not only by the first waves of deindustrialization of the Rust Belt and the movement of industry and manufacturing to the low-tax, antiunion regions of the South but also by the massive public investment of tax dollars that flowed into defense contracts and allowed for entire landscapes of employment based on military production.[18] Amid the growth and prosperity of Sunbelt production, the landscapes of suburban social reproduction also tended to reinforce the entrepreneurial logics of Sunbelt capitalism. In the context of Charlotte, North Carolina, Lassiter characterizes a predominant Sunbelt ideology: "Suburban identity politics based on consumer status, taxpayer rights, and meritocratic individualism."[19] Suburban neighborhoods were constructed as private enclaves shaped by the racial politics of real estate exclusion. Apart from public schools, and the legacies of massive public infrastructure and roads, suburban Sunbelt residents often imagined that their lives could be entirely reproduced outside of the public realm—private housing, private transportation, and privatized consumption.

While automated refineries offer a classic example of Marx's discussion of the capitalist application of technology against workers in the realm of production, in this chapter, I explore the constitutive sociotechnical and ecological role of refineries in fragmenting working class power in the *realm of social reproduction*. It is this realm, reproduction—in relation to, but nevertheless more important than production—that must be the focus if we are to adequately understand the decline of working-class politics in the United States that began with the Taft-Hartley Act of 1947 and continued on through the McCarthyism of the 1950s, the crisis of the 1970s, and the rise of neoliberalism.[20]

As one of the authors of the Taft-Hartley Act and arch opponent of unions and the New Deal, Senator Robert A. Taft, put it, "the basis of the American way of life has been equal opportunity to improve one's condition by one's own effort."[21] The central argument of this chapter is that refineries provided an ecological basis, and consequently the supplementary materiality, for reproducing the imaginary of an individuated condition, or "life," that is improvable solely by one's own effort and entrepreneurial capacities. Refineries, and their petroleum products, saturate the landscape of suburban social reproduction—from gasoline-fired automobility to vinyl-sided homes and petroleum-based food commodities. Just as refineries produced their own set of discrete fractionated products distilled and cracked from crude oil, petroleum products provided the material basis for the appearance of *fractionated lives,* each tidily contained and controlled within the private spaces of the car, the home, and the body. As such, refineries actively constitute the ability of millions of individuals to ask the core question posed in chapter 1: "What will I make of my life?" For some people living in postwar America (particularly in the Sunbelt), the answer to this question included, of course, a job and a place of work, but this work was seen only as a means to an end. The *product* of one's own efforts, or one's own entrepreneurial capacities, was expressed through a material geography of social reproduction centered on privatized spaces for a nuclear family, a single-family home, a yard, and an automobile (or two or three). As I discussed in chapter 1, while this is often framed as a geography of consumption, or a consumer society,[22] Foucault argues that entrepreneurial subjectivities are essentially *productive,* where an individual appears as "an entrepreneur of himself; being for himself his own capital, being for himself his own producer, being for himself the source of his own earnings."[23] It was one's own ability to produce and reproduce this respectable geography of "success"—to pay a mortgage and other bills, to raise a respectable family—that stands in as evidence (positive or negative) of one's own entrepreneurial capacities. The fractionated products spewing from petroleum refineries are literally an explosive underpinning of particular lived practices and structures of feeling that supplement this imaginary of entrepreneurial life. As I will explore in the rest of the chapter, while the core to a politics of entrepreneurial life is the appearance of autonomy and atomized effort, the oil industry was careful to promote a narrative that reminded American consumers that the materiality of that life was inseparable from the multiple petroleum products distilled and cracked from the hydrocarbon assemblages of crude oil. In order to trace more concretely the role of refineries in shaping the reproduction of entrepreneurial life, it is important first to review some basics about petroleum refining and its associated products that reveal particular barriers and problems in the material transformation of crude oil.

Fractionating Hydrocarbons: A Primer

Petroleum (Latin for "rock oil") seeps above the earth naturally in many different parts of the world, and its use value is contingent on the social conditions of particular historical moments. Historians have traced the use of petroleum to long before Colonel Edwin Drake drilled for oil in Pennsylvania in 1859: to ship-caulking, flame-throwing weapons, and medicinal uses by a number of cultures throughout history.[24] Native Americans in parts of Pennsylvanian were associated (rightly or wrongly) with "Seneca Oil," which was marketed to cure everything from rheumatism to constipation.[25] Yet crude oil by itself is of limited use. Key to the contemporary use of petroleum is the refining process of fractional distillation. In addition to small parts of nitrogen and sulfur, crude oil is mostly a complex assemblage of different kinds of hydrocarbon molecules that vary according to the type of crude extracted in a particular region. Fractional distillation allows producers to segment a given amount of crude into a variety of hydrocarbon *fractions* from light gases with lower boiling points and fewer carbon molecules to heavy, tar-like substances with extremely high boiling points and more carbon molecules.[26] As fractions boil off they are channeled through a network of pipes where they are either reliquefied or captured as gaseous products.

Although the process of distillation has been traced back to ancient Egypt and China for lamp and heating oil,[27] petroleum refining in the nineteenth century coalesced with modern chemistry to produce a certain kind of knowledge of distillation as a molecular process of chemical transformation. A Yale University chemist named Benjamin Silliman Jr. is credited with explaining in molecular terms how refining techniques could be applied to petroleum to produce high yields of the illuminant kerosene.[28] At a moment of crisis in the global stocks of whale oil (the famous illuminant of the first half of the nineteenth century), the first petroleum boom in the 1860s was focused on the mass production of kerosene from crude oil.

The majority of refiners set up rudimentary distillation towers to transform crude into kerosene as quickly and haphazardly as possible.[29] With kerosene representing a middle fraction in a given barrel of oil, the lighter fractions (gases, gasoline, and naphthas) were simply flared off into the atmosphere, and the heavier tar-like materials such as bitumen (a key ingredient in asphalt) and petroleum coke were scraped off the distillation tower and disposed of in nearby water systems.[30] Yet the existence of such wasteful by-products naturally led many to seek out marketable outlets for them. As the petroleum boom proceeded on a mountain of waste, chemists and engineers began to imagine a given barrel of crude as not simply a profitable means to kerosene, but rather as a vertical hierarchy (see Figure 9) of different hydrocarbon molecules that could each be transformed into marketable products. Indeed, Silliman claimed that the residual or waste products of the refinery process should not be ignored. He emphasized, "The crude product contained several distinct oils all with different boiling points . . . my experiments prove that nearly the *whole* of the raw product may be manufactured without waste."[31] While kerosene—and later gasoline—was still the most profitable product, a given barrel of oil began to be imagined as containing not one but hundreds of petroleum products. As early as the late 1870s, heavier fractions were being marketed as lubricants, waxes, petroleum jelly, and even chewing gum.[32]

For much of the history of refining, the yield of the most valuable product (kerosene in the late nineteenth century and gasoline for much of the twentieth) was dependent upon the particular kind of crude oil, which varies by region.[33] For example, light crude oils yield the largest proportion of light fractions, such as gasoline. Frustration with low yields for certain crudes forced refiners to devise "cracking" methods for turning what used to be considered "waste" into more valuable products. The first development of thermal cracking allowed refiners to use extreme pressure and heat to break up heavier hydrocarbon molecules into smaller, lighter ones. During the 1920s alone, refiners in the United States increased gasoline yields from 25 to 39 percent using thermal cracking.[34] The 1930s saw the first widespread development

Wide Fractions ->	Narrow Fractions ->	Refined Products
Petroleum Gases	Natural Gas	1. Methane
	Natural Gas Liquids (NGLs)	2. Ethane
		3. Propane
		4. Butane
Light Ends	Naphthas	5. Light naphtha
		6. Heavy naphta
Gasolines		7. Motor gasoline
		8. Aviation gasoline
Middle Distillates	Kerosenes	9. Jet fuel
		10. Gas turbine Fuel
		11. Kerosene
		12. Diesel fuels
		a) Automotive diesel
		b) Marine diesel
		13. Light fuel oil
		a) Home heating oil
		b) Industrial fuel oil
Heavy Ends	Heavy Fuel Oils	14. Residual fuels
		a) Bunker fuel oil
		b) Heavy fuel oil
	Specialty Products	15. Base oils and lubricants
		16. Waxes
		17. Bitumen
		a) Asphalt
		b) Road oil
		c) Emulsion fuels
		18. Petroleum coke
		19. Carbon black

(left margin, top: Lighter Fractions; left margin, bottom: Heavier Fractions)

FIGURE 9. PETROLEUM PRODUCT FRACTIONS.
The very process of refining itself necessitates that crude oil is separated into multiple "fractions." The challenge for the petroleum industry was to seek out marketable outlets for them. Adapted from Downey, *Oil 101*, 170.

of the use of chemical catalysts (such as aluminum chloride) to allow hydrocarbon molecules to break up more quickly at lower temperatures. As gasoline yields depended less on the quality of the crude oil itself, the further development of catalytic cracking in the United States created exceptionally high yields of gasoline in U.S. refineries. Even today, while global averages stand at 26 percent, the average U.S. refinery yields 44 percent gasoline from its crude feedstock.[35] Thus cracking allowed refiners more flexibility to produce the kinds of products most in demand at particular moments. For example, During winter refiners switch to "max distillate mode" to produce the highest volume of heating oil, and during the summer driving season, refiners switch to "max gasoline mode."[36] Furthermore, cracking itself produced its own particular waste by-products that were subject to investigation of possible marketable outlets. One of the major by-products of cracking is the production of olefins (ethylene and propylene) that do not occur in nature and became the vital feedstock for the production of petrochemicals and plastics.[37]

Undertaken in what are colloquially referred to as "crackers," the development of cracking technologies both increased the scale of operations and intensified the centralization and concentration of capital in the refining sector. As depicted in a Sun Oil refinery in the 1940s in Toledo, Ohio (Figure 10), the average refinery today requires vast amounts of territory—at least one thousand hectares and often more[38]—to accommodate the complex set of processes necessary in the transformation of crude: desalting, dewatering, distillation, cracking, blending, coking, and waste disposal. This need for territory suited the Gulf Coast of the United States, as refineries were able to purchase vast amounts of land from formerly slave-owning plantation owners.[39]

To say that refineries have an environmental impact is an understatement. The complex process inevitably leads to leaks, spills, and the

FIGURE 10. SUN OIL REFINERY, TOLEDO, OHIO, CA. 1940S.
Refineries are expansive industrial geographies that not only consume vast amounts of space, energy, and water but also contain risks of spills, fires, and explosions. Photograph courtesy of the Sun Oil Company and the Hagley Museum and Library.

flaring of greenhouse gases (and other air pollutants not linked to climate change).[40] The process of crude transformation deploys highly flammable materials through intense amounts of heart and pressure, making deadly explosions and fires a necessary evil of operations.[41] The products and wastes of the refinery include known carcinogens such as benzene and arsenic that lead to severe burns, skin irritation, chronic lung disease, psychosis, and elevated cancer risks among workers and nearby communities.[42] The chemical industry—much of it reliant on feedstock like ethylene and propylene derived from cracking processes at refineries—has the third-highest level of toxic chemical releases (behind metal mining and electric utilities) and is first in the cancer-causing "dioxin or dioxin-like compounds" as recorded by the Environmental Protection Agency.[43] The 150-mile stretch of refineries and chemical plants along the Gulf Coast, also known as "Cancer Alley," has become the epicenter of the environmental justice movement, where communities struggle with oil companies and government technocrats to prove scientifically that the concentrated levels of cancer and death all around them are a direct result of oil and chemical pollution.[44]

The gasoline combusted in an automobile doesn't even begin to take into account the energy required along the oil commodity chain. Refining is the most energy-intensive stage in the process of transforming crude into petroleum products.[45] In fact, some suggest it is the most energy intensive of any industrial sector in the United States.[46] An estimate using United Nations data suggests that a single refinery in the United States consumes the electricity equivalent of 30,633 households.[47] Refineries also require huge amounts of water for the generation of steam and cooling towers. It takes an estimated 1.53 gallons of water for each gallon of crude processed.[48]

A precondition of a petroleum-intensive social formation is, of course, substantial refining capacity. Some of the most prolific domestic producers of crude oil are forced to import refined petroleum products because of their lack of domestic refining capacity (e.g., Iran imports 40 percent of its gasoline).[49] Thus refining capacity and the domestic capacity to produce petroleum products has an uneven geography. As Table 2 illustrates, the United States has far and away the largest refining capacity in the world, but other industrial countries' petroleum consumption levels are roughly parallel to their refining capacity. Much of it constructed with federal financing, the refining capacity of the United States was increased approximately 40 percent to fuel the World War II effort.[50] Moreover, after the war, the American-directed Marshall Plan solidified Europe's oil consumption through the financing of substantial refinery construction.[51]

Table 2. Global Refinery Capacity and Crude Oil Consumption

Country	Refinery charge (input) capacity (million barrels per day)	Refinery capacity as a percentage of global total	Oil consumption (million barrels per day)
1. United States	17.4	20.4	20.9
2. China	6.3	7.4	7.7
3. Russia	5.3	6.2	2.9
4. Japan	4.7	5.5	5.2
5. South Korea	2.6	3.0	2.6
6. Germany	2.4	2.8	2.6
7. Italy	2.3	2.7	1.7
8. India	2.3	2.6	2.7
9. Saudi Arabia	2.1	2.5	2.1
10. Canada	2.0	2.3	2.0
Global total	**85.4**	**100**	**85.7**

Source: Downey, *Oil 101*, 75, adapted from International Energy Agency data, 2007.

Although Europe was then able to produce petroleum products, it could not produce petroleum (crude oil) within its territories and was forced to import nearly all its oil from the United States and increasingly from the newly developed supergiant oil fields of the Middle East (much of it developed by American oil companies). Thus the United States emerged from World War II as a perfected petro-capitalist social formation with immense material infrastructure for the mass production and consumption of petroleum.

Flexible Crude—Refineries as History

Crude oil is such a slow-forming substance it is almost ahistorical, the product of millions of years of sunshine expressed in unoxidized marine plant life.[52] On the other hand, refineries can be seen as particular expressions of the historically specific relations between petroleum and society. Thus the use value of crude oil as expressed in refining processes is contingent on the historically specific politics and culture of capitalism at a given moment. The ecology of postwar suburban mass consumption contained its own historically specific bundle of refined petroleum products. But since the word *war* is inclusive in the phrase "postwar," it bears remembering the ways in which the war economy actively constructed the historical conditions for postwar capitalism in the United States. During World War II, oil was equated with the war effort. "Oil is ammunition. Use it wisely" was the tag line of government programs of gasoline rationing and appeared in many different oil advertisements.[53] The oil industry promoted representations of the refinery and its vertical set of petroleum products as a prototypical war machine, providing not only aviation gasoline, explosives, and "paint for military equipment," but also providing for peace and "the needs of tomorrow."[54] The centrality of oil to war was increasingly tied to its centrality to civilian life. A 1943 memo from James H. Tanham lays out the postwar "marketing" plans for the Petroleum Industry War Council: "The petroleum industry deserves a better public opinion. If properly handled, there probably never was a better time to undertake this work. There is nothing inimical about the prosecution of the war and this job. Both have to do with protection of a way of life, wholly American, against enemies without and within the country."[55]

After the substantial boom of petroleum consumption by the U.S. military, the concerns of the industry shifted to the social construction of a "postwar" American landscape that also was fundamentally dependent upon petroleum. As a Conoco Oil Company annual report put it in 1945, "the advent of peace has not found Continental's marketing organization unprepared."[56] The next year it claimed: "At the beginning of the first full peacetime year there was some question as to whether civilian consumption of refined petroleum products would be sufficiently large to replace the no longer existent military requirements. . . . Fortunately, the conversion to a peacetime basis was accompanied by an unprecedented demand for petroleum products hampered only to a superficial extent by a restless labor situation."[57]

Indeed, as it turned out, the war helped accelerate the catalytic cracking revolution. Since catalytic cracking of heavier hydrocarbon molecules into lighter ones actually increased the octane rating of fuels, the federal government underwrote a massive 527 percent expansion of catalytic cracking capacity between 1941 and 1945 to expand the production of high-octane jet engine fuel.[58] Thus, given that "the postwar expansion of the industry depended upon the sale of gasoline,"[59] U.S. refineries emerged from the war with the ability to produce higher-octane gasoline per barrel of crude oil than ever before. And again, the expansion of cracking capacities during the war allowed for a massive expansion of olefin production, which became the foundation of the petrochemical and plastic industries.[60] Thus refineries took crude oil and historicized it into a set of hydrocarbon fractions particular to the moment.

During the 1950s, oil companies were eager to actively produce a vision that a multiplicity of fractionated petroleum products effectively *saturated* the whole of living, a set of practices linked to particular visions of freedom, domesticity, and health. In October 1957, a television special celebrating the seventy-fifth anniversary of Standard Oil made the case for oil and "this thing called progress." The host informed the audience,

> We Americans take so many things for granted. Especially this thing called progress. We seldom stop to think about what has made all these things possible . . . most of all the American system of free competition. . . . [M]ost of the rubber we use in this country does not come from trees, it's made from oil, manmade fibers are derived from oil, asphalt roads, medicines, all made from that incredible chemical wonderbox petroleum. But most important, oil is energy—energy to lighten man's toil and to increase his time for leisure and study; and tonight in celebrating the birthday of Standard Oil Co. New Jersey, we also salute the entire industry, because this is oil progress week . . . a week devoted to reviewing the oil industry's accomplishments—and planning the contributions to the comfort, prosperity, and security of our nation.[61]

A year earlier, the mouthpiece of the oil industry—the American Petroleum Institute—released a film unique to the Cold War mentality of the time called *Destination Earth*. In this film, a faraway "red" planet, stricken by totalitarianism, mass conformity, and technical stagnation, sends a space traveler to explore planet earth. He just happens to land in the United States. He discovers automobiles are not simply the privileged transport of a selected few but are affordable to "almost everybody." Stunned by the open access to ideas in the local library, the space traveler studies how this came to be. He discovers that "the big secret is, of course, oil!" out of which emerges "a whole galaxy of things to make life better on earth . . . the result—a higher standard of living in the USA than in any other country on the whole planet." But oil cannot do this by itself, explains the astounded extraterrestrial; "the key to making oil work for everybody is *competition* . . . [with not] just one but thousands of oil companies all competing with each other."[62] Thus life itself—and the material standard of living—was constructed as only possible through the logics of competition and the materiality of oil.

As these examples illustrate, petroleum products became key to the construction of a "free" society in opposition to communism. In both these particular representations, the ethic of competition is projected upon an innovative petroleum industry (the uncompetitive nature of which is shown in the previous chapter). Left unsaid are the ways in which the logics of competition and entrepreneurialism saturate the construction of an oil-fueled life. According to its boosters, oil represented the key ingredient to a society of competition predicated upon the atomization of individual competing subjects. Petroleum products became the condition of possibility of an individuated freedom to control space at three critical scales of lived experience—mobility, the home, and the body itself.

The Ecology of "Mobile Privatization"

I argued in chapter 1 that in the United States petroleum has helped fuel the process of a transition from the formal to the real subsumption of life under capital. Just as Marx recognized coal-fired steam engines and other machinery as constitutive of the real subsumption of labor in the realm of production, the expansion of machinery into everyday life should also be seen as an active force in the process of the real subsumption of life under capital where life is viewed as a product of entrepreneurial energies and choices—in short, *life as capital*. In the realm of everyday machinery, the most important is undoubtedly the automobile or, more concretely, the oil-fired internal combustion engine. Compared with the steam engine, the internal combustion was more compact and, as the name implies, contained the spark-plug-ignited combustion of air and fuel in a small chamber.[63] The compactness of the engine, however, depended upon an extremely energy-dense fuel like gasoline to power a heavy steel automobile over long distances for a single driver. Considered a drawback in the nineteenth century, the volatility of gasoline proved a key, explosive underpinning of internal combustion. While the steam-powered locomotive marks the important historical break between muscle-powered mobility and automatic high-speed mobility over space—the ecological "annihilation of space by time" in Marx's terms[64]—the internal combustion engine, along with cheap mass production and working-class struggle for higher wages, allowed for an unprecedented expansion of individuated mobility over the course of the twentieth century. As I mentioned in chapter 2, public transit in the United States began a precipitous decline in 1923, but the most sustained expansion of automobility occurred during the post–World War II period. Along with the increase in suburban housing, between 1945 and 1955 automobile registrations doubled from 26 million to 52 million and increased 62 percent on a per capita basis; only to increase another 65 percent per capita between 1955 and 1975.[65]

Space is both socially and ecologically produced.[66] The lived practices of energy consumption actively make possible specific spatial configurations of residential settlement, transportation networks, and the global flows of commodities. As an emerging literature on automobility has emphasized,[67] cars allowed what Raymond Williams described as "an at-once mobile and home centered way of living: a form of mobile privatization."[68] This "mobile privatization"—the generalization of internal combustion engines to wide spectrums of individuated consumers—was predicated upon the combustion of dense, fossilized petroleum. The internal combustion engine actively internalized this autonomy as an individuated sense of freedom and *power* over space in comfort. This internalized power to make space—materialized through the car—appears as a direct product of one's entrepreneurial efforts not only to make the money to afford the car but to *choose* the kind of car that suited one's specific identity and needs in life. Thus the internal combustion engine allowed for a privatized command over and experience of space that became constitutive of American conceptions of freedom, the open road, and the crafting of what Cotton Seiler calls "autonomous subjects."[69] The social relations of production that made the purchase of that car possible were underemphasized in favor of the individual's own entrepreneurial capacities, which were constructed as the "real" force behind the brute material force of the internal combustion engine. The quality of car—its style, its power, its number of cylinders, and its time spent increasing to 60 miles per hour—all stood in as evidence of an individual's work ethic and life choices. As automobiles were themselves increasingly bought on credit installment plans—increasing from 35 to 62 percent of all car purchases between 1947 and 1960[70]—the car became an increasing expression of life as capital, life as a series of investment choices and debt financing to *make a life for yourself.*

The extension of fossilized "mobile privatization" to increasing sectors of the population allowed for the dramatic dispersal of the geography of social reproduction between home, work, school, and leisure activities. The process of suburbanization effectively expanded the *scale* of urban life from walkable cities and narrow tentacles of public streetcars to a vast sprawling "megalopolis" with roads and residential developments emanating in every direction.[71] In fact, in 1949, the Bureau of the Budget (now the Office of Management and Budget) was forced to scale up the definition of the city to include the wider suburban rings that together created a "standard metropolitan area."[72] Illustrating the "victory" over space promised by General Motors in 1939, the amount of space traversed measured in passenger miles per capita increased over 97 percent between 1945 and 1955 to nearly 3,000 miles per year and 4,825 by 1975.[73] While during much of industrial capitalist history the mass of workers walked to work (with muscle power), by 1960, nearly 65 percent of the population drove to work[74] and by 1969 the Nationwide Personal Transportation reported that the average journey to work was 9.9 miles.[75] With automobility, long commutes—though never preferable—became an option if the right circumstances emerged for a perfect neighborhood for one's life. In a cartoon appearing in a 1958 issue of *The Saturday Evening Post,* the gendered dimensions of social reproduction were expressed through the figure of the increasingly frazzled mother relegated to the role of "taxi driver" (she waves in solidarity to a taxi in the street), shuffling children and breadwinning male workers through the vast spaces of everyday life.[76] Moreover, automobility expanded vacations into road trips and, on a more everyday basis, expanded the spaces of leisure time to include a wider set of choices—malls in the suburbs, nature parks on the outskirts, arts in the city—leading to a desire to effectively manage leisure time as a well-planned series of *destinations* where the question "What are you going to do?" increasingly became "Where are you going to go?"

More important than a simple extension of the scale of everyday life was an increasing entrepreneurial view of space as a vast, open territory subject to individual choices over where to live and spend leisure and vacation time. Typical of the Cold War anxiety to offer evidence of the superiority of "the American way of life," the November 1956 special issue of the magazine *House Beautiful* was titled "Report to the World on How Americans Live."[77] It included an article titled "The Key Ingredient in America Is the Freedom to Be Enterprising, to Create a New Business, a New Way of Living."[78] The story featured a couple with a successful small business and focused on *their home* as the expression of that success. But this particular story had wider implications. It was "the story of Mr. and Mrs. Everybody of the U.S.A . . . the story of opportunity Unlimited, the story of deciding how and where you want to live and work and then proceeding to do so."[79] The *choice* of where to live and work represents the qualitative (and sometimes quantitative) metric of an individual's entrepreneurial capacities connoting both one's own success in raw material terms and a family's ability to invest in the "human capital" known as children, as the quality of education and schooling came to correlate with the property values (and, thus, fiscal revenues for schools) of a given neighborhood.[80]

Founding lifestyles upon a finite resource like petroleum was not much of a concern in a nation with massive petroleum resources and gasoline purchases only making up roughly 3.5 percent of overall consumer expenditures.[81] As mentioned in the previous chapter, the whole notion of petroleum conservation did not even confront the expanding geography of automobility predicated upon long-distance commutes (if one chose), joyrides, and continent-spanning road trips. Fossil fuel underlies the logic to the famous Chuck Berry song that proclaimed, "Riding along in my automobile . . . no particular place to go." Average fuel economy for passenger vehicles and motorcycles actually declined between 1945 and 1975 from 15 to 14 miles per gallon.[82] In the 1950s and 1960s, what mattered most was a vehicle's power, as the auto companies commenced a "horsepower" race, each promoting bigger and bigger automobiles with inefficient eight- cylinder engines.[83] As Conoco's 1955 annual report indicated, the cultural mania over powerful cars translated into the refinery process: "The horsepower race among automobile manufacturers spurred the octane race among refiners of motor fuel."[84] Spurred by the catalytic cracking capacity installed during World War II, and as seen in Sun Oil's placard at gas stations (see Figure 11), refineries and oil companies each attempted to market their gasoline as more powerful than the other. It did not bother many that high-octane fuel is generally less energy efficient. In today's age of climate change, Humble and Oil's 1962 advertisement (see Figure 12) conveys a bitter irony: "Each day Humble supplies enough *energy* to melt 7 tons of glacier." The goal was *power* no matter the consequences.

The ecological basis of the vast geography of individuated choice over where to live and travel was predicated upon not just the gasoline to actively fuel automated mobility but also a wider set of petroleum products that provisioned and lubricated the infrastructures of suburban mobility. Oil companies were careful to point out that it was petroleum that allowed for not only this *power* to traverse space but also a whole set of material supplements to the car–road assemblage that actively constituted the experience of mass automobility. An Esso Oil (later Exxon) advertisement from 1950 (Figure 13) reveals the ways in which refined petroleum products were seen as distinct elements that helped construct the idea of a single life as evidenced by Esso's tagline, "Petroleum helps to build a better life."[85] Life itself is produced from not just one but multiple petroleum products. The imagery of an antiquated muscle-powered, horse-drawn carriage lodges petroleum into an imaginary of progress defined *as speed and power* to traverse space. Compared to the discombobulated expression of the horse carriage rider—forced to submit to the living whims of animal muscle—the necessarily *white* car driver (and his family) is cool, calm, and in control of his own machine powered by nonliving fuel. A

historical experience of roads "that were mostly ruts and mud" allowed
Esso to also situate *asphalt* as a central material element in the construction of a smoother, less bumpy riding experience. Asphalt is a composition
of sand, gravel, and 5 percent of the petroleum product bitumen, which
helps bind the pavement together when laid and cooled.[86] Bitumen, often
referred to as the "bottom of the barrel,"[87] represents one of the heaviest
fractions of the refining process and found its market expanding steadily
from 157,000 barrels per day in 1949 to 522,000 in 1973.[88]

Another Esso ad claimed, "The miles just seem to float by when you
travel on quiet, safe, and easy-to-drive highways."[89] Indeed, unacknowl-
edged, taken for granted *mileage* seems to be the core of the particular
spatial imaginary of freedom so central to "the American way of life."
No doubt, the building of the interstate highway system starting in 1956
helped secure the asphalt market for many years to come.[90] Finally, if there
is any function of a petroleum product that has few substitutes, it is as a
source of *lubricants*.[91] Another of the heavier fractions of a given barrel of
crude, lubricants are "needed to protect engines at higher speeds." Thus oil
not only powers the car and smoothes the riding experience but also powers the machinery itself. Petroleum products both fueled and provisioned
the very *idea* of being in control of space, the road, and everyday mobility.

Oil advertisements like these attempted to remind drivers that their
individual power to conquer space could be "taken for granted" and was,
in fact, impossible without the "important role that petroleum products
are playing in the development of better living standard everywhere." This
particular strategy served to make petroleum products the foundation of
entrepreneurial life, where life was imagined as what you make of it, but
without petroleum your individual ability to make anything would vanish.

The Real Subsumption of Home

In the chapter of *Capital* on "Primitive Accumulation," Marx discusses
precapitalist forms of private property wherein "the worker is the free
proprietor of the conditions of his labor, and sets them into motion himself: where the peasant owns the land he cultivates, or the artisan owns
the tool."[92] From the perspective of capital, this form of private property
had to be annihilated because the "fragmentation of holdings and the
dispersal of other means of production" would not allow for the sufficient concentration of social labor and productive forces adequate to the
expansion of capital. If allowed to continue, it would constrict a "society
in narrow limits" and, quoting Pecqueur, "decree universal mediocrity."[93]
The solution, as Marx describes, is the dispossession of peasants and other

FIGURE 11. "FUEL POWER TO FIT HORSEPOWER."
A Sun Oil gasoline station placard. The 1950s witnessed a cultural obsession with "horsepower," massive V-8 engines, and high-octane motor fuel. Photograph courtesy of the Sun Oil Company and the Hagley Museum and Library.

EACH DAY HUMBLE SUPPLIES ENOUGH ENERGY TO MELT 7 MILLION TONS OF GLACIER!

This giant glacier has remained unmelted for centuries. Yet, the petroleum energy Humble supplies—if converted into heat—could melt it at the rate of 80 tons each second! To meet the nation's growing need for energy, Humble has applied science to nature's resources to become America's Leading Energy Company. Working wonders with oil through research, Humble provides energy in many forms—to help heat our homes, power our transportation, and to furnish industry with a great variety of versatile chemicals. Stop at a Humble station for famous Esso Extra gasoline, and see why the "Happy Motoring"! Sign is the World's First Choice.

HUMBLE
OIL & REFINING COMPANY
America's Leading Energy Company

(Esso)

FIGURE 12. "ENOUGH ENERGY TO MELT 7 MILLION TONS OF GLACIER!"
In the postwar era, the voracious consumption of energy was celebrated rather than criticized. Unwittingly prophetic, this Humble/Esso ad from 1962 boasts about the capacity of fossil-fuel combustion to melt glaciers.

"free proprietors" of the land, tools, and other means of producing a livelihoods for themselves and forcing them into wage labor that would then lay the material conditions for a higher form of society beyond capital.

Yet, somewhere along the way, Marx's admittedly modernist conception of capital laying a progressive history for emancipatory futures got short-circuited through a kind of *reconstruction* of a fragmented geography of wage workers as free proprietors whose "freedom" and "ownership" were wholly relegated to the *means of social reproduction*—specifically the mass dispersal of single-family homes, each with a parcel of land. The real subsumption of life under capital replaces free proprietorship of productive tools and conditions of labor with a world of freedom away from work—a "life" imagined as free despite its reliance upon and subjection to the whim of commodity relations. Postwar suburbanization in the United States should be seen as a construction of a kind of neopeasantry[94] where *politics* often becomes constrained within "narrow limits" focused on the family, private property, and anticollectivist sentiments. Key to this politics of privatism was a vision of life itself as a material geography of the home as property made possible through atomized entrepreneurial choices and individual energies. The previously mentioned issue of *House Beautiful*

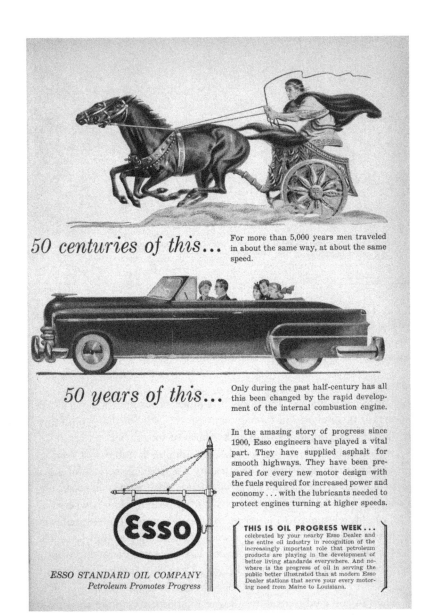

50 centuries of this... For more than 5,000 years men traveled in about the same way, at about the same speed.

50 years of this... Only during the past half-century has all this been changed by the rapid development of the internal combustion engine.

In the amazing story of progress since 1900, Esso engineers have played a vital part. They have supplied asphalt for smooth highways. They have been prepared for every new motor design with the fuels required for increased power and economy ... with the lubricants needed to protect engines turning at higher speeds.

ESSO

ESSO STANDARD OIL COMPANY
Petroleum Promotes Progress

THIS IS OIL PROGRESS WEEK ... celebrated by your nearby Esso Dealer and the entire oil industry in recognition of the increasingly important role that petroleum products are playing in the development of better living standards everywhere. And nowhere is the progress of oil in serving the public better illustrated than at modern Esso Dealer stations that serve your every motoring need from Maine to Louisiana.

FIGURE 13. "PETROLEUM PROMOTES PROGRESS."
This 1950 Esso ad contrasts the bygone eras of muscle-based mobility with the modern command over space guaranteed by oil-fired automobiles. Petroleum provides not only the fuel but also the engine lubricants, tire materials, and asphalt for the roads.

featured an article titled "The People's Capitalism" that situated private property as "basic to our republic" where "every American [is] his own capitalist."[95] Another article celebrated God's new temple as private property, "man's home among the trees—on its own plot of land, independent, individual, and in harmony with the restoring rhythms of nature."[96] But a home is what the individual makes of it. Another article offered as evidence of the dictum "no man need be common . . . no life ordinary . . . we offer the home of a man, who sells nothing but his labor as a house painter and his wife, who practices as a private nurse."[97] Their unique and beautiful home is meant to stand in contrast to their modest, and some might consider dulling, occupations, to prove that "people are aspiring upward in varied and individual ways."[98] It is their entrepreneurial hard work, meticulous savings, and attention to architecture and design that made such a home possible. It is implied by Foucault in *The Birth of Biopolitics* that entrepreneurial life is not as much about mass society—a society of homogeneity and conformity suggested by the Frankfurt School[99]—but rather about the individual capacity to make life your specific product characterized by the particularities of your work ethic, occupation, and lifestyle.

Even more than the car, the single-family home is the most perfect expression of an individual wage worker's *life as capital,* the style and location of the home being a specific material indicator of one's own capital (savings) and wage-earning capacity. In contrast to the free proprietor who owns his own means of subsistence, however, this form of private property and ownership is completely subsumed within commodity relations. Through the housing reforms described in the previous chapter, thirty-year mortgages meant, for many, *a life of debt.* The FHA programs along with the GI Bill ("homes for vets") allowed for a literal explosion of postwar single-family housings in the expanding metropolitan spaces of American cities. In 1935, the FHA insured 23,397 single or multifamily home mortgages; by 1950 that figure had risen to 342,576 units.[100] After declining through mass foreclosures during the 1930s, home ownership skyrocketed from 43.6 percent to 61.9 percent between 1940 and 1960.[101] The vast number of housing starts was a *constant* in the postwar period— from 216,000 in 1935, to 1.3 million in 1947, to 1.6 million in 1955.[102]

Ignoring the ways in which it lifted the United States out of depression, James Howard Kunstler declares that suburbanization represents "the greatest misallocation of resources in world history."[103] This is true from an ecological perspective, but as it turns out, the dispersal of individual nuclear families over vast spaces is also a nearly impossible arrangement from a *private* perspective concerned with social reproduction. As many feminist–Marxists have detailed,[104] reproducing the conditions of living in the household requires considerable *work* such as cooking, cleaning, yard maintenance, repairs, and child care. Privatizing the responsibility for reproductive labor to a single household and, usually, a single woman, is at odds with much of history when such forms of work were shared through wider social ties of kinship and community.

The postwar expansion of single-family housing in the suburbs created substantial anxiety that "the American way of life" actually entailed too much work to maintain the appearance of cleanliness and family prosperity that the suburbs were supposed to guarantee. While the internal combustion engine was the machine that guaranteed the mass *dispersal* of low-density, single-family housing throughout a vast, sprawling metropolis, a whole host of household machines were marketed as the key time-saving ingredients to efficient household work and more leisure time for mothers and their families—automatic dishwashers, laundry machines, vacuum cleaners, and so on.[105] Just as machines in production allowed technology to be imagined as solely "an attribute of capital," the mechanized household allowed individuals to conflate the power of these machines with their own powers as entrepreneurs actively making a privatized living space. Each household was conceptualized as its own private factory with a "budget"—money coming in and expenditures going out on the capital equipment necessary to reproduce both living labor and the household itself.

Although oil did provide a considerable amount of heating oil to warm the space of the household, the energy required to power this set of everyday machineries was provided not as much by petroleum as by electricity. An ad for the electric utilities from 1958 created the notion of "housepower . . . to help you live better electrically. . . . Today's all-electric living makes light work of so many household tasks." Four out of five homes, the ad warned, "suffer from *low* housepower."[106] While the burning of some of the heavier petroleum fractions as fuel oil in electric utilities did make up a small proportion of the fuel powering the electric power sector, oil's energetic qualities were mostly for the transportation sector.[107] In order for the petroleum industry to promote its products as the new key to "modern living" and its associated everyday machineries, it had to remind consumers of the *materiality* of innumerable refined petroleum products that not only made the home's structure possible but also, in their own way, helped lighten the workload. Thus the industry attempted to call attention not only to gasoline but to the multiplicity of products saturating the entire household.

One way to link petroleum products to everyday household machinery was through lubricants. In the mid- to late 1950s, Esso launched a pervasive ad campaign that attempted to illustrate the multiple ways that "Esso research works wonders with oil." One showed the figure of the male home improvement worker with an electric saw: "You probably never thought of it because you never have to—but thanks to permanent, sealed in lubricants, a great many of the motors in your home never need oiling. These 'lifetime lubricants' in your home workshop motors, in vacuum cleaners, refrigerators, washers and air conditioners are another dramatic example of how Esso research works wonders with oil!"[108] Indeed, the sense that "you never have to" think about the material processes that make an individual life possible was essential to the construction of the heroic entrepreneurial life as constructed through individual efforts.

The material infrastructure of the home itself was linked to a vast number of petroleum products whose material properties helped create the appearance of an individuated or *fractionated* life. The Esso campaign claimed petroleum led to many "little things that add up big . . . but nothing is little if it makes life better, and that's what we're doing here with oil."[109] An ad campaign from Shell in 1956 titled "From A to Z—An Alphabet of Good Things about Petroleum" provided an exhaustive list of things and practices of social reproduction linked to petroleum. *H* was for "Home": "Oil research helps with quick drying paints, no polish floors, durable plastic table tops, and weather defying asphalt-shingled roofs. In many ways, your home is a house that oil built."[110] And all these things can be derived from the chemical properties of flexible crude oil that could be multiplied through the refining process. *H* was also for "Hydrocarbon": "Because crude oil is almost 100% pure hydrocarbons, Shell scientists are hydrocarbon experts. They know how to rearrange the carbon and hydrogen atoms to get exciting new compounds not found in nature. Hydrocarbons are the broad base for the 1,001 good things oil brings you."[111] This multiplicity of products derived from refining combined to reduce the toil of household work. Figure 14 shows *M* was for "Mother," which speaks of "Mother's little helper—oil."[112] The goal of this ad is to implicate oil within a set of consecutive practices that combine to make and remake the everyday life of a housewife and her family— cooking, cleaning, shopping, and even sleeping in what I can only assume are petroleum-based fabric sheets. Oil was framed as the thread holding together this seemingly disconnected series of practices of social reproduction. Without oil, life, family, and everything else *could not be reproduced.*

Of all petroleum-based products, plastics were probably the most celebrated for their contribution to easy modern living. The plastics industry was revolutionized by the petrochemical industry when refiners discovered that cracking petroleum gases like ethane created a synthetic chemical compound of ethylene. Ethylene is versatile and can be combined with other molecules to create a whole host of thermoplastics like polyethylene (seen

FIGURE 14. "HOUSEWIFE, COOK, CHAUFFEUR, HOSTESS, TEACHER, GLAMOR GIRL—SHE DOES DOZENS OF JOBS WELL . . . WHO'S RESPONSIBLE FOR SO MANY OF THESE NEW TIME-SAVING PRODUCTS? MOTHER'S LITTLE HELPER—OIL." The key to the idea that "petroleum helps to build a better life" is the implication of a multiplicity of petroleum products in nearly every aspect of daily life. This Shell Oil ad from 1957 reveals the mother's reliance on oil from morning until night.

in plastic bags) or vinyl chloride (seen in everything from music records to raincoats).[113] The malleability and durability of petroleum-based plastics revolutionized material life.[114] As a cultural historian of plastic put it, "plastic offered an unprecedented degree of control over individual things—allowing extravagance of form to coexist with precisely engineered function."[115] As such, plastics became central to an imaginary of life made through "aspirations for a casual life of leisure."[116] A 1960 article in *Good Housekeeping* titled "A New Way of Life in One Word—Plastics" attempted to offer a report on "how these gifted materials can influence *your* life, present and future."[117] The italicization of "*your*" invokes the ways in which life was individuated as a singular project in search of management and control. Plastics were promised as "stubbornly durable. And with their whisk-clean properties, they cut down housework hours, keep maintenance expense to the bone." A plastic-inundated house was also perfect for children (an idea that sounds somewhat horrifying today in our current age of concern over plastics and chemical exposure): plastic rooms were ideal "for youngsters to live in and grow in—with maximum dignity for them and a minimum of drudgery for their mothers."[118]

Eventually the *home itself* was built with plastic. In the 1960s, the chemical industry introduced colored vinyl siding as yet another plastic item that was marketed as durable and maintenance free in order for a carefree homelife. The *New York Times* reported: "In addition to completely eliminating the need for outside painting . . . vinyl siding will not dent under the impact of heavy hail, thrown rocks or heavy objects. The high strength is also completely impervious to warping, and highly resistant to cracking or splitting."[119] Polyvinylchloride (PVC) plastic is its key material ingredient and has been linked to dioxin and other toxic exposures not only for workers in the chemical industry but also throughout its life cycle.[120] Since 1994, it has been the leading product on the market—competing with brick, wood, and aluminum—making up 34 percent of exterior siding on new single-family homes in 2009.[121]

When reviewing many petroleum advertisements in the 1950s, it becomes clear that they are promoting a very particular vision of home replete with imagery structured through uneven relations of race, gender, and class. Men work, woman stay at home, and *everyone is white* and lives in a single-family home with a garage, children, and sometimes pets (dogs and cats and all-white children make numerous appearances in the "Esso research" ad campaign). Furthermore, the imagery of a petroleum-fueled life is completely relegated to practices of social reproduction, mainly in the household or spaces of leisure and transportation. This particular vision of life is a life *in opposition to work*, where work is the often tedious interruption of one's real life of family, home, and leisure. If the realm of work is spoken of at all, it is only in relation to a heroic petroleum industry and its role in lightening modern labor. In the Shell "A to Z" campaign, *F* is for "Father": "Fix it! And Daddy does. Today's Dads, freed from the 12-hour workday have time to be with their kids—to lead, to share, to comfort, to fix. One reason—machines powered by oil have cut man's work week in half."[122] Of course, a supposed increase in time for leisure in suburban geographies is part of the constructed privatized responsibility of entrepreneurial life—to have the time to effectively manage your life, your children, and your home, with no need for outside help or any form of collective solidarity. Moreover, if life is best managed as an entrepreneurial project left to the freedom of individual private control, it only follows that *production* or work should be controlled according to the dictates of private entrepreneurial capital and its particular imperatives.

Crafting the Body with Petroleum Products

Automobility and privatized homelife were very much structured through a set of embodied, corporeal practices, but petroleum products were also purported to infiltrate, in a positive fashion, the very biology of bodies themselves.[123] The presupposition of capitalist production is, of course, a class of bodies cut off from the means of bodily reproduction—and the most important of these is food. Through the dust bowl and uprooting of masses of homesteading farmers, the Great Depression was in many ways the death knell for subsistence farmers in the United States who had considerable control over their own means of life and food.[124] The twentieth century in the United States can be read as a dramatic transformation of a geography of food producers into food consumers. In 1910, 34.9 percent of the working population in the United States was involved in agricultural production. By 1940, it had dropped to 23.2 percent; in 1960, to 8.7 percent; in 1990, to 1.9 percent.[125] Of course, a consumer market for food is an important part of the critical process of "primitive accumulation" or the severance of the working population from the means of producing their own livelihood.[126] If Aglietta described the Fordist "social consumption norm" as "characterized by the domination of commodity relations over noncommodity relations," the Fordist wage worker's relation to food is no different.[127] The new model of land ownership was based on a "yard for the kids" and maybe a small garden, but food was mainly accessed through the commodity form.

Although many increasingly relied upon food as commodities, another general trend is a decreasing proportion of income spent on food. Of course, this frees up the postwar consumption norm to concentrate on a host of other nonfood commodities—much of it wrapped up in the home–automobile nexus. The key to the real subsumption of life under capital is the construction of a realm of freedom subsumed in commodity relations. Between 1900 and 1960, food expenditures declined from 44 percent to 27 percent of consumer expenditures in the United States.[128] A lot of this decrease has to do simply with rising incomes (giving consumers more money to spend on other commodities), but it also has to do with a large-scale process of what Goodman and Redclift call the cheapening of the food system.[129] This has to do with the way in which food is produced. In 1978, one commentator summed up the developments of postwar American agriculture as "the use of land to convert petroleum into food."[130] Since World War II, the American food system has been completely *fossilized*, or has grown to rely on fossil fuel inputs at each stage of production, distribution, packaging, and consumption.[131] This is especially true of agricultural production where mainly biological forms of energy (muscles) were replaced by inanimate fossil machine power and energy-intensive synthesized chemical inputs (fertilizers and pesticides) in place of natural ones (manure).

This was achieved through three critical petroleum-based mediums: diesel-fired tractors, fertilizers, and petrochemical pesticides. The savings in human labor provided by the oil-fueled tractor are impressive: "by 1960 the tractor reduced annual labor use by at least 3.44 billion man-hours of field and chore labor from the level required using horse power technology. . . . This was the equivalent of approximately 1,720 thousand workers."[132] This not only decreased the amount of labor needed on farms but also allowed single "family farms" to control and monitor agricultural production single-handedly on extensive plots of industrially produced corn, soybean, and cotton plantations. Distinct from gasoline and the internal combustion engine, diesel is a heavier fraction that is not only more energy efficient but also easier for refineries to produce.[133] Second, the greatest energy input in American agriculture is nitrogen fertilizers. As Smil recounts, whole patterns of twentieth-century food production and consumption may have hinged on the discovery of nitrogen ammonia synthesis by German chemist Fritz Haber.[134] This process not only requires more energy than any other facet of the agricultural production process (over three times the energy needed to construct agricultural machinery); it also requires voluminous amounts of the natural gas (some of which is produced from crude oil refineries and gas separation plants in crude oil extraction sites). One report estimates that synthetic nitrogen fertilizer production accounts for around 1 percent of total global energy consumption.[135]

Such rampant fertilizer use has not come without costs, however. Scientists have discovered a marine "dead zone" in the Gulf of Mexico near the end of the Mississippi River induced by substantive runoff of fertilizers from the "corn belt" of Iowa and other farming regions along the river.[136] Third, although less energy intensive, petrochemicals became central to the production of a whole array of pesticides and herbicides that became controversial for their toxicity but reinforced a monoculture approach to agricultural production.[137]

In the postwar period, the fossilization of agricultural production alongside rising incomes allowed for dramatic increases in per capita meat consumption.[138] The key commodities to consider in this respect are what Goodman and Redclift refer to as the "corn-soya bean-livestock complex."[139] Fossil-fuel-produced corn and soy beans provide not only inputs in a variety of processed food commodities in all American supermarkets (from high fructose corn syrup in Coca-Cola to the partially hydrogenated soybean oils in Doritos) but, more important, the cheap animal "feed" composed of corn and soy for the cheap production of meat on a large scale. Opening up disposable income to fill the increasingly expansive homes of the postwar period, the fact that consumers spent *so little on so much food* was paramount. Fordism was about not only homes and cars but also a certain "standard" of food consumption. This "standard" required levels of meat consumption previously unseen in the history of human life.[140]

Tearing 35 percent of the population away from land-based food production obviously shifted food narratives from concerns with property and land control toward discourses of consumer choice.[141] Again, during the 1950s, the petroleum industry crafted a message that situated petroleum products as the critical ingredients in the diets of Fordist consumers. Seen in Figure 15, another Esso advertisement claimed, "An oil discovery that helps you *eat* better!" with images of healthy fruits and vegetables made possible through "a brilliant new chemical . . . hailed as one of the most versatile and effective fungicides in existence." The discourse of oil helping "you eat better" reinforced the increasing commodified logics through which sustenance was increasingly framed as a matter of *choices*. Not only was food cheaper, but the family *diet* was increasingly managed by the household through a navigation of the increasingly complex and multiple food commodities on the market. A new decidedly biopolitical discourse made causal linkages between particular food choices, quantifiable nutrition values, exercise, and the health and longevity of the body itself. And one's own body increasingly became an expression of one's own entrepreneurial responsibilities to manage a diet and craft healthy food choices. Fat became constructed

FIGURE 15. "AN OIL DISCOVERY THAT HELPS YOU *EAT* BETTER!"
Oil led not only to fuel and materials but to the very stuff of bodily reproduction—food and medicine. This Esso ad from the mid-1950s glorifies the role of petrochemicals in modern food production. Photograph courtesy of the ExxonMobil Historical Collection, the Dolph Briscoe Center for American History, University of Texas at Austin.

as the result of a certain lack of individuated self-discipline.[142] While proletariat life was structured through a precarious struggle to obtain the bare minimum of food calories (and often less), entrepreneurial life made food and sustenance a matter of life management. And the petroleum industry attempted to remind consumers that its products were at the center of this newfound power to craft the body in healthy ways. The Shell "From A to Z" campaign claimed G was for "growing": "Better foods and medicines make your kids the healthiest growingest [sic] kids in history . . . products made from oil help assure good health and vitality for coming generations."[143]

The oil industry marketed a whole host of products that were meant to enhance the body's stylistic presentation, such as cosmetics, synthetic fabrics, and aftershave lotion, but oil's most vital contribution was framed in the world of medicine. In a 1964 article by a Shell researcher in *New Scientist*, titled "Plentitude from Petroleum," the author situates petrochemicals as a key to a new biology of living bodies: "Petrochemicals will . . . be used more and more in the field of public health. . . . Here, as in the field of plastics, science has discovered potent new methods of analyzing and synthesizing complex molecular structures. . . . The future control of diseases in plants and animals will be based on increased understanding of the biological activity of specific chemical structures."[144] The Shell "From A to Z" campaign offered repeated reminders of petroleum's contributions to medical progress. A was for "Antiseptic": "Petroleum is an important medicine too."[145] Another ad claimed, "Shell makes possible many new anesthetics, antibiotic solvents, and other medical marvels to help all of us live to riper old ages."[146] Oil could also target specific organs: "Shell chemicals make important heart drugs pure and potent."[147] Simply the proliferation of plastics made petroleum the presupposition of a whole host of medical equipment.

The entanglements of medicine and petrochemicals allowed the industry to craft petroleum as the condition of possibility of continued life itself, the material ingredient of effective *biopower*. This makes political opposition to the industry a threat to the biopolitical vitality of the population as a whole. The biopolitical logics of derision aimed at those who would challenge the health effects of petrochemicals was starkly revealed on public television in 2001. A documentary by Bill Moyers, "Trade Secrets,"[148] made use of substantial historical archival research of the chemical industry's secret documents to make clear that the industry had substantial knowledge of the contribution of chemicals—most notably polyvinyl chloride—to the cancer and death of their employees.[149] In striking similarity to the tobacco indus-try, the documents revealed efforts to cover up such evidence in order to avoid financial liabilities. The documentary offered contextualizing interviews from scientists and medical professionals concerned with the health effects of the proliferation of petrochemicals in everyday life. In a personalizing moment, Moyers himself was tested for the presence of synthetic chemicals and eighty-four were found. When the program aired on public television, it was followed by a roundtable discussion featuring two representatives from the chemical industry, one environ-mental activist, and one environmental scientist concerned with the health effects of petrochemicals.

In one of the tensest moments of the conversation, one of the industry advocates, Terry Yosie, the president of the American Chemistry Council, issued clearly planned remarks:

> Mr. Moyers you had your own body tested and this was shown to the viewers. What was not shown to the viewers was that the products that we make probably saved your life. From what I read in the news-papers you had a very serious heart operation in about 1994; you had a blockage in an artery leading to your heart. When your Doctors dis-covered this problem and advised you and provided the professional counseling and expertise that made it possible for you to recover to the robust man that you are today, they were using our products. . . . They diagnosed your problem using technologies that we helped develop. When they operated on you they used surgical instruments that we helped develop. To ensure that you did not contract a subse-quent infection post-operation you were given medicines; in addition you were probably given medication afterward to ensure your continu-ing return to health. I believe that your state of well-being today was directly dependent on the benefits that our industry provided to you and to every American.[150]

The vague use of "technologies" and "our products" stood in for the unnamed but assumed multiplicity of petrochemical products—mostly plastics for medical equipment I assume—that made Moyers's heart sur-gery possible and allowed him to recover to "robustness." The framing of petroleum products as key to "the benefits that our industry pro-vided you and to every American" acts a biopolitical trump card for any form of contestation of industry practices. Even as synthetic chemi-cals circulate within our very bodies, petrochemicals are crafted as the supplementary materiality of all the medical infrastructures that allow chemical-laden life to go on. Opposing petroleum, as it turns out, is opposing the whole basis of entrepreneurial life—the freedom to make a life for yourself, to use your individual energies to bring together the medical commodities necessary in preventing premature death. Lack of access to such petroleum-based medical products would, of course, interrupt the atomized life project of disciplined productivity setting the stage for a twilight of leisure and retirement.

Conclusion: Refining Suburban Politics

Figure 16 reveals the material politics of Esso's ad campaign. The figure of a successful, well-dressed couple in the shadow of a vast industrial chemical plant sums up the entire campaign to *make visible* the dependence of life on a multiplicity of refined hydrocarbon products. It situates the chemical plant as constitutive of a successful and glamorous life. As social anxiety over the environmental and health effects of petro-capitalism has intensified since the 1950s, the petroleum industry is happier today to set aside refineries and chemical plants as part of the many invisible networks of socioecological interchange that make certain lived practices possible. In this chapter, I have attempted to show how the petroleum industry both materially and ideologically situated the vast array of petroleum products at the center of a particular vision of entrepreneurial life. This view of life is not particular to postwar American capitalism and, of course, has its roots in what Max Weber called "the protestant work ethic" and a whole proliferation of bourgeois promises of the way capitalist competition leads to self-improvement and rags-to-riches opportunity.[151] What is historically specific to postwar American capitalism is the unprecedented extension of this view of life to millions of middle- to upper-income suburban home and automobile owners, not to mention the "other America" living in impoverished rural areas and inner cities that might have aspired for such a life. As I detailed in the previous chapter, this cultural politics of life should be viewed mainly as the product of struggles over the appropriate "standard of living" for masses of capitalist wage workers. But there is no question that these struggles produced a particular vision of life that was contingent on the vast hydrocarbon assemblages of crude oil. In the postwar period the oil industry was indeed keen to make such entanglements visible. What is most striking (and somewhat preposterous) is how quickly a vision of life as produced through *public* and *collective* energies (government housing, labor and infrastructure commitments) was transformed into a *privatized* vision of life as simply a product of individual efforts and choices. Perhaps the greatest contradiction of the New Deal was the way

December 10, 1955

ESSO RESEARCH works wonders with oil

Wonderful new fibers that oil helped make

Next time you hear Dacron⁵ or nylon . . . think of Esso Research, too. Wonderful man-made fibers like these are made with the help of the kind of chemicals produced from oil through Esso Research! Wherever you see the Esso name, you know *great research* is behind it! **ESSO RESEARCH** (ESSO)
⁵DuPont trade mark for its polyester fiber.

FIGURE 16. "WONDERFUL NEW FIBERS THAT OIL HELPED MAKE."
During the 1950s, chemicals were acclaimed as a pathway to "better living."
In a juxtaposition that we would find odd today, this Esso ad situates elegance
and style *alongside* the imagery of a petrochemical plant that made the clothing
possible. Photograph courtesy of the ExxonMobil Historical Collection, the
Dolph Briscoe Center for American History, University of Texas at Austin.

in which it committed public energy to construct a *privatized* geography of social reproduction. Before long, much of popular common sense simply forgot about the public basis of a privatized existence.

This cultural political amnesia about the transformative power of public works and redistributive economic policies began to create a solid political force throughout the newly laid suburban tracts in the postwar era. As Mike Davis put it, "the ballast of capital's hegemony in American history has been the repeated autonomous mobilization of the mass middle strata in defense of petty accumulation and entrepreneurial opportunity."[152] During the nineteenth century this "mass middle strata" was composed of the free proprietors and petty commodity producers whose interests in private property aligned with capital. Yet many of these proprietors produced some of their own subsistence and were not fully subsumed within commodity relations for processes of social reproduction. During the postwar period, the unrelenting process of suburbanization laid a *political bloc* of waged bodies who more and more viewed their own material surroundings—a house, a car, a yard, their own bodies—as solely a product of their own efforts and thus their own responsibility to manage and maintain. These entrepreneurial efforts were mostly managed through commodity relations—mortgages, car payments, and grocery bills—that made life more and more about budgets, investments, and financial planning: life as a business negotiated through the commodity form.[153]

Much of this suburbanization occurred in the "Sunbelt" of the American South and Southwest. It was here that capital fled from the unionized landscapes of the soon-to-be "Rust Belt" of the Northeast and upper Midwest. Davis situates "cheap energy" as a key feature in a new postwar "union resistant geography of American industry": "Cheap energy [was] a key factor in allowing industry to disperse in search of malleable, non-union labor."[154] As refineries themselves shed a unionized labor force through automation, refined products supplemented the material structures of suburban feeling in the Sunbelt and beyond. Making use of the fractionated products produced by refineries, Americans began to view the life of mobility, home, and the body as a fractionated singularity reducible to individual choices and efforts. With the materiality of life appearing so private—private homeowners drove private cars to private workplaces—it is no wonder suburbanization engendered a politics of "hostile privatism"[155] that was defined by its disdain for taxes, government, and any notion of "the public." As social reproduction was shot through with the political imagery of freedom, property, and entrepreneurialism, the politics of capitalist production translated easily into a neoliberal celebration of markets, the private sector, and the beneficence of the profit motive.

This geography of privatism *was laid* during the postwar period, but its political effects became mobilized to a sufficient electoral majority by the end of the 1960s. In Davis's correct view, "the seventies witnessed the most rapid and large-scale shift in economic power in American history."[156] It is during this decade that oil figured centrally in debates over inflation, the cost of living, and concerns with the limits of American hegemony in the face of "foreign" competition and resource ownership. It was these debates that helped produce the rise of an antigovernment neoliberal discourse as a political force against New Deal liberalism in American politics. The role of suburbanites as the popular force behind such a political rise can help us recontextualize Foucault's remarks in 1978: "I think the multiplication of the enterprise form within the social body is what is at stake in neoliberal policy."[157] I will now move on to this volatile decade, the oil shocks, and the entrenchment of neoliberal hegemony.

CHAPTER FOUR

Shocked!

"Energy Crisis," Neoliberalism, and the Construction of an Apolitical Economy

The time when everything seemed easy is over, the time when you could believe that human energy like natural energy was unconditionally and endlessly at your service: when filling stations blossomed enticingly in your path all in a line with the attendant in green or blue or striped dungarees, dripping sponge at the ready to cleanse a windscreen contaminated by the massacre of swarms of gnats.[171]

—Italo Calvino, *The Petrol Pump*

Levittown Ablaze

The 1970s oil crisis was a "shock" in the wake of the postwar period of relative prosperity and suburban mass consumption. It would be difficult to find a landscape that represents the suburban boom of postwar American capitalism more than Levittown, Pennsylvania.[1] Constructed by the famous suburban developers Levitt and Sons, the development housed several white families—the attempt of a black family to move to the neighborhood in 1957 ignited a race riot[2]—whose mostly male breadwinners worked in a nearby U.S. Steel factory. Levittown was the expression in landscape form of the postwar class accord between capital and labor that began to disintegrate in the 1970s. In the long summer of 1979, this larger disintegration was symbolized on these very streets. On Saturday, June 23, a convoy of independent truckers converged on the Five Points intersection in Levittown (which contained four gasoline stations) to publicize their nationwide strike. The motorized occupation was meant to be a peaceful protest over high fuel costs and government restrictions over speed and load limits. Representing what environmental historian Mark Fiege calls "rural populism," the truckers projected characteristics like "hard-working, virtuous anti-authoritarian, and staunchly autonomous." The truckers, who had grown to become cultural icons of independence and rebellion in the 1970s, believed their rigs not only could make fewer deliveries under speed limits but were meant to "operate most efficiently at 70–75 mph."[3] In fact, they went so far as to wield "55 miles per hour" signs altered into swastikas to represent conservation measures as totalitarian forms of state control.[4] In solidarity, and equally frustrated over gasoline shortages and long lines at the pump, "scores of enthusiastic Levittowners lined the streets to cheer on the convoy."[5] When one trucker fired up the crowd and was taken to the ground and beaten by police, the once peaceful protest quickly turned violent. Different accounts number the protesters between 1,500 and 3,000, many of which were teenagers who "torched cars, destroyed gas pumps, and pelted police with rocks and bottles."[6] The police force—many of which were reinforcements sent in from Philadelphia—fought back brutally, as many peaceful protesters were struck by clubs or bitten by attack dogs. Thus the protest quickly evolved to combine rage over limits to gasoline with outrage over police brutality.[7] Chants erupted of "More Gas Now!," "No Gas, My Ass!,"[8] and "To Hell with Shell!,"[9] all representing the popular refusal to accept limitations of gasoline, which had more and more become seen as a necessity of everyday life. As one protester put it, "I'm frustrated by it all, like everybody else. We want to get gas without waiting in line."[10] Three weeks after the riots, Jimmy Carter delivered his famous "malaise speech," which blamed the stagflation and energy crises of the 1970s on a "a crisis of confidence . . . as crisis in the growing doubt about the meaning of our own lives and the loss of a unity of purpose for our nation."[11] The speech of course came to symbolize the fall of Carter's presidency and the rise of Reagan with his "optimism" about American might and refusal to accept the discourse of sacrifice.

Thus the eruption of riots in 1979 at gasoline pumps in Levittown, Pennsylvania, can be seen, in the words of one historian, as "symbolically marking the close of the postwar period."[12] Of course, what made the violence in Levittown so remarkable was the veneer of normalcy and security that the suburbs were supposed to offer—as opposed to "other" urban geographies wherein violence is expected.[13] Conservative columnist George Will asked in *Newsweek*, "Social disorder in Levittown? The postwar era really has ended."[14] As one Levittown resident recounted the event in 2011, "Levittown is a solid, middle-class working town which I believe is representative of the rest of our country, and the country was angry."[15] The riot expressed the underlying contradictions of the postwar class consensus based not only on cheap oil but also on high wages, an increasing standard of living for middle-upper-income blue-collar workers, and exclusionary geographies of suburban white privilege.

When oil was scarce, working-class consumers viewed it as just another threat to their way of life, along with attacks on wages and benefits in the workplace, demands of austerity from government, and escalating inflation. Indeed, in line with the equation of government speed limits with Nazism, the politics of the 1970s more and more focused on a demonization of "Big Government" whose taxes and restrictions threatened the freedom of average citizens. The solution to the shackles of Big Government was the market. As a historian of the 1970s put it, "increasingly, all sorts of Americans, even those with dreams of radical reform, looked to the entrepreneur and the marketplace as the agent of national progress and dynamic change."[16] While labor politics, government intervention, and energy were all seen as vital to the construction of "the American way of life" in the 1930s and beyond, during the 1970s it was precisely these forces that were suddenly constructed as problematic threats to that very way of life.

In this chapter, I suggest that popular understandings of the "energy crisis" tended to reinforce the shift to neoliberalism.[17] If there was one utterance from the riot that reflects this larger popular interpretation, it was the quip "No Gas, My Ass!" Poll after poll revealed that the majority of Americans believed the energy crisis was "fake" or "contrived" by a variety of forces including the oil companies (construed as monopolist profiteers), oil sheiks, and the government itself (through oil price controls).[18] Most believed that oil scarcity was not based in any physical limits but was, as Ronald Reagan claimed in an op-ed, a form of "politically inspired scarcity."[19] Thus the energy crisis of the 1970s represented not so much a crisis of scarcity but rather, as a *Fortune Magazine* editorial put it, "a crisis for the whole free market system." The editorial goes on: "The cutbacks may soon entail rationing and allocations of gasoline and fuel oil, and these, too, would be bad news for those who believe in an economic system governed by the free play of supply and demand."[20] In fact, the crisis centered upon a whole set of actors and institutions that were construed as the antithesis of the free and fair competition of the market.[21]

Most Americans, however, were not concerned with abstract theories of supply and demand but with a notion of "fairness" within the logic of entrepreneurial life. A supplementary cultural politics that underlies such a view of "life" is the imaginary of an "even playing field" of competition wherein market subjects are assured that wealth and privilege only flow to those who earn it. The rise of neoliberal political hegemony must grapple with the popular meanings of competition. Foucault states: "The society regulated by reference to the market that the neo-liberals are thinking about is a society in which the regulatory principle should not be so much the exchange of commodities as the mechanisms of competition. . . . It is a matter of making the market, competition, and so the enterprise, into what could be called the formative power of society."[22]

The popular interpretation of the energy crisis was not only that it wasn't "real" but that it was unfairly rigged by a set of actors whose position in the market was both monstrous and unearned. The centralized and large organizational power over the market wielded by "Big Oil," "Big Government," and "Big OPEC" appeared discordant when compared to the decentralized, hardworking, taxpaying, suburban geography of everyday life epitomized by what Richard Nixon referred to as "The Silent Majority."

Thus the rise of neoliberalism during the 1970s created a popular terrain of common sense around the construction of an *apolitical economy* wherein any visible form of power over the market—labor strikes, price controls, the redistribution of wealth—was construed as an unfair "political" attempt to capture wealth by virtue of connections with special interests, rather than individual tenacity and "hard work." Through the logic of entrepreneurial life the market must appear as an impersonal and decentralized geography of free and fair competition where the life chances of all individuals are negotiated through an even playing field. Therefore, the free market and deregulatory ideology of neoliberalism found popular purchase through the interdiction of politics from the impersonal and abstract forces of the market and the price mechanism. While such idolatry of the free market circulated in multiple geographies, it is no coincidence that it found purchase within the dispersed geographies of private property owners in the suburbs. Of course, this decentralized suburban geography was made possible through petroleum products and the materiality of everyday social reproduction in American suburbs tended to reinforce an idealization of a free market. Before exploring this specifically neoliberal politics of the 1970s energy crisis, it is necessary to provide some larger historical context. As it turns out, the oil shocks of the 1970s are rooted in some very basic aspects of the materiality of oil—its finite nature combined with the uneven geography of deposits.

Fossil Fuels and the Specter of Exhaustibility

Ever since William Stanley Jevons classically posed *The Coal Question* in 1866, the politics of fossil fuels has always anxiously confronted the materiality of exhaustibility.[23] As capitalism became more and more dependent on fuels that were limited to stocks of subterranean deposits, the vexing predictive question of when they start "running out" has recurred time and time again. In the United States, concerns among geologists about petroleum supplies date back at least to the 1920s and probably before, but the 1970s energy crisis witnessed an expansion of concerns with the finiteness of fossil fuels into the popular imagination.[24]

Most analysts consider the 1973 oil embargo as the signal moment of "energy crisis" with the quadrupling of oil prices, gasoline lines, and geopolitical turmoil.[25] Yet two other very important events happened earlier—two events that guaranteed the embargo would have the particular effects that it did. First, hindsight reveals that 1970 was the peak of U.S. crude oil production at 9.6 million barrels per day.[26] The United States was the number one global oil producer until the mid-1960s and, in fact, consistently remains the number three global producer to the present day. Nevertheless, the United States has never produced as much crude as it did in 1970. After the peak of U.S. production became recognized for what it was, it vindicated petroleum geologist M. King Hubbert who predicted as much in 1956.[27] Since this vindication, a whole cottage industry of peak oil theorists—and their detractors—have speculated and vigorously debated the impending peak of global oil production.[28]

Second, 1972 marked the end of a postwar American capitalism based on substantial oil production capacity. Indeed, as discussed in chapter 2, it was the *overcapacity* of U.S. production fields that sent oil markets into crisis in the 1930s and necessitated the elaborate set of institutions to manage and curtail the production of oil in alignment with projected (and always increasing) consumer demand. In March of 1972 the TRC and the Louisiana Conservation Commissioner set all wells to 100 percent of their Maximum Efficient Rate of Recovery.[29] Thus, rather than restraining production below capacity as was the custom from the mid-1930s, U.S. producers were allowed to produce as much as they could. As the *New York Times* reported, "the action came after executives from the nation's largest oil companies gave rosy forecasts of growing market demands in 1972. But they said domestic production simply could not meet more than a fourth of the 800,000 to 900,000 more barrels a day the nation would use this year than it did in 1971."[30] The lack of spare capacity within the territorial boundaries of the United States created great uncertainty within world oil markets, which depended upon the United States—and specifically Texas—as the so-called swing producer who could step up production in moments of crisis.[31] For example, during the Suez Canal crisis of 1957, and again during the 1967 Six Day War, attempts by the Gulf oil states to counter Euro-American-Israeli imperialism through oil cutoffs were thwarted by U.S. producers increasing exports across the Atlantic.[32] In 1973 and 1974 the United States could not play such a role. The peaking of U.S. production and disappearance of spare capacity came as an abrupt surprise. As Vietor recounts, "scarcely anyone recognized the decline in spare capacity until it had occurred."[33] As late as 1968, the industry mouthpiece *American Petroleum Institute* estimated the United States contained nearly 2.5 million barrels per day of spare capacity.[34]

Thus in 1972 it appeared the United States had reached its geological limits. Of course, it was during the same year that the Club of Rome issued its now infamous *The Limits to Growth,* which kicked off a decade fixated on scarcity and the finite nature of nonrenewable resources (like fossil fuels) upon which modern industrial capitalism depends.[35] A 1974 editorial in the *New York Times* titled "An Age of Scarcity" claimed that "abundance" is only a "modern idea." In the context of the postwar consumer boom the inevitability of scarcity has become less abstract and more commonsense—"It is not neo-Malthusian doctrine but mere common sense that impels men everywhere to come to terms with a new age of scarcity."[36] Critics of the psychological and spiritual emptiness of the "consumer economy" and suburban lifestyles proliferated throughout the 1950s and 1960s,[37] but only in the 1970s did it appear that "the American way of life" was threatened by an external force of natural limits. As early as 1972, an editorial declared, "the energy crisis . . . threatens the American way of life, at least that life that means color television, frostless freezer, self-cleaning ovens, and electric grills, knives, combs and toothbrushes."[38] While the last chapter showed its celebration, the centrality of energy powering a whole set of automatic machines and social reproductive practices was suddenly problematized. The multiplicity of petroleum products provided the materiality underneath an individualized vision of control over the stuff of life—space, the home, the body—but the 1970s witnessed innumerable events that put this control over life into question.

More than other commodities, the scarcity of oil—with its pervasive embeddedness in all forms of everyday practice—signaled a larger crisis.

While there were shortages of many commodities in the 1970s, one editorial stated, "Not wheat, nor newsprint, nor beef came close to discommoding as many Americans as do gas[oline] and oil."[39] The commonsense view of oil scarcity was expressed in countless letters to newspaper editors and politicians. One letter to the editor nervously contemplates the subterranean finitude of petroleum: "everybody knows that sooner or later the oil inside the earth is going to play out and then what are we going to do? Can you imagine a world without automobiles? How can the modern world survive without oil?"[40] The very survival of the modern form of "life" was at stake. A 1973 political cartoon depicted "Automobilicus Americanus—1893–1973" on display in the museum of natural history.[41] After the decade of scarcity, individuals came to dreary conclusions. One letter from 1981 blames the profligacy of U.S. consumption: "We have grown fat and obese and sickly by our consumption. Like the fat man, our arteries are clogged—with traffic, smog, noise, plastic, radiation—and our vitality and mental health are suffering."[42] The imaginary of finite fossil fuels was also rooted in a corresponding discourse of energy nationalism, which produced anxiety over increasing reliance on energy not found within the territorial boundaries of the U.S. nation-state—the problem of "foreign oil."

Foreign Oil and the Territoriality of Dependence

One of the most basic geographical problems with petroleum (and other mineral resources) is that deposits are unevenly distributed and materially fixed in space. As David Harvey has long instructed, such spatial fixity always stands in contradiction to the *motion* of capital, labor, and money under capitalist social relations.[43] The fixity of mineral resources in particular spaces is one reason for the "geopolitical fetishism," discussed in chapter 1, wherein oil is viewed as a strategic object of competition between rival nations and companies. Critical political geography has long argued that the most basic territorial structure of mainstream geopolitical discourse is the distinction between "inside" and "outside."[44] This distinction provides the basis for a whole normative language and anxiety over the territoriality of where oil happens to exist—domestic "inside" oil (good) and foreign "outside" oil (bad). Since oil was so central to life, dependence upon "outside" oil became synonymous with insecurity, as a whole nation's population was assumed subject to the whims of "foreign" politics. Moreover, oil's fixity in space (and declining reserves within the U.S. territory) created increasing geostrategic discourses where access to oil for the reproduction of American life was equated with national security, or what was eventually termed "energy security."[45]

It is important to understand the historically shifting narratives surrounding the problem of "foreign oil," because it has not always had the same discursive power that we recognize today. During the postwar period, the geopolitics of petroleum governance in the United States were worked out to construct a Fordist national oil regime wherein mass oil consumption was largely provisioned by domestic production. It is fashionable to trace U.S. dependence upon "foreign oil" to 1945 when FDR had his famous meeting with Saudi King Saud on an American warship along the Suez Canal.[46] But this meeting was about securing Saudi oil not for American consumers but rather for U.S. oil capital, which by 1948 include the companies we now call Chevron, ExxonMobil, and Texaco (now Chevron) forming the Arabian American Oil Company. With its Americanized enclaves, U.S. oil workers exploited domestic and migrant workers in the Saudi oil fields to mainly export oil to Europe and Japan and not the United States.[47]

As discussed in chapter 2, the Fordist national oil regime depended on a series of institutional arrangements—state prorationing, the Interstate Oil Compact, and federal projections of demand—to keep prices stable and high enough to protect a variety of high-cost independent oil producers. But the spatially fixed and finite nature of U.S. petroleum reserves necessarily stood in massive contradiction to the postwar Fordist regime of accumulation itself based around booming economic growth—growth both in monetary terms of gross national product and in *biophysical* terms of always-increasing demand for materials, energy, and the concomitant production of waste. The prospect that domestic "inside" oil supplies would not be sufficient to satiate rising consumer demand was certainly acknowledged and fretted over by intellectual and political elites. Most famously, the Paley Commission Report of 1952 advised the Truman administration that the United States would become increasingly reliant on foreign sources of oil and a whole host of other finite raw materials.[48] Yet amid the boom of postwar prosperity, suburbanization, and the dramatic expansion of car culture, such concerns were not widespread within popular culture. Indeed, one of the most common narratives about the energy crisis of the 1970s was that the United States was completely "caught unawares" and "shocked" by their sudden and brutal reliance upon foreign sources of energy.[49] In retrospect, commentators suggested the exclusive use of domestic supplies during the postwar period meant a policy of "drain America first."[50]

Foreign oil was seen as a problem long before the 1970s, but the concern was mainly articulated by a coalition of independent, high-cost domestic oil producers.[51] With clear memories of the crisis in East Texas, these producers feared that prices would collapse if cheap foreign oil was allowed to flood the domestic market. Precisely because of the actions by state prorationing agencies to restrict output and keep prices high, oil produced from Venezuela to the Middle East was considerably cheaper to produce. Although estimates varied, Prindle suggests that in 1960 an average barrel of crude in the Middle East cost $.20 to produce, while the U.S. level averaged $1.75 (a number that may itself be reflective of proration policies).[52] Not only was foreign oil cheaper, but the fields were so prolific that if tapped they would very quickly unleash massive amounts of oil onto the market. For example, in 1955 the average production per well in barrels per day was 5,090 in the Middle East, 176 in Venezuela, and only 13 in the United States.[53]

Thus until the 1970s, "foreign oil"—especially the massive reserves in the Middle East—was constructed as a grave but narrow and sectoral threat to the domestic U.S. oil petroleum industry. International companies—and even independent refiners—always had a strong incentive to import this cheap oil and capture markets in the United States. Insofar as the United States *could* provision itself domestically with *high-cost* oil, it needed to construct a nationally circumscribed "market" that would shield domestic producers from low-cost foreign oil. This required a massive institutional project to "fix" the U.S. oil market—both "fixing" the market in the sense that a contest is "fixed" and "fixing" the market in space.[54] The production of oil was not governed by a decentralized network of free buyers and sellers, but by centralized system of allowances and exemptions serving to allocate supply to projected demand within the U.S. national territory.[55]

The contradictory tendencies of this arrangement revealed themselves very early on in the 1950s. Table 3 shows the level of imports and the percentage of imports quenching demand throughout much of the postwar period. The year 1948 should be seen as the watershed year in which the United States became a net importer of crude oil. The slow and steady increase in imports both in raw numbers and as a percentage of demand was considerable. As domestic consumption needs increased throughout the postwar period due to the expansion of suburbanization, the export of U.S. oil declined precipitously (except during international crises in 1957 and 1967) as more and more oil was needed for domestic consumption. Between 1945 and 1960, U.S. crude oil exports declined from 33 million barrels to 3.1 million barrels.[56]

The pace, however, could have been considerably greater without the installation of a mandatory import quota program in the later years of the Eisenhower administration that remained in effect between 1959 and 1973. Under pressure from domestic independents, this program attempted

Table 3. Total Imports and Imports as a Percentage of Domestic Consumption in the United States, 1945–74 (selected years)

Year	Imports (millions of barrels)	Percentage of imports/ consumption
1945	–69	–4
1950	199	8.5
1955	321	10.4
1960	590	16.8
1965	833	20.2
1970	1,154	21.9
1971	1,351	24.9
1972	1,654	28.8
1973	2,199	35.5
1974	2,150	36

Source: Bohi and Russell, *Limiting Oil Imports*, 22–23.

to fix the level of crude imports at 12.2 percent of domestic demand, but a complicated set of exemptions by refineries and geography ensured that the level was higher than that. Nevertheless, Bohi and Russell estimate that if the program had not been instituted, imports would have constituted 61 percent of domestic consumption in 1970.[57] The same analysts even go as far as to claim that the program was coordinated "against the best interest of the original major company importers," concluding that "the political power of oil may be great, but based on the record of the mandatory quota program, the power is not found in the international giants of the industry."[58] The program mainly served the politically vocal and dispersed domestic independent producers. The import quota program represents an attempt to—in David Harvey's terms—"re-schedule" the crisis of the petro-capitalist United States from the 1960s to the 1970s.[59] The program served to mollify the contradictory tendencies inherent within the entire system of prorationing—namely, the maintenance of national high-cost producers in the face of a global geography of low-cost production.[60]

Only in the 1970s did the concept of "foreign oil" become problematized from the perspective not of just oil producers but also consumers. Americans were not worried about foreign sources of coffee, bananas, or increasingly manufactured consumer goods, but oil's saturation of social reproduction and centrality to ideas of life, home, freedom, and mobility made dependence on foreign oil seem unduly precarious. Such dependence fit squarely within a wider narrative of American decline marked by the erosion of global hegemony during the 1970s.[61] Ever since, leaders have continued to promise an energy system contained within American borders in the name of "energy independence." Indeed, Richard Nixon's first major speech after the Arab embargo initiated a new "Project Independence," which unrealistically promised American independence from foreign oil by 1980.

Among politicians and intellectuals, the oil crisis was represented as a great geopolitical confrontation between the United States and Europe and the rising power of OPEC and the oil-producing countries. The effective use by the Gulf oil states of what was called the "oil weapon" seemed to reverse the many centuries of Euro-American global domination.[62] It was the mere assertion of power by non-Western countries that was seen as so shocking and unacceptable. On a more popular level, the politics of oil were shot through with a racialized politics of anti-Arab xenophobia. As seen in Figure 17, political cartoons inundated American newspapers with highly caricatured images of obese Arab oil men cynically plotting their next draconian imposition of pain on American consumers. This form of "popular geopolitics" found its purchase through anger over U.S.

FIGURE 17. "LOUSY CAMEL—WE'LL HAVE TO GET RID OF IT."
Part of the "shock" of the 1970s oil crisis for Americans was the audacity of "other" nations to actually exert power over their own oil. One result was the proliferation of xenophobic imagery of Arab oil men in cartoons such as this. Cartoon by Pat Oliphant, Copyright 1975 Universal Uclick. Reprinted with permission. All rights reserved.

exports to these very nations.[63] Just after the embargo, a Texan man wrote President Nixon's energy advisor, John Love: "In 1973, King Feisal [*sic*] and other 'sheeted sheiks' are cutting our oil off while we continue to ship drill pipe and other drilling equipment to the Arab states."[64] By the second oil shock of 1979, country music star Bobby Butler released "Cheaper crude or no more food," which echoed a long-standing neomercantilist sentiment that the United States fed the world and thus could cut off food supplies as retribution. The folksy lyrics suggest a vindictive geopolitics of "us" versus "them": "If they don't lower the price of crude, we're gonna cut off the food. And give about a week they'll sing a different tune. Crude oil prices have gotten so high it has gotten hard to survive, and I bet those Middle Eastern countries are havin' a laugh."

One letter to Nixon's energy czar in 1973 presciently summed up the song's message, which emphasizes that ultimately food is more important than oil for *life itself*: "Tell the Arabs, 'You drink *your* oil and we'll eat *our* grain."[65] As I will detail later, the primary objection emerging from popular discourse was that Arab nations were unfairly intervening within the marketplace. Yet for most Americans, the energy crisis was less about geopolitical confrontation and foreign policy and more about the "shock" of gasoline lines and limits to everyday geographies of social reproduction combined with spiraling inflation, or what was called "the rising cost of living."

Freedom on Fumes: Gasoline Lines and the Geography of Limits

During the winter of 1973–74, and again in the summer of 1979, consumers witnessed winding lines at gasoline pumps in different parts of the country, limits on how much gasoline could be purchased, and outbursts of violence between and among consumers and gas station attendants. One attendant in Bradenton, Florida, was killed by being crushed between two cars when an eager driver propelled the car in front of him forward into the victim.[66] In Pennsylvania, Bruce Hibbs obtained a 12-gauge shotgun, joining "a number of operators who are toting guns to protect themselves."[67] Theft from gas stations and automobiles themselves was not uncommon. No longer taken for granted, access to gasoline appeared as a Hobbesian "war of all against all."[68]

The geopolitical narrative of dependence and insecurity translated well to the everyday struggle for gasoline. Just as the Arab embargo was represented as a lack of U.S. control over distant spaces, the gasoline shortage was characterized by a sudden and dramatic limitation to the privatized command over space central to the postwar vision of entrepreneurial life. Thus

Richard Nixon's "Project Independence" on national territorial terms paralleled the loss of independent control over everyday life during the gasoline
shortage. For many short on gasoline, the most pressing concern was how to
traverse the new suburban geography marked by vast spaces between home
and work. This new geography made private automobile commuting the only
option, and therefore the sudden lack of gasoline was framed as an unjust
threat to livelihood. As one writer from infamously suburban Southern California put it to President Nixon's Energy Office, "many thousands of us have
no public transportation to get to our jobs and rely on our cars. I have to
travel 70 miles a day round trip to work and no bus could get me there. I
must drive, and soon I'll be unable to buy gas *or* afford it. This *isn't right!*"[69]

Apart from getting to work, the limits on gasoline threatened the entire
expansive geography of household provisioning and social reproduction. A
letter from a suburban Long Island housewife laid out the impossibility of
life under gasoline shortages: "We live on Long Island and cannot walk to
food stores, banks, doctors, etc. Forget pleasure riding—how do I feed my
family if it is six miles round trip to *one* supermarket and about the same to
our doctor, upon whom we literally depend on to survive?"[70] Perhaps most
alarming was the inability to traverse the space between home and doctor
or hospital. Another woman from North Carolina with a sick child had her
gas stolen from her tank. She explained the ordeal in a letter to the editor:
"My gas indicator registering on empty, I tearfully explained to the attendant my plight. To no avail, he annoyingly told me he was not selling any
gas until the proper time. He . . . explained he had already turned away at
least 25 folks with the same hard luck story—sick kid, stolen gas."[71]

This was a crisis not only of space but also of the dialectical relation
between space and time. The most visceral aspect of the crisis was marked
by lines—that is, time spent waiting. Of course, the Darwinian struggle
to obtain gas took place outside the workplace and within the terrain of
life and freedom so central to postwar prosperity. The *New York Times*
reported that one mother of five children would wake before five o'clock
in the morning to attempt to beat others to the pump. She claimed to feel
"like a hunter who has been out and gotten his supplies for the week."[72]
A widely read article in *Time*, "Gas Fever: Happiness Is a Full Tank,"
depicted a housewife waiting in line knitting a scarf: "Housewives in hair
curlers knit sweaters at the wheels of their station wagons in the predawn
blackness of Miami."[73] The time spent in line cut into time not working
and this so-called free time was also filled up already with the vast duties
of privatized social reproduction.

At stake were the very time–space rhythms of what was known as leisure, specifically the temporal space of freedom known as "the weekend."

In a story focused on the plight of exurbanites, the *New York Times* laid out the commonsense association between leisure, automobility, and the weekend: "Americans' leisure-time activities, particularly those on the weekend, have long been dependent on their cars, and there are indications that a drastic revision of those activities is taking place in some places."[74] Shortly after the embargo, news reports circulated that the Nixon administration was considering a ban on Sunday driving. A citizen from Bayonne, New Jersey, wrote to Nixon, "Some of us can only use our car on Sunday, because of working during the week, and only have this day to visit our children out of town."[75] One letter writer from New York City boasted that he uses public transit for work during the week but reserves the weekend for recreation and oil-powered escape: "We drive to escape the caverns of the city; and mass transportation is insufficient for such purposes. Such a ban would amount to the complete elimination of recreation outside the home."[76] In the exurban fringe, one isolated individual lamented, "Before the energy crisis . . . I'd visit friends or go to see my brother or play golf, shop around town. Now I stay home and work around the house. . . . What the hell kind of life is it to just work all the time and not have any recreation or vacation even."[77] Indeed, removal of plentiful gasoline raised new questions about the nature of life and work in the suburbanized United States. As seen in Figure 18, an ad for long-distance telephone service offered a techno-spatial fix to the new limitations over space confronted by American drivers on the weekend—"Fill 'er up" with phone conversations rather than face-to-face visits with family and friends.

Certainly the experience of the first oil shock was discombobulating. But a more important political question is how the crisis itself was explained. Who or what was blamed? Central to the popular understanding of the oil crisis was wider outrage over what was bemoaned as the rising "cost of living."

Life's Cost

I know where my inflation comes from; from the gas that you give me!

—Archie Bunker to his Son-In-Law,
Michael Stivic, *All In the Family*

The hit television series *All in the Family* centered upon the cracks in the pillars of postwar social reproduction during the 1970s—a bigoted male breadwinner (Archie Bunker) threatened by the social and political upheavals of the 1960s. In 1974, the first four episodes of the fifth season were titled "The Bunkers and Inflation." The saga detailed the

Fill 'er up this weekend.

You can still take "pleasure trips" on the weekend, even though there's a fuel shortage. You can go by Long Distance—this way you save fuel and money too. Dial-direct rates are especially low all day Saturday...and Sunday until 5 p.m.

So, pick a place and take a spin this weekend.

Long Distance is the next best thing to being there.

FIGURE 18. "FILL 'ER UP THIS WEEKEND."
Gasoline shortages represented a crisis to the time–space rhythms of everyday life in the postwar United States. This Bell telephone ad from 1974 promised a technological fix for those who lacked the fuel to physically visit their friends and family.

increasing cost of living for the Bunker family in the face of a strike at Archie's plant and the necessary entrance of his wife Edith into the work force. Without Archie's wages, bills mount, gender roles are destabilized, and Archie is forced into the tasks of household maintenance and social reproduction.

The story arc that holds the four episodes together is the strike, and interestingly it is the strike itself that is constructed as an utter calamity for the Bunker family because of the loss of wages. As an avowed old "trade union man," Archie makes his hostility to the "young hothead" strikers plain: "There's a right way to strike and a wrong way to strike, and the right way is don't strike!" The plot represents the remarkable turnaround in the four decades between the Great Depression and the 1970s. The threat to the life of the Bunker household was, in a phrase, *political claims on the market*—labor strikes. Once central to a vision of a "better life" and fairness in American political economy, labor unions were now constructed as corrupt, greedy, and illegitimate interests groups whose wage demands served to push prices upward and harm ordinary consumers.

The Bunkers' battles with inflation fit squarely within a larger narrative in the 1970s over the rising cost of living. During a decade of widespread anxiety and concern over economic decline, several polls indicated that the rising cost of living was the primary concern of the majority of Americans.[78] Inflation was constructed as a universal threat that affected all consumers everywhere, threatening both their incomes and savings. The entrepreneurial vision of life as a business was reinforced through an escalating set of money costs and a vicious cycle of price increases outstripping wage increases. In August 1971, President Nixon's economic stabilization program—which included the abrogation of the international gold standard—included the establishment of the Cost of Living Council (COLC), which was tasked with controlling wages and prices on an economy wide basis.[79]

Obviously direct government control of prices and wages did not fit nicely with the vision of a free market. According to the utopic vision, the "free market" was supposed to be "self-regulated" by impersonal, quasi-natural forces of supply and demand.[80] Inflation was often seen as being generated by personalized forms of market intervention. As a COLC pamphlet, *Inflation: On Prices and Wages and Running Amok*, explained in 1973, inflation was caused by a particular form of "market power": "In some activities, big corporations and big unions seem able to push prices and wages up even when demand is steady or going down. They are able to do this because competition to provide the goods and services is limited or restricted in some way. Economists call this 'market power.'"[81]

Throughout the 1970s, the escalation of inflation was attributed to various forms of market power by large and visible organizational forces whose presence in the economy was seen as unfairly institutionalized and threatening to competition. Three forms of political intervention were isolated. First, the Keynesian commitment to full employment, government spending, and social services was constructed as inflationary by enlarging the money supply. Although from a strict monetarist perspective, it was the "printing" of money and simple expansion of the money supply that was the *sole* cause of inflation, several analysts sought to conflate monetary with fiscal policy.[82] In 1977 as he prepared for another run for president, Ronald Reagan suggested as much in a radio commentary: "Inflation is caused by one thing—government spending more than government takes in."[83] Unwittingly, government efforts at welfare and justice—even if well intentioned—contained an "inflationary bias." As the head of President Ford's Council of Economic Advisor, Alan Greenspan, put it in 1975, "the inflationary environment that prevailed throughout the 1960's and that carried the seeds of eventual recession stemmed from an overly optimistic view of our supply capabilities. Governments strongly committed themselves to ameliorate social inequalities at home and abroad and to achieve an ever rising standard of living. However morally and socially commendable, these commitments proved to be too ambitious in economic terms—both in what they actually attempted to achieve as well as in the expectations they raised among the public."[84]

Second, as with the Bunker family, labor unions were constructed as a primary driver of "cost-push inflation" through the assertion of their own "monopoly power" over the price of labor power. Such power over the market served to push wages higher than they "should" be in a competitive market and thereby pushed up prices up along with them. As neoliberal Austrian economist Gottfried Haberler put it, labor unions represented an outright contradiction of a properly competitive economy: "It should be observed that in a competitive economy with flexible wages and prices there would be no such thing as a cost or wage push. Cost or wage-push inflation implies monopolies, or more generally absence of competition. I shall concentrate on labor monopolies, that is labor unions."[85]

Thus high wages—once seen as the key to a virtuous Fordist cycle of high productivity, profits, and "effective demand"—were now seen as the cause of inflation and economic decline. Thus the politics of the 1970s tended to focus on the need for austerity and belt tightening. As labor historian Jefferson Cowie puts it succinctly, "the old disease of low wages in the thirties was now the new cure for bloat in the seventies."[86]

Third, as previously mentioned, there was perhaps no more visible intervention than the COLC's *direct* wage and price controls in 1971 via the appointments of a separate "Price Commission" and "Pay Board." President Nixon insisted these dramatic forms of market intervention could only be temporary: "We will continue price and wage restraints until inflationary pressures are brought under control, but we will not make controls a permanent feature of American life."[87] Direct controls were represented as the exact "other" of a free market economy. As conservative economist Alan Reynolds put it in the *National Review*, "frozen wages and prices prevent the smooth, continual adjustments which free markets would otherwise make in response to government's inept management of debt and money."[88]

Overall, inflation was itself blamed on *politics*—that is, the assertion of political claims upon what is meant to be an apolitical naturalized realm of the market. As seen in Figure 19, the COLC pamphlet made this clear with the image of protesters in the streets simply asking for "More money now!" Any politicized attempt in the market was seen as a violation of the abstract rule of value in a properly competitive economy. And obviously, the image of street protesters most overwhelmingly implicates workers and unions as a primary cause of inflation, whose interventions in the market are *necessarily* politicized. As a commentator in the *National Review* put it, labor-induced inflation could only be solved by depoliticizing the price of labor power, the wage: "We need a method of removing wages from politics."[89] One letter to Nixon's energy office stated, "History has proven that only a free market in wages and prices will stop inflation."[90]

Government spending, unions, and price controls were all seen as paradoxical attempts at economic betterment that had the unwanted side effect of exacerbating inflation, but after the Arab embargo of 1973, oil price increases were elevated to the primary driver of inflation in the public imagination. Like government, unions, and price controls, oil's role in the rising cost of living was seen through the assertion of particular forms of interference with market forces.

The Ubiquitous Commodity

Naomi Klein argues that the "shock doctrine" is imposed on particular societies during moments of political and economic crisis, and the notion

FIGURE 19. "MORE MONEY NOW!" Increasingly during the 1970s, inflation was blamed on "political" interventions with the marketplace. In a Cost of Living Council pamphlet on inflation, political protest for "more money" (by workers one must assume) is itself seen as inflationary. From Cost of Living Council, *Inflation: On Prices and Wages and Running Amok* (Washington, D.C.: Government Printing Office, 1973), 14.

of an "oil shock" fits within the larger crisis of the 1970s.[91] It was oil's unique centrality to social reproduction as whole that created the imagery of an oil shock, or what Daniel Yergin called at the time "an oil-induced economic crisis."[92] Oil was constructed as a ubiquitous commodity—not only as central to the multiplicity of everyday practices that constitute "life" but also as an input to virtually every stage of economic activity, not the least of which was the transportation of commodities, which had shifted dramatically toward diesel-powered trucking in the postwar period. As Nixon's appointed "energy czar" and strident neoliberal William Simon explained, "petroleum is a unique commodity, entering into almost every facet of our economy, as the fuel for heating our residences and other buildings, as the fuel for transportation of goods and people and as the raw material for a myriad of products like fertilizer and petrochemicals. It is hardly an exaggeration to say that petroleum has become the lifeblood of our economy."[93]

Petroleum's pervasiveness meant an increase in the price of oil permeated through the prices of all commodities and thus was seen as a singular force causing inflation and recession and eroding the capacity to make a living. In December of 1973, the *New York Times* declared the onset of "The Energy Recession," and commentators began to hypothesize a one-to-one relationship between oil price increases and the decline of economic statistics.[94] Writing in *The New Republic*, Charles L. Shultz claimed, "About one third of the rise in unemployment over the past year can be traced to [oil price increases]."[95]

The imaginary of an "oil shock" corresponds nicely to what Michael Watts calls "commodity determinism."[96] Watts uses this concept to critique the so-called oil curse wherein oil-endowed nations are automatically beset by state corruption, nondiversified economies, violence, and war.[97] Oil shock discourse explained economic crisis as a naturalized product of commodity price increases and underemphasized the concurrent power shifts within the broader American political economy. Thus the focus on the oil shock stood in as an external explanation for the dramatic declines in living standards during the rise of what David Harvey calls neoliberalism as the "restoration of class power."[98] Yet more important than the vision of an externally induced crisis was how the "crisis" itself was explained—and, as it turns, it wasn't seen as a real crisis at all.

"Energy Crisis? Phooey!"[99]

While many naturalized the oil shock as an inevitable product of geological scarcity, the vast majority saw the oil crisis as not natural but politically "contrived." As one letter put it, "the 'energy crisis' is phony and a hoax on the people."[100] In fact, it became rare to see the phrase "energy crisis" *without* the accompaniment of scare quotes, indicating the ultimately contested nature of and skepticism over the reality of the crisis itself. As part of a series of panel discussions put on by the neoliberal American Enterprise Institute, one 1974 program was simply called "Is the Energy Crisis Contrived?"[101] Like the major explanations of the drivers of inflation, many blamed forces of "market power" whose institutional presence in the economy allowed oil prices to be rigged for the benefit of special interests. As stated previously, the most obvious villain—and the easiest target for xenophobic rage—was OPEC, specifically the Persian Gulf producing states, who unabashedly announced their presence in the market as a cartel with political interests. As one op-ed summarized, "the Arabs play . . . [a] . . . special mixture of politics and economics."[102] Like the politics surrounding inflation, it was this *mixture* that offended the logic of a free and fair market. It was the use of a vital commodity to advance political goals that informed the idea of "the oil weapon." The oil weapon—one headline called it "stronger than armies"[103]—was seen as an "extra-economic" form of violence imposed upon ordinary consumers.

Yet several polls revealed that the majority of Americans felt that it was not OPEC that was primarily to blame, but the private oil companies.[104] The blame for the oil companies emerged out of a long history of popular disdain for "Big Oil" originating with the muckraking exposé of John D. Rockefeller and Standard Oil by Ida Tarbell in 1904.[105] In the 1970s, books like *The Seven Sisters, The Brotherhood of Oil,* and *The Control of Oil* all depicted a story of a world oil market controlled by a handful of multinational oil companies.[106] As one letter to Nixon's energy czar exclaimed, "All appearances lead to the conclusion that this crisis has been foreseen and purposely augmented, if not engineered by the international oil cartels, to make their grip on the economy more secure."[107] The most vocal critics of "Big Oil" were on the political left. Highly visible was consumer advocate Ralph Nader, who described the energy debacle as "the most phony crisis ever afflicted on a modern society."[108] He charged specifically that "the energy crisis was orchestrated for political and economic benefit by the oil industry."[109]

Like the disdain for the monopolies known as labor unions, the popular rage against "Big Oil" was also rooted in the accusation that the oil companies were "monopolists" who unfairly rigged the marketplace for their narrow gain. One reporter observed a school bus that ran out of gas with a fourteen-year-old shouting out the window, "You see what happens when a couple of monopolistic oil companies take over?" Bumper stickers were circulated that read, "The oil companies are hoarding oil to raise prices."[110] The fact that high oil prices in the 1970s also generated record oil profits did not dampen suspicion of the oil companies. One citizen wrote to Nixon's energy czar, "It is appalling to me to go to my local service station and discover a 3 cent per gallon jump in one week, and then to read in *Time Magazine* that Exxon showed a net profit increase last year of 80% to $638,000,000."[111]

Of course, the logical solution to this was the reassertion of "competition" in the marketplace. Even Ralph Nader conceded as much in his recommendations to energy czar William Simon in congressional testimony: "[Simon] should be concerned with devising ways to break up the oil monopolies and with bringing some competition into the industry."[112] More everyday reactions concentrated on the idea of "fairness" and the imaginary of an even playing field of the marketplace. One letter suggested, "Give the oil companies a fair margin of profit, but do not allow the monopolistic practices of the major companies to continue."[113] Ordinary consumers believed that the oil companies' position in the market was unfair in comparison to their own: "Where are the incentives for the overburdened middle class? . . . they [the oil companies] get a 15% price increase while the forgotten consumer is supposed to be satisfied with a 5.5% salary increase that has to cover unlimited price increases on all the necessities of life. Where is the equity in that?"[114]

The logic of market fairness centered on the tried and true distinction between "big" and "little" forces in the market. Countless letter writers identified themselves as simply "the little guy" or just an "average citizen" whose fate was stacked against the big forces of oil monopolies and the government that served them. As one letter to the editor put it, "it appears that the average working class citizen's vote has lost all economic power and the policy of the federal government is now determined by corporate board room decisions."[115]

While "Big Oil" remained a convenient scapegoat for the forces on the political left, the rising power of the political right attempted to put the focus on the machinations of "Big Government." One letter to the editor in the conservative paper the *Orange County Register* stood apart from the more populist rage against "obscene" oil profits: "We must stop blaming all our problems on 'big' industry (the productive segment) and start looking at the growth of government (the unproductive segment)."[116] Indeed, Ronald Reagan concretized his position on energy during the 1980 campaign with the catchy slogan "Our problem isn't a shortage of oil. It's a surplus of government."[117] And the oil crisis provided a clear terrain through which to locate the monstrous power of government in the marketplace—price controls. While most of the wage and price controls instituted in 1971 were lifted in 1973, price controls for domestically produced oil persisted until 1981 and kept domestic oil prices slightly lower than imported oil. While many efforts were made to "decontrol" oil prices throughout the 1970s, it became politically difficult because of the perceived inflationary impact of higher oil prices. A *Los Angeles Times* editorial warned, "Instant decontrol will deliver a jolt not just to consumer pocketbooks but also to prospects for national economic recovery."[118]

From the emerging free market perspective, the price controls provided an easy explanation for shortages.[119] Conservative critiques were right to emphasize the mystifying bureaucratic complexity of the price controls themselves based on complicated distinctions between "old" and "new" oil and inland versus coastal refineries. The key was to locate the controls as the *cause* of shortages. The story tells how bureaucratic efforts to allocate supplies created the very shortages they were charged with solving. It became common dogma that the gasoline lines were not at all attributable to the Arab embargo but rather to government price controls. Writing in 1979, neoliberal economist Milton Friedman and his wife Rose laid it out in characteristically simple terms: gasoline lines were caused by "one reason and one reason alone: because legislation, administered by a government agency, did not permit the price system to function. . . . The smooth operation of the price mechanism—which for many decades had assured every consumer that he could buy gasoline at any of a large number of service stations at his convenience and with minimal wait—was replaced by bureaucratic improvisation."[120]

The price mechanism stood in as a naturalized force against the *politicized* interventions of government in the market. High prices would both discourage consumption and encourage more production. As the conservative magazine *The National Review* put it, "if prices were allowed to rise, they would encourage new supplies and discourage waste. Rationing simply replaces these smooth adjustments with arbitrary political decisions."[121] Conservative thinker William Buckley reasoned, "You are much better off reducing the amount of gas spent by raising the price of gasoline than by setting up a giant bureaucracy engaged with the impossible job of adjudicating everyone's claim to gasoline."[122] Government involvement in energy amounted to the politicization of what should be abstract, apolitical market forces. One letter to Nixon's energy czar put it plainly: "No man or group of men in government is able to allocate resources as wisely as the entire market adjusting to meet altered demands."[123]

Certainly this free market critique of Big Government resonated with some "average" Americans. One letter put it plainly: "The obvious solution to the energy crisis is to let the free market work it out on a supply and demand basis."[124] Again, the problem was rooted in the personalized intervention into a free and fair market. Price controls were pinpointed: "Let's get rid of price controls and remove all the other shackles government has on the producers of energy. They can then increase production so much that the whole world will be amazed."[125] Yet the more common sentiment simply did not distinguish much between "Big Government" and "Big Business"—both were commonly seen as symbiotic forces stacked against "fair competition" for average workers. This was based on a perception that both the government and big industry had obtained unearned privilege within the market while the average workers struggled to get by on the basis of their own hard work and tenacity. "We're sick of government officials kowtowing to all the big interests in this country while the individual is struggling to make ends meet and getting nowhere fast."[126] Indeed, according to the logic of entrepreneurial life, the individual's capacity to make a life for himself or herself was thwarted by these larger forces skewing what should be an even playing field: "Please make the corporations and government officials aware of how badly they are treating the common man, because of their greed for power and money or both."[127] The scale or "bigness" of government and industry simply was not comparable to the modest everyday geographies of suburban (and urban and rural) social reproduction.

Thus, regardless of one's political perspective, the commonsense sentiment was that the energy crisis was contrived by a set of *political* forces intervening in the marketplace—OPEC, oil monopolies, and (perhaps the most important concretization of "the political" in capitalist society) government bureaucrats. These forces belied the ideology of an "even playing field" that structured the vision of a competitive market composed of individual entrepreneurs. The "other" of this politicized market was of course an *apolitical economy*—a market imaginary wherein power is *decentralized* and prices fluctuate not as the result of "Big" forms of "market power" but rather of millions of "little" individual choices. Over the course of the 1970s, this imaginary of the decentralized apolitical economy mirrored the suburban geography of oil-powered privatism.

Suburbanization and the Silent Majority of the Market

The very idea of a competitive market is based on a *geographical* imaginary of a decentralized price mechanism. As Friedrich Hayek put it, "to split or decentralize power is necessarily to reduce the absolute amount of power, and the competitive system is the only system designed to minimize by decentralization the power exercised by man over man."[128] In the ideal, perfectly competitive market, the movement of prices is determined by millions of diffuse choices whose aggregate force constitutes what Hayek called "the impersonal and anonymous mechanism of the market."[129] This vision of the impersonal market stands in contrast to the villain of neoliberal thought—"collective and 'conscious' direction of all social forces to deliberately chosen goals."[130]

During the 1970s in the United States, political power shifted rightward through a popular critique of all forms of "collective and conscious" interventions into the marketplace.[131] This critique rests on the expurgation of politics from the realm of the economic, or the construction of an apolitical economy wherein any visible form of power over the market—labor strikes, price controls, the redistribution of wealth—was construed as an unfair "political" attempt to capture wealth through privilege and not individual tenacity or "hard work." Taxes, welfare systems, affirmative action, and busing all were seen as skewing the competitive playing field.[132]

This critique of public intervention in the market found popular purchase through a middle- to upper-income stratum of mostly white homeowners concentrated in the suburbs, most importantly, rapidly suburbanizing Sunbelt megametropolitan areas like Atlanta, Charlotte, Dallas, Houston, and Phoenix.[133] At the end of the volatile politics of the 1960s, Richard Nixon coined the term *the silent majority,* which appealed to this mass of suburbanites who felt distanced and alienated from the highly visible political struggles against war, colonialism, racism, sexism, and environmental destruction. Indeed, the mass social protests of the 1960s were characterized by their wholesale rejection of so-called middle-class suburban life.[134] The civil rights and women's movements called attention to the exclusionary nature of New Deal liberalism and its celebration of the white male breadwinner. Antiwar protests revealed the "golden age" of postwar prosperity was predicated upon brutal subjugation of the "Third World."[135] Countercultural experiments included back-to-the-land movements that attempted to sever the postwar construction of life as only realizable through commodity relations.[136]

For those actually living the "American dream" of suburban home ownership these protests were not only seen as an attack on their way of life but also exhibited the very form of "politics" that was beginning to be villainized as a threat to the ideal of an apolitical economy. The "silent majority" is often linked to Nixon's "Southern strategy" of harnessing the overt racism of the formerly democratic South hostile to the civil rights agenda.[137] But, as Matthew Lassiter argues, the "Southern strategy" was not as much based on backward, rural, George Wallace–style racism but was more properly a *suburban strategy* that harnessed ideologies of "a middle-class outlook expressed through the color-blind language of consumer rights and meritocratic individualism."[138] While overt racism was pervasive—indeed I read far too many letters that championed the energy-saving solution of ending the extra mileage of school busing[139]—the competitive imaginary of "the even playing field" tended to downplay structural disadvantages based on race or geography. Thus key to this "middle class outlook" is what Edsall and Edsall term "conservative egalitarianism," which was "based on an idealized concept of 'equal opportunity' and reinforced by free market economic theory."[140] It is this vision of a free and fair competitive market that "provided the intellectual justification for the abandonment of the interventionist and redistributive policies that had characterized the New Deal order."[141]

Of course, at the core of "meritocratic individualism" is the wider logic of entrepreneurial life to exercise what Hayek called the power "to shape their own life . . . [and] . . . the opportunity to choose between different forms of life."[142] According to the suburban silent majority, their entrepreneurial life projects were individual and privatized affairs that were only threatened by the various forms of public intervention in the marketplace. As one letter to Nixon from a white suburban father in Charlotte, North Carolina, put it succinctly, "I have never asked what anyone in government or this country could do for me; but rather kept my mouth shut, paid my taxes and basically asked to be left alone."[143] Thus the *silence* of the silent majority was key to the construction of life as a privatized affair that stood in contrast to the vociferous world of *politics* whose very goal was to capture resources not through the normal circuits of meritocratic individualism but through institutionalized channels of public privilege in government.[144] The suburban silent majority, and its "ideology of hostile privatism,"[145] was hostile toward not only government welfare programs but *all forms* of politicized privilege in the market, including the monopolistic power of "Big Oil." Of course, Big Oil's power was only secured through its coalition with "Big Government." Hostility to government, taxes, and the critique of Big Oil is only a product of a deeper process of the everyday production and reproduction of life in the suburban geographies of the United States. As I've argued, it is important to understand that oil itself—and the multiplicity of petroleum products oil affords—powered and provisioned a particular material geography of everyday life. Cheap gasoline in particular represents one of the key bases to an entire geography of privatized automobility and low-density suburban residential settlement. Only with the fuel to power the dispersal of individuals across the dispersed sites of social reproduction was such "sprawl" possible.

Therefore, there is a material ecology underpinning the *decentralized geography of suburban life,* and this decentralization mirrored the vision of the impersonal and decentralized market. In contrast to the centralized site of the city—with its public spaces and volatile political eruptions—the suburban decentralization of the population allowed for the idealization of an *apolitical* economy based on the decentralized forces of the price mechanism. From the perspective of dispersed homeowners, the power of market actors should be as modest as their own, and wealth, epitomized by the home and the car, needed to be seen as a product of competitive, entrepreneurial efforts, not institutionalized privileges. Again, key to this idealization is *silence,* or the removal of politics from what is supposed to be an "impersonal and anonymous market mechanism." The silence of the silent majority is only silence in the public realm of politics—freedom, choice, and life itself are all located in the *privatized* spaces of home, leisure sites, and the automobile that connects them. The materiality of oil-based life made it appear that this life was purely the product of the individual and that life itself could be "left alone" from the machinations of the public. Oil-powered life did not *guarantee* these neoliberal ideologies (there were certainly plenty of suburbanites who were antiwar and strong supporters of civil rights, women's liberation, and environmental protection[146]), but it created a *lived geography* conducive to a politics of privatism against the public sphere.

The decentralized geography underpinning the silent majority of the market was precisely what was seen as under threat during the 1970s. If freedom was materialized through privatized command over space, the energy crisis ushered many forms of control and coercion limiting that freedom. One letter to the editor mocked the 1970s sentiment that Americans must live with "less": "Yes, we must live with less—less of the bureaucrats and less of the giant multi-nationals controlling our lives, our assets and our future generation's lives and assets."[147] One editorial by Butler Schafer in the *Orange County Register* theorized that the political construction of "threats" was central to the legitimation of government domination: "Without [threats], people may become accustomed to living their own lives and making their own decisions without the divine intervention of the state. Such a 'threat,' I suggest, is being promoted as 'the energy crisis' a 'threat' we are told, that can be overcome only though increased political control over our lives."[148]

This threat of control was expressed as a threat over geographical patterns of life. A 1979 advertisement by automobile interests depicts a wholesome image of leisure—a family fishing (Figure 20). It reads, "Try getting it there without a car or truck." By depicting the government regulations as an imminent threat to the geography of leisure, the ad enrolls the consumer to "help us protect your freedom to drive." Ironically, several letters expressed the opinion that they *favored* gasoline rationing because it would allow consumers themselves to *choose* how to use their own gasoline as opposed to politicized determinations of "essential" versus "nonessential driving": "I am opposed to any form of gasoline allocation that pre-determines my selection of its use. The restriction of gasoline use for recreational pursuits is an infringement on my basic right of freedom to choose."[149]

More viscerally, the energy crisis was seen as a threat to individual life projects whose years of hard work and tenacity were based on the assumption of plentiful cheap fuel. One letter speaks of a woman's saving plans to "make a lifetime dream come true. I bought my camper in July in order to see my country up close." Again, the threat to this life project was pinpointed upon political interventions: "I will not be restricted as long as my taxes support parks and highways. I bought a camper to go places, and will not let an irresponsible government direct its use or hamper my

Try getting it there
without a car or truck.

Not so many years ago, only a privileged few could own and keep a boat on America's lakes and waterways. Today, almost every place for boating in America is accessible to almost everyone. Thanks to the automobile.

The automobile and our national network of streets and highways have become the world's best system of transportation.

Getting your boat to where you can enjoy it is only one measure of what the automobile does for you. Where you work and live, where you shop and go to school—almost everything you do, you do better because of the automobile.

But don't take it for granted. There are people in government, and others, whose *only* answer to our environmental and energy problems is to restrict use of the automobile.

We want continued improvement — not restriction. We want to see the car and our highways become an even more efficient system of transportation.

Join with us. Write to us. Tell everyone you can how important your automobile is to you. Because, if you don't speak up today, your freedom to drive may be restricted tomorrow. (NADA)

New car and truck dealers of America
8400 Westpark Drive, McLean, Virginia 22102

Help us protect your freedom to drive.

FIGURE 20. "HELP US PROTECT YOUR FREEDOM TO DRIVE . . . THERE ARE PEOPLE IN GOVERNMENT, AND OTHERS, WHOSE *ONLY* ANSWER TO OUR ENVIRONMENTAL AND ENERGY PROBLEMS IS TO RESTRICT USE OF THE AUTOMOBILE."

For many the "energy crisis" was seen as a contrived threat to justify more government control of everyday life. In this 1979 ad from the New Car and Truck Dealers of America, auto companies claim a shared interest with private car owners against government regulation that endangered a spatial experience of freedom.

plans."[150] Another letter complained of COLC price controls that threatened the writer's business: "I am, you might say, a self-made man. . . . My wife and I have worked since then, day and night, year round, like slaves to build this business up and bring to the level it is at today."[151] The sudden and dramatic *manipulations* of the market threatened the whole imaginary of self-made life.

Overall, the crisis of the 1970s focused on an escalating set of political controls over everyday forms of freedom and choice. The politics of oil-powered privatism that emerged from the geography of suburban life focused on the elimination of all forms of political control. In the face of increased control and unfair forms of organizational privilege, the only logical response was the elimination of market controls (deregulation) and the freeing of the forces of competition. By the end of the 1970s, Ronald Reagan rose to political power through the idealization of the market against all forms of political control in energy policy: "The greatest problems in the energy field came about with government's involvement in the marketplace, regulation, price-fixing and so forth, and I think that today the answer lies in the marketplace."[152] The freeing of competition in the marketplace resonated with the popular interpretation of the energy crisis as contrived by uncompetitive forces. Just as the decentralized geography of homeowners wanted to be "left alone" from the invasive tentacles of Big Government, it was "common sense" that private industry should be afforded the same freedom.

Aftermath: Oil and Power in Reagan's America

> [There was a] . . . just irritation with those that used liberal
> phraseology in defense of anti-social privilege.
>
> —Friedrich Hayek, *The Road to Serfdom*

The language of fair competition and free markets resonated with large cross section of American society, but as even Hayek acknowledges is possible, in reality neoliberal hegemony was exercised more as the deployment of state power on behalf of private capital. The myth of neoliberalism is, of course, a vanquished state, but as Foucault suggests, neoliberalism means that "government must accompany the market economy from start to finish."[153] After the election of Ronald Reagan in 1981, this became particularly clear in relation to the oil and energy sector. He appointed James Watt, who demonstrated hostility toward environmental policy and restrictions of private extractive capital on public lands, secretary of interior. Harnessing the decentralized imaginary of neoliberal freedom, Watt claimed that environmental regulation "is centralized planning and control of society" akin to Nazi- or Communist-planned societies.[154] Overall, Reagan instituted the classic neoliberal strategy of deregulation by fiscal evisceration—that is, imposing massive cuts on the agencies charged with regulation, such as the Environmental Protection Agency. As Watt himself claimed, "we will use the budget system as an excuse to make major policy decisions."[155] Vice President George Bush chaired the Presidential Task Force on Regulatory Relief, which, Daniel Faber explains, "quickly compiled a hit list of 'burdensome' regulations that it had solicited from business, trade associations, state and local governments, and other local organizations."[156] Faber claims the largest requests came in reference to environmental regulations, and the petroleum complex of industries surrounding refineries, chemical plants, and oil transportation companies were some of the most vocal. Moreover, as many commentators have noted, the shift to financialization after 1980 has been the hallmark of neoliberal capitalism based on more predatory forms of speculative accumulation.[157] In 1983, as part of a larger deregulation of finance under Reagan, the New York Mercantile Exchange began to allow the trading of crude oil futures, which quickly catapulted oil traders as primary drivers of the price of crude oil.[158] While futures markets are often justified as a means for players to hedge risks and provide stable price information, after 1983 the price of crude oil became subject to intense bouts of volatility not seen since the 1930s. This volatility became the basis of huge windfalls for those financial speculators who bet on the "right" price movements.

In the wake of the 1970s, the shift of American politics toward free market ideology and deregulation of industry should come as no surprise. The decade was marked by the rise of highly organized think tanks, like the Heritage Foundation, spouting neoliberal logics that, as Timothy Mitchell points out, were built and expanded with oil money from the likes of the Koch Brothers and Richard Scaife of Gulf Oil.[159] Political Action Committees (PACs) were constructed with the express purpose of lobbying government officials for probusiness policies.[160] The role of the oil industry in shaping the growth and success of the Republican Party through contributions to the Republican National Committee is well documented.[161] In the popular imagination this has cemented "Big Oil" and "Big Government" in an unholy alliance, but perhaps more important was the role of the millions of independent oil producers and royalty owners who became formidable sources of financing and votes for GOP congressional candidates across the Sunbelt in Texas, Louisiana, and Oklahoma.[162] Recent statistics suggest that 67 percent of the domestic oil industry has few employees or fewer, 46 percent of domestic production is done by independents, and there are a staggering eight million landowners who receive royalties from the oil and gas industry.[163] This represents a far more decentralized source of financial and electoral power for the GOP. During the 1980s, vice president of the Independent Petroleum Association of America (IPPAA) William Anderson launched a program of "Political Wildcatting" that did not form PACs but endorsed nonincumbents "more sympathetic to the goals of the independent petroleum industry."[164] He suggested that taking a risk on probusiness freshman candidates was akin to wildcatting for oil: "So just as you've got to continually be putting in new wells all the time, you've got to continually be putting new freshman classes in all the time."[165] Anderson's IPPAA endorsement would instantly attract "thousands of contributions from independent oilmen—and from other sectors of the business community as well."[166] As Raymond Vernon explained, "the strength of the independents, then as now, rested in part on the fact that they were well distributed over the face of the United States and could rally formidable Congressional support for any position they took."[167]

Thus the rightward shift of American politics could not happen with the financial and organizational power of "Big Oil" alone. It required not only the decentralized popular energy of the suburban silent majority but also the dispersed coalition of independent oil producers and royalty owners who delivered both money and millions of votes. What connected "little oil" producers to the "little guys" owning suburban homes was a vision of a "free" society composed of individual enterprises that only asked for the fair opportunity to compete on an even playing field with everyone else. Yet the neoliberal revolution was also based on a massive, upward redistribution of wealth. Most working-class Americans have witnessed in the period since 1980 eroding standards of "life," mounting debt, and increasing job insecurity. Under these conditions the necessary relations between cheap oil and "life" become more pronounced. In fact, cheap oil became a matter of life and death in more ways than one.

CHAPTER FIVE

Pain at the Pump

Gas Prices, Life, and Death under Neoliberalism

Pain at the Pump

The 1970s decade of shortages and perceived scarcity seemed to indicate the end of the era of petroleum profligacy. No one in the 1970s would have expected the subsequent collapse of energy prices and evaporation of popular concerns for energy conservation in the 1980s and 1990s. Yet by the mid-2000s, discourses of "oil crisis" returned. While the focus on scarcity and the imminence of "peak oil" resurfaced, the everyday geographies of oil crisis were not so much about limits, shortages, and lines for gasoline but rather the ordinary violence of the market expressed through rising prices. Those who could pay were not worried about acquiring gasoline, but for the vast majority the price of gasoline continued to produce anxiety and, as the *New York Times* put it, "[inspire] intense emotion."[1] The price of oil and gasoline have increasingly become a kind of social barometer—rising prices produce anxiety and falling prices relief—reported on as often as the weather. Anyone who watched nightly news telecasts in the United States could not avoid the pervasive reporting on high gas prices, in which disheveled consumers griped about the outrageous prices. In fact, given the importance of oil to the twentieth-century construction of "life" in the United States, what could be called "pain at the pump" discourse suddenly associated gasoline with pain, suffering, and even death. An October 2005 cover story of the *AARP Bulletin* was titled "The Big Hurt: High Gas Prices Take a Trickle-Down Toll."[2] As seen in Figure 21, the cover depicted a man in a life and death struggle with a gas pump itself. Between 2007 and 2008, a period of record high gasoline prices, ads for the modestly fuel efficient Chevy Malibu (33 miles per gallon) and very inefficient SUV Chevy Tahoe portrayed sentient gas pumps sabotaging drivers when they leave their car by locking their doors, deflating their tires, and detaching their boats from a rear hitch. The slogan of the campaign simply stated, "Gas Pumps Hate Us." In the summer of 2011, Phillips 66 ran a commercial featuring a hospitalized man in a coma. His sobbing wife sadly remarks, "I never even got the chance to tell him, he won Phillips 66 gas for life." The man quickly

FIGURE 21. "THE BIG HURT."
Over the last decade, high gasoline prices have often been equated with metaphors of pain, suffering, and even death. In this 2005 cover of the *AARP Bulletin Magazine*, a man struggles with a gasoline pump's efforts to strangle him.

jumps out of bed, rips off his IV, and proclaims, "I have a reason to live!" Other ad slogans, like Gulf's "*Life* . . . one mile at a time" and Ford's "Life on full" chose to avoid the more morbid aspects of oil addiction and hammer home the inextricable dependence of life on oil.

No matter what side of the political spectrum, the "outrageous" price of gasoline appears to represent the apex of everyday oppression, a symbolic gauge of everything wrong in the United States—from the subprime housing crisis to the failed war in Iraq. Even Moveon.org—the flagship liberal Web-based organization—has complained of the suffering of gas-gouged consumers "just in time to crimp summer vacation plans."[3] One particular interpretation of this outrage over "high" gasoline prices is a pervasive cultural sense of entitlement to profligate energy consumption patterns. After all, because of its substantially higher gasoline taxes, European countries have coped rather well with high gasoline prices for decades. From this perspective, the American public is easily caricatured as spoiled oil junkies unable to adjust their behavior to increasing geological and geopolitical realities. In this chapter, however, I propose a different interpretation. Pain at the pump discourse is not simply because of American "excess" and "profligacy" but is rather about the increasing economic insecurity and anxiety under neoliberalism. As others have recognized, under capitalism generally, and neoliberalism specifically, pain and suffering is experienced as much through the market, or what Moishe Postone calls an "abstract form of domination," as it is through direct, face-to-face coercion.[4] To be sure, by the 2000s the patterns of life and living in the United States demonstrated a wanton disregard for energy efficiency, but overall, life under neoliberalism is characterized not by excess but by eroding wages, mounting debt, longer work hours, and nonexistent job security. Only in this social context can clamoring for cheap gasoline be understood.

Furthermore, the furor directed toward "price"—the realm of exchange—must be situated as a long-term historical product of the capitalist organization of life itself around access to commodities. As discussed in chapter 2, the reforms of the 1930s provided state support for an "American way of life" in the realm of social reproduction centered upon high wages, home ownership, and prodigious access to energy, but this way of life was only *comprehensible* through the wage relation wherein access to the means of life is necessarily mediated by the commodity form. The New Deal promised a life of freedom, but neoliberalism revealed the perils of freedom only accessible through the abstract forces of the market. As the social supports for this way of life began to erode starting in the 1970s, the violence of commodity-dependent life became more and more expressed through outrage over things like gas prices.

Of course, many have tracked the erosion of wages and incomes for the majority of working people in the United States,[5] but if there was one reprieve from falling incomes it was what David McNally and others call a "consumption deflator" whereby cheap consumer goods help make up for eroding incomes.[6] The emergence of export-oriented industrialization in a variety of locations across the global south—where low wage workers are never expected to consume the goods they produce—allowed for a global regime of "wage compression." Likewise, during the 1980s and 1990s, there was a relative collapse of not only oil prices but a whole host of other agricultural goods and raw materials (see Figure 24). Thus, while the 1970s witnessed skyrocketing prices for energy, food, and other necessities making up the value of labor power, the subsequent two decades were characterized by a full-scale capital offensive against the working classes supplemented by an "ecological deflator" of cheapening energy, food, and other raw materials of the consumer economy. Just as cheap consumer goods were produced through the sweat and blood of the low-wage global industrial proletariat, cheap ecologies relied on a global regime of resource dispossession, overproduction, and local and global forms of ecological crisis. Whatever gains were made in the 1970s through higher fuel efficiency standards and fuel switching were quickly overwhelmed by cheap prices and the rise of an unabashed SUV culture, intensified suburban and exurban sprawl, and the rise of so-called edge cities on the outskirts of metropolitan regions.[7] By the 2000s, rising food and energy prices disrupted already eroding socioeconomic conditions, and thus led to the proliferation of metaphors of pain, suffering, and death.

Despite its convincing rationale from the perspective of struggling workers, the implication of a populist refusal to accept high energy prices has wide-ranging and disturbing implications. As I will illustrate, the commonsense hatred for high energy prices in general, and high gasoline prices in particular, served to pathologize any coherent energy policy to curb massive levels of U.S. oil consumption. More specifically, energy policies themselves were often discussed in neoliberal terms of universally hated *taxes*. Overall, the discursive construction of energy reforms as a tax allowed for a profound level of paralysis in the face of climate change, escalating geopolitical entanglements, and spectacular local/regional disasters (e.g., the BP oil spill). Moreover, the insecurity of life under neoliberal class rule[8] led to implicit consent for the imperial control of global oil flows—if only it promised cheaper prices.

Once again, it is important to first confront the ways in which the materiality of oil itself shapes the politics of oil. In the case of outrage over gas prices, consumers are by and large navigating a larger landscape of *gasoline stations* as central "pit stops" within the wider geography of suburban sprawl and automobility.[9] The landscape of gasoline stations has a lot to do with the *liquid* properties of oil itself.

Liquid Landscapes

> In America, every puddle, gasoline rainbow.
>
> —*Built to Spill*

In the United States, gasoline consumption is one of the most banal ways in which nature–society relations interface with the geographies of everyday practice. As resource geographer Gavin Bridge puts it, "refueling the car is one of the relatively few moments when one becomes conscious of the material resource flows that undergird both personal and corporate economic activity. Pump in hand, connected fleetingly by a streaming umbilical cord of gasoline directly to the material substances of the earth, the familiar boundaries between self and other, human and nature begin to look a little less certain."[10]

The materiality of oil matters in the making of the gas-fueled subject. Oil is the *liquid* fossil fuel. Unlike bulky coal or indiscernible gas, crude oil is an incredibly cooperative substance fueling the "time-space compression" of global transportation and commodity circulation. As petroleum economist J. E. Hartshorn puts it, its propensity to *flow* cannot be underestimated: "Once it has reached the surface, it can be moved more cheaply than any other fuel over long distances . . . its readiness to flow naturally remains the dominant physical factor in all the myriad actions of this industry's technology."[11] On the other hand, with this advantage comes great risk. Recall Edith Penrose's warning quoted in chapter 2 that oil is inherently "volatile and dangerous" and therefore is "best managed if allowed to flow continuously."[12] Thus, like the relentless flows of capital, oil works best when *in motion*. Yet the easy flow of oil must be managed by sociotechnical networks that monitor and attempt to, but cannot, prevent the inevitable litany of spills and explosions at the wellhead, pipeline, refinery, and even the gasoline station.

The gasoline station is partly a product of these biophysical qualities. First and foremost, the diffuse geography of gasoline stations is itself a product of oil's liquid propensity to flow. Oil is extracted in relatively few places, but from the point of extraction a dense network of pipelines, tankers, and eventually gasoline pumps is what make gasoline's ubiquitous availability possible. Indeed, on the interstates of the United

States, the exception is the unavailability of fuel in places like Nevada, where drivers are properly warned of "no fuel" for one hundred miles. Just like crude oil, there is a history of *overproduction* of gasoline stations, and a landscape of abandoned stations and their toxic legacy is pervasive across the United States. Peaking at about 183,000 in 1972, the number of gasoline stations in the United States fell to fewer than 100,000 by 1997.[13]

Gasoline is also prized for its particular *volatility*, which provides the explosive force driving the internal combustion engine. This volatility was originally a problem, as the fuel would ignite unexpectedly, creating a possibly destructive form of "engine knocking."[14] This led to the development of lead-based "antiknocking" additives. Of course, once the public health consequences of lead were discovered, the industry scrambled to develop petrochemical alternatives such as methyl tertiary butyl ethyl (MBTE). By the mid-1990s, public health concern intensified about the cacogenic and neurotoxic effects of MBTE as it was found in groundwater aquifers across the United States.[15] In the interim, yet more antiknocking alternatives have been developed in the form of ethanol, which come along with their own concerns surrounding the ecological and social effects of increased agro-fuel production from corn in the United States.[16]

Because of gasoline's liquid properties, gasoline stations contain multiple opportunities for spills and more pernicious forms of everyday seepage. Indeed, any consumer of gasoline immediately recognizes how difficult it is to return the pump to its stand without some gasoline leaking. Stations all have underground fuel storage tanks and a network of pipes (the fuel is pumped from underground) that, over time, are prone to leakage and consequent contamination of groundwater supplies. In 1984, as the Environmental Protection Agency estimated that one-quarter of underground gasoline tanks were leaking, Congress passed legislation mandating public cleanup "when tank owners could not be found or resisted a cleanup order from government."[17] Between 1984 and 2005, the Environmental Protection Agency had undertaken cleanup of some 412,657 gasoline station sites across the United States.[18]

Apart from the materiality of gasoline itself, from the driver's perspective, the liquid landscapes of cheap transportation fuels are mostly discernible through the realm of market exchange and price. While big box retailers pervade the sprawling suburban landscape with the promise of a multiplicity of cheap products, the prices posted at gasoline stations represent concrete nodes in the iconography of capitalist value.[19] The moments viewing streetscapes pervaded by gas prices and experiencing the meter's rise as one fills up offer pure quantitative measures that allow everyday consumers to calculate the shifting value of labor power.

As seen in Figure 22, the gas station displays themselves illustrate the multiple value standpoints from which to approach the commodity form. First, as already suggested, the constantly fluctuating exchange value of gasoline attracts the most attention. However, the station itself is also literally surrounded by American flags. This suggests that gasoline, as a use value, is shot through with *meaning* and, more to the point, (geo)political meanings aligned with what Mark Billig calls "banal nationalism"— that is, an ordinary moment through which individuals enact practices of shared national identity centered upon gasoline-fired automobility.[20] In other words, gasoline, as a use value, is not simply useful because it allows travel between two points on an isotropic plane, but because it literally enables particular visions of freedom, mobility, and "the American way of life." Names of gas stations can suggest these use values (I've seen Petro-USA, Freedom Fuel, and Liberty), but this one is simply named "Valu." This notion of value is not referring so much to the gasoline itself but rather to the *value of labor power,* through which gasoline is but one of what David Harvey describes as "the intersection[s] of that particular bundle of use-values necessary for the labourer's survival."[21] The value provided by cheaper fuel necessary for life allows for greater proportions of the value of labor power to be devoted elsewhere.

The cultural politics of outrage over "high" gas prices is about much more than the apparently obvious and quantitative realm of prices. These discourses are also about the meanings and use values of the commodity gasoline. The meanings surrounding value circulation correspond to what Geoff Mann calls "the politics of measure."[22] He argues that domains often considered purely quantitative and economic are saturated with cultural political struggles over the meanings and practices putatively measured through quantitative indices. In his words, "measure . . . is precisely this node or knot that constitutes the space in which value is politicized, and the politics of measure consists in not only the struggles in that space but also the struggle to produce those spaces, to tie knots in the thread of value where there had previously only been slippery appearances."[23]

Thus the rise in price from $2.00 to $4.00 per gallon does not merely suggest a strain on a quantitative budget spreadsheet but also qualitative concerns over the maintenance and reproduction of everyday geographies of home, work, leisure, and ultimately national identity. Moreover, populist clamoring for lower prices ends up generating political interventions within the circuits of value production to increase production and force this commodity to trade at its "normal" (low) prices (e.g., fostering the

FIGURE 22. VALU GAS STATION, WORCESTER, MASSACHUSETTS.
Gas stations are a central part of the iconography of capitalist value. Their prices are one of the most visible parts of a commodified landscape, but the inclusion of American flags also invokes connections between gasoline and American national identity. Photograph by Matthew T. Huber.

political will to convince OPEC to increase production or expand offshore drilling domestically).

Yet it is the quantitative matrix of exchange value that reorients and destabilizes the bundle of use values making up the historically specific and moral aspects of the value of labor power and "the American way of life." The "pain at the pump" discourse in the mid-2000s constantly referenced the effect of high gas prices on an expected "bundle" of commodities needed for the social reproduction of labor power. In the 2006 film *Dan in Real Life,* the main character watches the prices spiral upward on the meter as he laments, "There goes Jane's college education, there goes Karen's." As gasoline prices skyrocketed in the summer of 2008, it became common to calculate wages—the expression of the value of labor power—in terms of gallons per hour. As one article from the *Charlotte Observer* explained, even after an increase, "the minimum-wage worker still has to work more than an hour to afford two gallons of gas."[24]

For workers living under neoliberal economic insecurity, high gas prices can upset the fragile underpinnings of everyday social reproduction. Another article, titled "Higher Gas Prices Leave Many Workers Running on Empty," cited research from a Florida State University Business School professor, Wayne Hochwarter. The research suggested that high gas prices led consumers to go without some of the "basics . . . such as heat or air conditioning" and caused worker "stress . . . [s]pecifically negative views of work and the company, sluggishness, antagonistic behavior, feeling overwhelmed and sadness were significantly higher for those indicating gas-price related effects on spending behavior."[25] Thus "pain at the pump" discourse reflected just one amid a cascading set of injurious trends under neoliberalism—stagnating wages, mounting debt, and increasing job insecurity. But such outrage at high gas prices can only be understood after a historic period of low prices for not only energy but all manner of natural resources.

Cheap Ecologies and Insecure Life

As labor historian Jefferson Cowie suggests, the 1970s were "the last days of the working class" in the United States.[26] The decade of stagflation and oil shocks set up the emergence of Reaganism and, more specifically, the large-scale neoliberal assault on unions, wages, and job security. On a symbolic level, Reagan's firing of the Professional Air Traffic Controllers Organization workers during a highly public strike portended the union and strike busting of the decades to come.[27] Figure 23 shows that since the

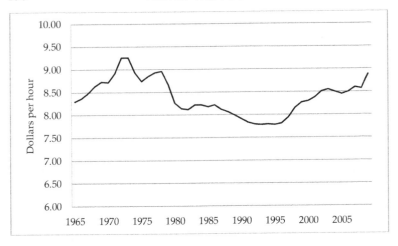

FIGURE 23. U.S. AVERAGE HOURLY EARNINGS (1982–84 DOLLARS) IN
PRIVATE NONAGRICULTURAL INDUSTRIES, 1965–2010.
Source: "Economic Report of the President," Table B-47 (Washington, D.C.:
Government Printing Office, 2011).

1970s, average hourly wages in the United States can best be described as
"stagnant." The decline in wages has been offset by the increasing prepon-
derance of dual-income households, longer work hours (at the household
level), and the explosion of household debt.[28]

In the context of an increasingly globalized capital–labor relationship,
these trends can be explained in the context of what David McNally
calls "neoliberal wage compression."[29] In other words, the explosion
of the global proletariat in combination with the increasing globalization of industrial capital (particularly to East and Southeast Asia) has
served to repress wages worldwide. McNally argues that this "wage
compression" was central to a global *revival* of capitalist profitability
and accumulation from the early 1980s onward. Moreover, capital's
increasingly global mobility—and threats of capital flight—has represented an ever-present warning to workers who dare to organize unions.
For David Harvey, this capitalist onslaught parallels a wider "restoration of class power" toward financial and corporate elites evidenced by
expanding income inequality overall and wealth redistribution upward
to the top 1 percent of the population in the United States (among other
parts of the world) not seen since the "roaring" twenties came crashing
down in 1929.[30]

These well-known patterns of neoliberal capitalism were not purely
a "social" process of capital's assault on the working class but must be

understood as a *socioecological* process tied to the production of materials, energies, and wastes central to the social reproduction of both capital and labor alike.[31] In the United States, overall declines in income and wages were supplemented by declining prices for food, energy, and consumer durables. Again, McNally points to the expanding global industrial geography of low-wage manufacturing as the basis for a general "consumption deflator," which indicates that "price changes for U.S. consumer durables—electronics, appliances, cars, and more—began to decline in the autumn of 1995."[32]

Yet the broader spectrum of the material goods more directly necessary for social reproduction (i.e., food and energy) witnessed spectacular declines much earlier. Using World Bank indexes for commodities in the food, energy, and metals categories, it is clear that after the "shock" of high commodity prices in the 1970s, prices rapidly collapsed in the early to mid-1980s and, although volatile, remained at a generally low levels throughout the 1990s (see Figure 24). As Figure 25 illustrates, these declines in commodity prices paralleled declining percentages of "consumer expenditures" devoted to food, gasoline, and utilities. Part of an overall decline in the postwar period, between 1975 and 1999 consumers went from devoting 23 percent to 15 percent of their incomes toward food. Figure 26 shows the collapse and two-decade slump in gasoline prices in the 1980s and 1990s. As Yergin reports, the cultural amnesia

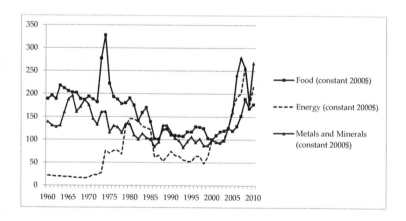

FIGURE 24. SELECTED COMMODITY INDEXES, GLOBAL PRICES (CONSTANT 2000 DOLLARS) (1960–2010).
Source: World Bank GEM Commodities Data, http://data.worldbank.org/data-catalog/commodity-price-data.

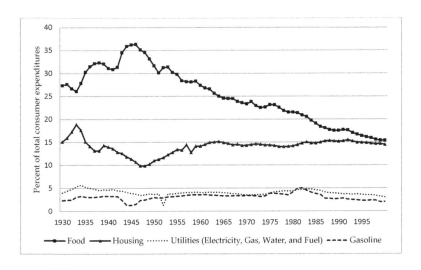

FIGURE 25. U.S. CONSUMER EXPENDITURES ON SELECTED CATEGORIES AS A
PERCENTAGE OF TOTAL (1929–99).
Source: Carter et al., *Historical Statistics of the United States Millennium
Edition*, Tables Cd154, 173, 186–90, 225.

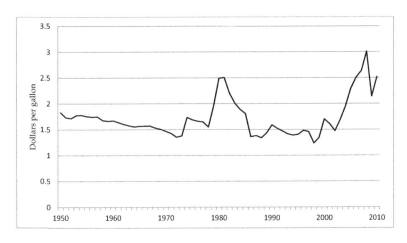

FIGURE 26. U.S. REAL RETAIL MOTOR GASOLINE AND ON-HIGHWAY DIESEL
FUEL PRICES, 1950–2010 (2005 DOLLARS).
Source: Energy Information Administration, 2011, http://www.eia.gov/
totalenergy/data/annual/txt/ptb0524.html

of the gas-line 70s was illustrated with gasoline being sold for zero (yes, zero!) cents per gallon at an Exxon station on the north side of Austin, Texas, in April of 1986.[33]

The experience of collapsing resource prices in the 1980s and 1990s is a common one in the political economy of natural resources. Rising prices, like those witnessed in the 1970s, are often followed by new investments in the technologies of exploration, development, and extraction of natural resources.[34] The boom is followed by a bust as new investments produce new supplies and, eventually, commodity surpluses or "gluts" cause rapid price collapses and "busts" (see chapter 2 on the 1930s).[35] During and after the 1970s, natural resource production entered a global regime of overproduction as neoliberal forms of governance encouraged export-based commodity production throughout the world.[36] For example, under the general aura of World Bank promotion of export-oriented development, Vietnam developed a dynamic coffee industry. The problem was that the Washington Consensus had the same advice for other nations (such as Brazil and Ethiopia) and consequently prices collapsed, decimating the world coffee market.[37] In the United States, the trauma of rising food prices and inflation in the 1970s forced Earl Butz (Nixon's secretary of agriculture) to abandon policies that kept land out of production and institute a "get big or get out" policy that rewarded *maximum* food production.[38] As prices for farm commodities predictably declined and crisis once again visited farm country in the 1980s, U.S. farmers could only survive through a complex system of direct monetary subsidies.

In the case of oil, the OPEC crisis led to an expansion of so-called non-OPEC oil in places like Alaska and, more important, offshore oil development in the North Sea and Gulf of Mexico. In the mid-1980s, frustrated with the inability to control member countries' production quotas, Saudi Arabia substantially expanded its own production to lower prices and punish uncooperative cartel members. The subsequent collapse of oil prices in 1986 exacerbated an already deep downturn in the U.S. oil fields of Texas, Oklahoma, and Louisiana. The crisis in the "oil patch"—reminiscent of the 1930s—led George H. W. Bush to take a trip to Saudi Arabia to beg them *not* to increase the flow of oil to the imperialist United States but rather to *decrease* their oil production to allow global prices to stabilize to the benefit of higher cost "independent" producers and small royalty owners.[39]

Low prices for natural resources, including oil, during the 1980s and 1990s represent their own kind of "ecological deflator," which served to (very partially) offset overall declines in wages and incomes. Yet after the 1970s, the "cheapness" of these resources could only emerge through a new regime of what has been called "global enclosures"—increased land and resource dispossession, the expansion of monoculture-style agriculture and industrial-scale mining across the world.[40] Overproduction was coupled with ecological devastation and livelihood displacement.[41] Thus on the one hand, in the United States "life" had become increasingly dependent on cheap ecologies in ways fundamentally disconnected from their deleterious environmental and social consequences. On the other hand, what James Ferguson calls "the neoliberal world order" produced common ground in the form of economic insecurity—migrant industrial workers in East and Southeast Asia, peasants dispossessed of their land in sub-Saharan Africa, and the workers in the new low-wage economy of the United States all—albeit in diverse and uneven ways—have experienced extreme dislocation to established patterns of social reproduction.[42]

Yet the cheap ecologies regime only lasted so long. After the recession of 2000–2001, rising gasoline prices—and commodity prices generally—became one more in a long line of injurious trends for workers under neoliberal capitalism. Like in the 1970s, a familiar list of villains emerged to explain the high prices—gouging oil companies, OPEC, and environmental regulation—but a new force specific to neoliberalism also took a large share of the blame: Financial speculation driven by crude oil futures traders on the New York Mercantile Exchange (among other global sites).[43] Overall, these theories reinforced the commonsense viewpoint that rises in energy prices were universally a bad thing. It was up to the forces on the neoliberal right to reframe this common sense into a standard villain of neoliberal ideology—taxes.

Energy Policy as Tax

> Gasoline prices are like a tax on our working people.
>
> —George W. Bush, April 22, 2008

In 1978, when Proposition 13 passed by a two to one margin in California, tax revolt populism spread throughout the nation against taxes in general and property taxes in particular.[44] In the view of entrepreneurial life wherein one's home/property is run like a business, property taxes were akin to a tax on small business. Inflation also pushed people into rigidly higher tax brackets, making rising tax rates seem all the more unjust.[45] Amid the more abstract forms of international economic competition and rampant inflation, taxes represented a cost of living with a concrete and visible actor to blame—the government. Moreover, disdain for taxes was fueled through outrage over where the tax money was going—specifically social and environmental programs. As Edsall and Edsall discuss, it was during the neoliberal 1970s and 1980s that "the meaning of taxes was . . . transformed. No longer the resource through which to create beneficent federal government, taxes had, for many voters, come to signify the forcible transfer of hard-earned money away from those who worked, to those who did not."[46] Edsall and Edsall further argue that the hatred of taxes—so central to the rise of the new right—specifically appealed to middle- to upper-income white homeowners who made racialized assumptions that taxes were a "cost to whites of federal programs that redistribute social and economic benefits to blacks and other minorities."[47] While many on the left might lament that the antitax fervor was not directed toward the real villain—military spending[48]—they underestimate the way in which the politics of entrepreneurial life is only legible through an imaginary of a competitive, even playing field of *individualized disciplined, hardworking subjects.* The linkage between taxes and the military industrial complex was obviously problematic, but the taking of money from hardworking individuals to give it to other individuals imagined as not working was constructed by forces on the right and suburban homeowners (among others) as the essence of injustice.

Long after the moment of the "tax revolt," it was on this platform that antitax forces, such as Grover Norquist's *Americans for Tax Reforms,* significantly shifted American politics rightward on the basis of one simple issue: "it's your money" stolen by government.[49] Moreover, the importance of antitax/government populism to the rise of the right in the United States belies the extent to which such political victories can be explained purely in terms of "cultural values" such as abortion, gay marriage, and gun rights.[50]

By the 1980s, the neoliberal populist anger toward taxes and "Big Government" slowly infiltrated more and more political debates, including those around energy and environmental policy. One outcome of the cheap ecologies regime of resource overproduction and global enclosures was continuing concern with ecological issues like acid rain, toxic waste disposal, and global warming. Despite stringent regulatory standards that many analysts attribute to dramatically cleaner air and water (in the United States at least), a critique developed around what was referred to as "command and control" environmental policy—that is, government mandates that force capital to abide by a certain level of pollution control. The libertarian think tank, *The Cato Institute,* explains, "Command-and-control regulations, which require regulators to determine exactly which technologies and what manufacturing methods are to be adopted for pollution control in every single facility in the nation, place an informational burden on public officials that is impossible to meet in the real world. . . . . Both common sense and experience tell us that individual plant managers are better equipped to discover the most efficient ways to control pollution at their facilities than are Environmental Protection Agency technicians and consultants."[51]

It was precisely this type of critique that allowed for the emergence of free market environmental policy on the one hand—the promotion of market-based environmental policies like pollution credit trading and wetland banking—and a wider notion of "green capitalism" on the other—the idea that rather than being inherently antiecological, the *profit motive* could be harnessed toward greater efficiency, less resource consumption, and green innovation.[52]

The cheap ecologies regime of overproduction itself lent credence to the idea that solutions lie in the market itself. Emerging orthodoxy on the left and right began to agree that the problem was natural resources were too "cheap." In the 1980s and 1990s, oil, food, and other raw materials were seen as so cheap that they encouraged overconsumption and distanced consumers from the "real" environmental costs of their consumption.[53] Specifically, "cheap oil" was seen as not only responsible for wasteful patterns of sociospatial development (i.e., suburban sprawl) but also directly generating geopolitical turmoil and ecological crisis. After 9/11, of course, "cheap oil" was blamed on generating terrorism and oil dictators. In a call to raise oil prices through a gasoline tax called the Real Patriot Act, Thomas Friedman puts it in his typical sweeping manner: "Not only would it mean less money for Saudi Arabia to transfer to Wahhabi clerics to spread their intolerant brand of Islam around the world, but it would radically improve America's standing in Europe, where we are resented for being the world's energy hog."[54] Thus the problem of "cheapness" according to neoliberal thought was that ecological and geopolitical costs were not reflected in market prices. The solution to cheap ecologies was to "get the prices right."

The problem of market failure and externalities was a long-standing one in the discipline of economics, but it took the conjuncture with neoliberal hegemony in the 1980s and 1990s for political momentum to develop around the idea that such costs could actually be accurately measured, quantified, and integrated into the price mechanism. In his influential *Earth in the Balance* (1993), Al Gore argued that it is important to "ensure that information is available in the marketplace about our environmental consequences of our choices."[55] For Gore, the most effective way to convey this information was through the price mechanism and "finding ways to put a price on the environmental consequences of our choices, a price that would be reflected in the marketplace."[56] The culmination of this new approach to environmental policy was the Clean Air Act of 1990, which installed a "cap and trade" system for sulfur dioxide that capped the amount of pollution overall but allowed coal-burning plants to trade pollution credits to those plants less able to install control technologies. Subsequently, the amount of sulfur dioxide decreased by some 31 percent, but questions still remain about the causal role of the free market system of pollution credits.[57]

The alternative to a cap-and-trade system is a "tax" on pollution. Given the popular antitax fervor of the age, it is somewhat ironic that many environmental policy thinkers looking to harness the price mechanism looked to taxes as the proper way to "internalize" costs. As the *New York Times* reported in 1993, "a new generation of environmental researchers, as comfortable with the theories of Adam Smith as they are with Darwin and Mendel, thinks taxes that penalize polluters could make the economy fitter and leaner, even as it makes the environment cleaner."[58] After Clinton's election in 1992, the *World Resources Institute* published an influential report titled "Green Fees: How a Tax Shift Can Work for the Environment and Economy."[59] The underlying logic of the report accepted the neoliberal premise that taxes are inherently bad—"People feel burdened by taxes because taxes are indeed burdensome"[60]—but twisted this premise to argue that we should only tax "bad" things like pollution: "Environmental charges that can raise revenues while improving environmental quality are more attractive than taxes that drive business and workers away."[61]

Thus in the environmental field, taxes emerged as a free market policy tool to harness the power of the price mechanism to transform consumer behavior. Given the widespread praise heaped upon incentive-based environmental policy, it is somewhat understandable that an "energy tax" became one of President Clinton's first legislative initiatives in 1993. The tax—constructed within an overall "deficit reduction package"—would be levied according to the heat content (British thermal units, or BTU) of different forms of fuel. Clinton announced the policy in his very first State of the Union address, "Our plan includes a tax on energy as the best way to provide us with new revenue to lower the deficit and invest in our people."[62] According to one policy analyst, "the hybrid Btu tax was brilliantly conceived in every way."[63] It would encourage cleaner fuels and was constructed to cushion the effects on the middle class.

Despite the rational logic of the policy *in itself*, the debate that ensued reveals the incredible political naïvety of the Clinton administration to bluntly call any policy proposal a tax. It did not take long for broad spectrums of capital—the API and the National Manufactures Association among them—to organize a massive "astroturf" campaign against the tax. Under names like "American Energy Alliance"—an amalgam of 1,650 organizations—energy-intensive capital hired direct marketing companies and spent one to two million dollars in twenty states "creating the impression of a mass movement."[64] Congress was inundated with phone calls and letters that were generated by these campaigns.[65] Mobil took out a full-page ad in the *New York Times* charging that the tax would increase the cost of manufacturing: "America's competitive position both here and in world markets would be damaged. And just at a time when a truly global economy is beginning to blossom."[66] The API estimated the tax would cost six hundred thousand jobs,[67] and before long the coalition of interests had renamed the BTU to "Big Time Unemployment."[68]

The problem was a fundamental contradiction between neoliberal environmental policy wonk enthusiasm for using taxes to harness the price mechanism and markets on one hand, and neoliberal *populist* hatred for any and all taxes on the other. While much of the critique of the BTU tax centered on jobs and competitiveness, the most overwhelming critique centered upon its cost on working, "middle-class" Americans. Given the popular disdain for taxes, any attempt to *raise* energy prices was easily caricatured as a liberal elite strategy (market based or not) lacking concern for the ordinary struggles of working Americans. One letter to the editor summarized the problem: "Radical environmentalists have never been known for their support for economic prosperity, and placing this new tax burden on the poor and middle class is merely their latest strategy to make us all more dependent on the State."[69] In this discourse, the energy consumer was framed as the chief victim of ill-advised government revenue generation. Another letter to the editor of the *Houston Chronicle* argued that the tax must not be seen as an energy tax on capital but fundamentally as a tax on *life*:

> The tax is not a tax on oil. If the tax is not passed, oil company profits and losses will not change. The tax is a tax on consumer use of energy. You as a consumer will pay to the government a tax on each Btu of energy you use whether it is oil, gas, electricity, coal, nuclear energy or any other type of energy that is sold. This will increase the cost of everything from toys and games to the basics of food and shelter. You will pay this tax every time you turn on your stove, run your refrigerator, iron your clothes, drive your car, water your lawn or

flush your toilet. There is nothing that you do or any part of your life that will not "pay" this tax.[70]

As in the 1970s, energy's centrality to everyday life allowed for price increases to be framed as inflationary. One letter bemoaned, "Since energy is a necessity for survival in our society, its effects will be inflationary."[71] The inflationary impacts of the tax would always ultimately reach the consumer as the personification of the entrepreneurial market subject. As the Mobil ad put it, "let's face it. In the end, the consumer always pays."

Just as this campaign was organized by energy-intensive capital—steel, chemicals, cement, and petroleum—the campaign focused on the anger of energy-intensive consumers in the suburbs who were seen as unfairly targeted by the tax. An API spokesperson suggested, "In general, it will penalize suburban and rural consumers at the expense of those who live in cities . . . it is neither fair nor equitable."[72] The *New York Times* ran a graphic titled "How the Energy Tax Would Affect Three Families"—urban, suburban, and rural. The suburban family would see their energy costs rise by $322, while the urban and rural consumers would merely see increases of $112 and $92 respectively.[73] Like so many other aspects of American politics, the debate over the energy "tax" revealed an antiurban bias.

Overall, the campaign against the BTU tax channeled the larger "tax revolt" energy, which focused its ire toward government spending. Before long, more fiscally conservative Democrats began abandoning the energy tax and proposed substantive cuts to "entitlements" like Medicare spending as an alternative way to reduce the deficit. Senator David Boren, a democrat from the oil state of Oklahoma, led the charge by suggesting, "We don't want to let the traditionally entrenched, big-spending liberals steal the momentum away from the President's commitment to deficit reduction."[74] Boren referred to the BTU tax as a "political tax. . . . [I]t was meant to be a hidden tax so that people wouldn't figure out they were being taxed. . . . If gasoline went up 8 cents, that wasn't a tax, that was some sort of thermal unit equivalency that you noticed at the gas pump."[75] The deficit-hawk wing of the Democratic Party reflected the larger rightward shift in the country as a whole undergirded by the populist construction of ordinary citizens versus government and taxes. One view was expressed by a letter to the editor from the Sunbelt city of St. Petersburg, Florida: "It's time to cut everything—Congress, the armed forces, space exploration, special interests' tax breaks, and giveaway programs to the rest of the world—by at least 30 percent. Then, and only then, will 'we' accept energy taxes, sales taxes and the other trial balloons. 'We' must see proof that our money is being spent wisely."[76] The scare quotes around "we" indicates a sense of reflexivity about the true univer-sality of populist rage against taxes, but the battle lines were clearly drawn between the people and a parasitical government.

In retrospect, it seems unbelievable that the Clinton administration would propose an energy policy with the accompaniment of the word *tax*. In the end, the BTU tax was scrapped and replaced by a 4.3-cent increase in the gasoline tax.[77] Ironically, as some pointed out, the gasoline tax hit poor and middle-class consumers more directly at the pump than the BTU tax, which targets the real source of energy profligacy in the indus-trial sector.[78] Despite the fact that taxing gasoline would do much to curb oil consumption and spur alternatives in the oil-dependent transportation sector, this modest increase was the last time the federal gasoline tax was raised. States tax gasoline from varying degrees, but the bottom line is that the United States has incredibly low taxes on gasoline when compared to other industrial countries. For example, averaging the state taxes, the United States taxes gasoline at the rate of $0.48 per gallon compared to $5.15 in Belgium, $4.88 in Germany, and $5.40 in France; consumers in most European countries pay more in *taxes* than those in the United States pay in total for a gallon of gasoline.[79]

Despite eroding transportation infrastructure (which the gas tax funds), the gasoline tax has become an untouchable political issue. As an infra-structure news website put it, politicians "won't touch the gas tax with a ten-foot pole. Why not? Because come election time, no one wants to be the candidate responsible for raising the most soundbite-ready and exe-crated tax on earth."[80] In fact, in the 2004 presidential campaign, George W. Bush ran a television ad with old-timey images of early twentieth-century automobility charging, "Some people have wacky ideas, like taxing gas more so people drive less—that's John Kerry." Despite the fact that Kerry had not supported such a tax in over a decade (because of the political implications), the ad estimated Kerry's tax would lead to $657 more in gasoline costs for the "average family."[81]

The contemporary political climate illustrates the extent to which *any energy policy whatsoever* is framed as a tax. Perhaps the greatest evidence has been the failure of President Obama's "Cap and Trade" leg-islation. Inspired by the 1990 Clean Air Act, the proposal is a hallmark of neoliberal environmentalism—cap pollution and allow free individu-als to exchange pollution credits on a market. As already stated, in the 1990s, such free market environmental policy tools were supported by forces on the right as more "efficient" than state-mandated pollution con-trol. Yet almost immediately, the legislation was denigrated by these same free market ideologues on the right as "Cap and Tax." The *Wall Street*

Journal editorial page described it as the "biggest tax in American history."[82] Calling it "Anti-Market" and "Anti-Consumer," The Heritage Foundation claimed, "Since 85 percent of U.S. energy demand is met by fossil fuels, taxing the lifeblood of the American economy would have disastrous consequences."[83] As part of the standard formula, the "average family" was purported to take a two-thousand-dollar increase in taxes per year.[84] The popular disdain for any legislation that implies higher energy costs is always rooted in the eroding conditions of life for the majority of working-class Americans. One letter to the editor form the Seattle suburb of Enumclaw, Washington, questioned the nature of "life" itself: "Have you tried to imagine life in the event cap-and-trade becomes law? . . . For lower and middle-income citizens, already struggling to make ends meet, the struggle becomes nearly futile."[85] Within the context of neoliberal insecurity and eroding conditions of life, further taxes and financial burdens make the reproduction of life almost unimaginable. The impasse reveals the political gulf between environmental technocrats who believe strongly that the only way to a green future is to raise the prices of energy-intensive commodities, on the one hand, and the millions of workers who rely on those very products for the basic reproduction of daily life on the other. Indeed, like in the 1930s, political struggle must center on new visions of life itself before energy consumption patterns can be transformed.

Living Imperialism, or the Logic of "Yes, Blood for Oil!"[86]

In 2006, a *New York Times*/CBS poll reported that 85 percent of those polled were opposed to an increase in the gasoline tax.[87] While the populist disdain for high gasoline and energy prices—whether through the market or taxes—is certainly understandable in the context of neoliberal class rule, the political implications starkly reveal the ecological and geopolitical contradictions of petro-capitalism in the United States. While Timothy Mitchell argues that the *idea* of democracy cannot be severed from carbon-intensive forms of social development, the overwhelming popular opposition to higher energy costs problematizes the capacity of "democracy" to solve the escalating set of emergent perils directly linked to the persistence of carbon-based capitalism—war, ecological crisis, and suburban sprawl.[88]

Amid the populist outrage over high gasoline prices, the United States invaded and occupied oil-rich Iraq. Evidence abounds that the war was at least in part about controlling some of the richest and untapped oil reserves in the world.[89] Of course, given very low prices in the late 1990s, it is far more likely that the oil industry would be more concerned with the uncontrolled tapping of plentiful Iraqi oil supplies. By 2003, more important than producing the oil for U.S. consumers (or anyone else) was the restriction and control of the supply of Iraqi oil to protect the first sustained price boom since the 1970s.[90] Indeed, it was Saddam Hussein's deals with French and Russian companies that threatened to unleash a glut of Iraqi oil onto global markets. Nevertheless, a month before the invasion millions of people around the world took to the streets to protest the latest episode of U.S. imperialism under the rallying cry "No Blood for Oil."

The political rhetoric around "No Blood for Oil" assumes that oil itself is a rather trivial thing—a mere luxury of an already extravagant "American way of life." Yet this idea of the triviality of oil belies its entanglements within a wider and unquestioned normativity accorded to the *use values* enabled through oil-based practices—home, family, freedom, and mobility. When access to oil is equated to these "American values," it does not take long for the "No Blood for Oil" logic to be flipped on its head to a logic of, in the words of Donald Trump, "Yes, blood for oil."[91]

As George H. W. Bush famously put it in reaction to talk of global environmental treaties at the Rio Earth Summit in 1992, "the American way of life is not up for negotiation."[92] The logic of "Yes, blood for oil" reveals more insidious implications of the equation of U.S. national security with access to petroleum—the "American way of life" must be defended. This posture serves to sanction unquestioned access to foreign petroleum reserves in the Middle East. This was confirmed by the vaunted man of "peace" Jimmy Carter through his "Carter Doctrine," which declared that any attempt to gain access to Middle Eastern oil "will be repelled by any means necessary, including military force."[93]

While antiwar activists rightly revealed the horrors of exchanging blood for oil, a more common sentiment suggested oil might be worth fighting for. As a solider serving in Iraq interviewed in the production of the 2006 documentary *The War Tapes*, Mike Moriarity, put it,

> You've heard people say—"we're over there for the oil . . . that's the only reason we're in Iraq—it's oil, it's oil, it's oil . . ." Well, listen—No . . . we're not there for the oil . . . If it were for oil, would that not be enough reason to go to Iraq? You bet your ass it would be. If you took oil away from this country tomorrow, what do you think would happen to this country? It would be . . . devastating. . . . So let's all stop crying about whether we had reason to go in there or not . . . it's a done deal—we're in Iraq. Support what it takes to make this thing work or shut up.

Here we see the crucial link between oil and the vitality of Americanness and the "devastating" consequences if that linkage is not upheld with—if necessary—military force. The implication is that *oil is worth fighting for,* even if it was politically convenient to disassociate the Iraq War as purely a war for oil. A 2005 op-ed from a professor from the Christian right Liberty University offered a critique of antiwar protestors and asked for President Bush to "explain—for future reference [because Iraq is *not* about oil]— why fighting for oil is not an inherently evil thing."[94] He claimed that such a hypothetical war would be about "economic survival. . . . And, that's OK. We have every right to survive. We have every right to fight for oil, just like Ancient Rome had every right to fight for grain."[95] Such discourses explicitly sanction wars for oil, but they are simply blunt expressions of a much wider and more pernicious *implicit* sanction of U.S. military strategies for oil that underlie the popular demand for cheap gasoline and energy. Indeed, the "strategic necessity" of the United States' continued imperial presence in the Middle East and beyond is often justified on the terms of "security" for the population.[96]

Again, the populist clamoring for cheap energy is not simply a story of greedy extravagance and American consumer excess but a reflection of already existing geographies of social reproduction—highways, low-density suburban developments—that make access to enormous quantities of energy a matter of *survival.* In the face of mounting debt and the relentless attack on wages, benefits, and the social safety net, access to food, energy, and housing becomes a daily struggle framed by the intensification of economic insecurity. While higher gasoline prices become "outrageous," the fighting of a war for oil can be seen by some as justified or even "common sense." Thus, while it is fashionable to blame U.S. inaction on climate change on political ignorance—politicians who refer to it as a hoax and, as of 2011, 53 percent of Americans who do not believe in its anthropogenic roots[97]—far more disturbing are the more entrenched and everyday forms of living, thinking, and feeling that make cheap energy a "commonsense" necessity of survival.

Conclusion: "Drill Here, Drill Now, Pay Less"

In the summer of 2008—a summer of record gasoline prices—Newt Gingrich wrote a book and started a campaign on the basis of a bumper sticker: "Drill Here, Drill Now, Pay Less."[98] While it was the phrase "Drill, Baby, Drill" that became the most memorable slogan of the presidential campaign, Gingrich's tagline exposes the underlying value logic of an energy policy based on expanding production—more production, lower prices for all. Gingrich recounts stories of pain in business, households, "meals on wheels charities," and churches—"Americans are hurting, and they're hurting bad . . . everyday folks just trying to earn a living, feed their families, and help others."[99] In the face of rising energy prices, domestic regulation of oil and gas production becomes an easy villain—what Gingrich calls "anti-energy left-leaning politicians"[100]—in explaining the lack of supply in the face of demand. Despite the fact that expanding U.S. production would probably do little to affect global oil prices, the "pain" consumers feel at the pump seems unreasonable when there is untapped oil within the "secure" territorial borders of the United States.

The fact is that—rather than spurring the "energy transition" many economists predict—rising energy prices help generate this populist support for expanding energy production from fossil fuels. Since 2008, the United States has massively expanded its production of shale gas and oil in places like Texas, Pennsylvania, and North Dakota.[101] In 2008, the *New York Times* posed the question "Will $4 Gas Trump a 27-Year Old Ban?," and George W. Bush responded by lifting a ban on offshore drilling.[102] It took the greatest maritime oil spill in U.S. history in the summer of 2010 to short-circuit the Democratic President Barack Obama's plan to dramatically expand offshore drilling off the Atlantic coast (a plan that seems destined to reemerge as the memories of the spill fades away). This massive production of fossil fuel promises to delay needed transformations toward non-fossil-fuel forms of energy in the face of the intensifying climate crisis.

The failure of the U.S. political system to respond to the challenges of petro-capitalism—war, climate change, and ecological crisis—is more complicated than the simple role of "Big Oil" in corrupting policy makers. It is about a specific regime of capitalism—a regime rooted deeply in the entire architecture of twentieth-century American capital accumulation—that has become structured around a cultural politics of entrepreneurial life. Overall, the social and spatial arrangement emerging out of the crisis of the 1930s is still relevant to understanding the contradictions inherent in the present. As chapter 3 shows, during the postwar period life was more and more constructed as a privatized project of individualized control over the spaces of the body, home, and mobility—a form of control inextricably linked with both massive levels of energy consumption and the increasing *commodification* of all forms of social reproduction. Yet since the 1970s, massive wealth redistribution upward and the eroding conditions of life for the majority of working-class people have not lead to the revival of the "public solidarity" politics seen during the 1930s. Rather, we have seen an intensification of a politics of hostile privatism wherein the *source* of economic insecurity is often blamed on forms of public solidarity— government programs, taxes, and wealth redistribution. In the realm of energy policy, any *collective* attempt to spur a much-needed energy transition becomes simplistically constructed as a "tax" on the private enterprises of "everyday folk." In the face of "Drill, Baby, Drill," popular rage against gasoline taxes, and any environmental restrictions on energy extraction, it is apparent that the question of an energy future has very little to do with technology and more to do with much more difficult *political* questions surrounding the problematics of populism, liberal democracy, and what kinds of social conditions can generate new and more collective imaginaries of life itself.

CONCLUSION

Energizing Freedom

When I began thinking about a project on oil and "the American way of life," I was fixated on the gas station, that central node of not only ecology and material exchange but ideology and politics. My first epiphany about the significance of the gas station to American politics took place around Minneapolis, Minnesota, in the spring of 2005 (I was on my way on the ultimate "escape to nature": a canoe trip in the pristine Boundary Waters of northern Minnesota and southern Ontario). It was a gas station with a simple title: *Freedom* (see Figure 27). This was a moment in history of tremendous cultural anxiety around oil consumption in the United States, not so much out of environmental concern but rather post-9/11 constructions of "foreign oil" and its supposed linkages to terrorism. Thus initially I found it quite ironic that a gas station could have the audacity to proclaim itself a site of freedom, with all oil's associations with various forms of unfreedoms—war, despotic petro-states, and social and environmental injustice along the oil commodity chain.

Indeed, the anxiety surrounding American notions of freedom at the gas station reached inane heights in February of 2007. A gas station opened in Omaha, Nebraska, with the name "Terror Free Oil." The gas station was the product of a citizen group calling for U.S. consumers to boycott oil produced in "terrorist" countries (i.e., the Middle East). The gas station claimed to only buy oil from companies (e.g., Sinclair and Hess) that obtain oil from the "safe zones" of the United States and Canada. Amid the publicity for such an audacious name for a gasoline station, it quickly came to light that such a claim was, in the words of an *American Petroleum Institute* economist, "absurd."[1] As it turns out, it is *impossible* to actually trace the origins of the oil that ends up in any particular gasoline tank. A spokesperson from Sinclair oil claimed

FIGURE 27. FREEDOM GASOLINE STATION, BLOOMINGTON, ILLINOIS.
Such gas stations promote an explicit connection between fuel and freedom.
There are different brand franchises of the Freedom gas station throughout the
United States. Photograph by Reecia Orzeck.

they *try* to only purchase oil that originates from the United States and
Canada, but "there is no way to know what oil from other countries has
gotten mixed in during transport through the pipelines—which Sinclair
does not operate."[2] Moreover, Sinclair admitted to purchasing oil on the
New York Mercantile Exchange, which is basically an "open market,"
and "the purchaser does not know where it's coming from."[3]

   Apart from the xenophobic nature of this initiative—and the ludicrous
assertion that environmentally devastating oil from the Albertan Tar Sands
does not contain its own kind of terror—the failure of the station to rightfully claim "Terror Free Oil" exhibits the paradoxical relations between
oil, consumption, and neoliberal notions of freedom at the core of this
book. At the heart of neoliberalism is the mantra that all individuals are,
as Milton Freidman famously put it, *free to choose.*[4] The celebrated field
of choice is, of course, the marketplace where free individuals make voluntary exchanges based on information about what the market has to offer.
The "Terror Free Oil" initiative is based in this fundamentally neoliberal
conviction that through consumption choices individuals can not only
shape the market but make a better world in doing so. It is this conviction
that shapes the manifold forms of "green consumption" that are themselves products of a historically specific era through which politics is seen

as most comprehensible—most possible—through market choices.[5] Yet the critics' objections that it is *impossible* to verify the level of "terror" in a given barrel of oil reveals the underlying problematic of neoliberal freedom. If freedom is ultimately exercised through the world of market exchange, commodity fetishism ensures that the social origins of those commodities will be obscured. More important, it ensures that life itself—as only accessible through the commodity form—will be subject to the abstract forms of domination specific to the value form under capitalism.

Yet, although the Minneapolis gas station Freedom appears a shaky proclamation in the oil-anxious decade of the 2000s, this book has set out to show the deep cultural and historical roots of precisely this linkage between energy and a particular *spatial experience of freedom*. In this concluding chapter, I will not only review the ways in which oil powers this specifically neoliberal vision of freedom but also speculate on the necessary role of energy in what Marx called the "realm of freedom" in a society beyond capital.

Energy and "the Realm of Freedom"

Oddly enough, in its project to create a life beyond work, Marx's vision of freedom corresponds to vision of oil-fired freedom wrapped up in "the American way of life." Especially in his later years, Marx located human emancipation in a world *beyond* work, or labor within "the realm of necessity":

> The realm of freedom really begins only where labour determined by necessity and external expediency ends; it lies by its very nature beyond the sphere of material production proper. . . . Freedom, in this sphere, can consist only in this, that socialized man, the associated producers, govern the human metabolism with nature in a rational way, brining it under their collective control instead of being dominated by it as a blind power; accomplishing it with the least expenditure of energy and in conditions most worthy and appropriate for their human nature. But this always remains a realm of necessity. The true realm of freedom, the development of human powers as an end in itself, begins beyond it, though it can only flourish with the realm of necessity as its basis. The reduction of the working day is its basic prerequisite.[6]

Importantly, this world beyond work was only made possible by the specifically capitalist development of the productive forces—along the lines of large-scale industry—which laid what he called "material conditions" for a society beyond capital.[7] This freedom is based on *material abundance* and, as Amy Wendling puts it, "an end to arduous human labor."[8] It is hard to imagine how this abundance would have been reached, in Marx's time or ours, without the use (or epic squandering, depending on your perspective) of the bounty of "buried sunshine" embedded in fossil-fuel energy. It is suggestive that Marx speaks of this "realm of freedom" in terms of "the least expenditure of energy."

Environmental and climate activists and other opponents of fossil-fuel energy are rightly uncomfortable considering the energy forms whose combustion has taken the planet to our current crisis as the "basis" or "material condition" of anything positive.[9] Yet it can't be emphasized enough that the world before fossil-fuel energy was a world where the class domination of the productive forces meant the domination of human muscles and the sweat and blood that comes from harsh manual work.[10] The age of fossil-fuel and automatic machinery held the possibility of relieving humanity from the toil of labor, but for Marx this possibility could only be reached if control over the productive powers of society was *not* in the hands of one part of society (capital) against another (the producers). In Marx's age, and ours, the incredible powers of fossil-fuel industrialism and the immense amounts of wealth generated have been narrowly appropriated by capital not for the purpose of serving human needs but rather for profit and "accumulation for the sake of accumulation."[11]

Thus from one perspective, the middle to upper strata of suburban homeowners scattered throughout the American landscape erected their own "realm of freedom" beyond the sphere of production and totally confined within the sphere of reproduction surrounding the home, family, automobility, and the geographies of leisure. Here is where "freedom" resides. But the incredible amount of energy necessary for this social form was not a democratic attempt to direct society's productive powers toward human emancipation. Rather, it was, as David Harvey reminds us, part of a larger *class project,* the larger neoliberal restoration of class power that has allowed for the redistribution of wealth upward toward a global elite.[12] As Gramsci pointed out, "if [a] hypothetical group of worthy men, notwithstanding the boundless material power which they possess, [does] not have the consent of the majority, they must be judged either as inept, or as not representative of 'national' interests."[13] Class power relies on consent, and it is difficult to imagine neoliberalism in the United States succeeding without the populist energy of the propertied masses of suburban homeowners in the Sunbelt and beyond who believed life success is a product of entrepreneurial effort, government was "the problem," and taxes were a form of politicized theft.

This vision of life is based on commonsense solidarity between privatized individual families and private capital. In the real subsumption of life under capital, *life itself* appears as a form of capital—managed through a household budget, debt financing, and investments. Yet capital itself requires the semblance of *atomized* market subjects, each competing with one another in the quest for profit and wealth accumulation. Under capital, wealth can only be appropriated *privately,* and it requires social and ecological forms that legitimate and reproduce *geographies* of private wealth appropriation. Oil, and other aspects of what David Nye calls "The High Energy Society," provides the material basis for this *privatized* geography of wealth accumulation centered on the home and automobile.[14] At the core of these geographies was the extension of the energy and power of capital—as expressed through large-scale machinery—to specific segments of the working classes. In effect, some parts of the working class were energized, afforded enormous power over machines, space, and everyday life in navigating the practices of reproduction. Critically, this was a specific form of energy and power— privatized power, individuated command over space in the automobile and a veritable mechanized factory of reproduction in the household. All these machines and productive powers lead to the belief that life could be reproduced entirely through the privatized forces and individual entrepreneurial capacities. This was no "false consciousness" but rather a logical facet of everyday practices of living, thinking, and feeling. It is quite simple to call attention to the social and public forces responsible for these geographies of social reproduction (e.g., public highways, public mortgage insurance, labor laws, and oil policies), but this does not contradict the fact that the power to traverse these spaces appears in the forms of machines that are constructed purely as products of an individual's own hard work, saving, and investing. Marx understood that in the nineteenth century industrial machines, and the science and knowledge that make them possible, "appear . . . as an attribute of capital," but he did not live to witness the twentieth-century industrialization of reproduction where machines appear as attributes of *individuals or households as capital.*[15] This subsumption of "life" under capital only becomes "real" through these broader social, technological, and ecological relationships.

Moreover, as seen in chapter 3, the *saturation* of everyday life with petroleum products—the unavoidability of oil—not only materially supplemented this vision of entrepreneurial life as capital but also turned its own logic, unwittingly, into a moral discourse on the *importance and benefits* of oil in providing the conditions of possibility for any particular individualized life project. Individuals may believe that the oil industry is corrupt, profiteering, or responsible for massive ecological destruction, but the logic of entrepreneurial life suggests that what matters most are *your individual life choices*—especially in the sphere of the market—and it is in those very practices one cannot help but purchase, use, and enjoy petroleum products. From plastics, to synthetic fibers; from asphalt to engine lubricants, life, home, travel, family, leisure, and *freedom*—are all rendered impossible without access to this one magical commodity, petroleum. Thus one can oppose the oil industry in the superstructural realm of "values," but the oil industry recognized the economic "base" was inextricable from petroleum products. Thus, according to the logic that what matters most is what you *do* with your "life," all forms of opposition were essentially ridiculed as *hypocritical* by the forces of oil capital.

The "American way of life" based on the realm of freedom beyond production was only afforded to a specific class spectrum that not only left out millions of workers throughout the urban and rural geographies of the United States but also the global geographies of production that, in effect, increasingly produced the material basis for this narrow "realm of freedom." From the *very beginning,* postwar American capitalism was about constructing its own exclusionary "golden age" of prosperity and suburban freedom through a global regime of resource extraction supposedly in the name of "free" private investment, but really in support of dictators and the use of terror against their own populations.[16] Oil is but one commodity, albeit a central one, whose production, transportation, and refining is shot through with unfreedom and injustice, injustice that directly allows for the specific geographies of mass oil consumption in the first place.[17] In the past, democratic experiments in resource sovereignty, like Mohammed Mossadegh's effort to nationalize Iranian oil in 1951, are met with ruthless repression (the British and CIA disposed Mossadegh in 1953 and installed the brutal reign of the Shah).[18] Today, the horrors of the Iraq War are only the tip of the iceberg of oil injustice. The United States' number-two supplier of petroleum in 2011, Saudi Arabia recently reached a thirty-billion-dollar weapons deal with the United States in the same month that a woman was beheaded for "being convicted of practicing sorcery."[19] In Nigeria, another top supplier (number six), whole landscapes of the Niger Delta have been poisoned by everyday oil spills and relentless flaring of natural gas into the air; resistance and efforts to affect community control over local oil resources have been met by savage state violence.[20] In Canada, the top supplier of U.S. petroleum, entire landscapes—some of which are the sacred grounds of First Nations peoples—have been contaminated, dredged, and disemboweled to produce dirty Tar Sands oil bound for the United States.[21] As mentioned in chapter 3, the refining and chemical centers of the United States in places like the Gulf Coast, New Jersey, and California are inundated with environmental justice struggles over occupational and community health. Overall, the freedom of "the American way of life" is not based on emancipation but domination, poisoning, and death.

As seen in chapter 4, access to oil is not only about fueling the geographies of consumption, but also ensuring that this oil has been produced and exchanged in a free and competitive market. Of course, the history of oil—from state prorationing in the postwar United States, to OPEC cartel, to financial speculation in crude oil derivatives today—has *never* conformed to the neoliberal imaginary of a free and competitive market. Yet the populist outrage at high gasoline and oil prices *expects* the state to work harder to produce the conditions for such an imagined (and utterly unrealizable) free market. Thus the political economy of oil has always been encircled by populist outrage based on a belief in a free oil market that really never has been or could be free.

"There Was No Room for Democracy in Industry"

While Marx's vision of the "realm of freedom" does involve large-scale industry and, thus, a massive deployment of energy, the critical difference is who controls the means of production. Marx's optimism about the capitalist development of the productive forces was based on hopes for a shift toward the *social control* of society's productive powers by the producers themselves in an emancipatory project. Neoliberal freedom was only legible through *ceding* control of the realms called the economy, market, work, and production to the despotism of capital and its imperatives of competition and accumulation. The postwar "capital-labor accord" was not so much about giving workers control over the production process as it was a concession of high wages (and the right to collectively bargain for them) in exchange for the maintenance of capital's total and authoritarian management of the production process in the interest of profits and efficiency.[22] As a historian of industrial relations put it, "businessmen made it perfectly clear that there was no room for democracy in industry."[23] Indeed, public opinion polls showed that Americans "were more preoccupied with the level of wages and time off from work than with working conditions and production processes."[24] The substantial and expansive freedom within the terrain of life—and its reproduction—allowed individuals to accept a nasty and brutish world of not only "work" but also politics—which was more and more equated with corruption and special interests. As Clark Kerr put it, postwar American industrialism provided for a new terrain of freedom: "Outside his working life the individual may have more freedom under pluralistic industrialism than in earlier forms of society. . . . There may well come a new search for individuality and a new meaning to liberty. The economic system may be highly ordered and the political system barren ideologically; but the social and recreational and cultural aspects of life diverse and changing."[25]

The capitalist distinction between production and reproduction explains the crux of the contemporary impasse around energy and climate concerns. We are continually told that the solutions to ecological problems lie in the reproductive arenas of consumer choice. In other words, we are supposed to lead "green lives" after coming home from work— our homes, our transportation, and our consumer choices become the only admissible expression of our political commitment to moving society away from fossil-fuel sources of energy. Meanwhile, outside of this political logic, the "hidden abode" of capitalist production continues to hang the sign Marx spoke of: "No admittance except on business." The mass production of commodities continues to be organized on a basis of the fossil-fuel energy regime and, more important, around production for profit over any kind of ecological sanity. When reform of capitalist production relations is brought up, it is only in the most neoliberal terms—through the establishment of carbon markets where producers can choose to emit greenhouse gases or not.

Yet for all the forms of freedom in social reproduction, this "accord" between capital and labor was a Faustian bargain. While the 1930s reconstructed many workers' lives around high wages, home ownership, and the public investment in infrastructure, it maintained a system in which life itself was only reproduced through access to wages, money, credit, and the abstract forces of the market. That is, it reproduced *waged life* wherein the bulk of the population not only remains severed from any access to or control over the means of production but also relies on wages as a mediator between life and the market. Quite predictably, by the 1970s, what David Harvey calls "the coercive laws of competition" produced a crisis of Fordism in which the pillars of postwar capitalism—high wages, unions, and the welfare state—were all seen as the cause of, not the solution to, crisis.[26] As seen in chapter 4, in the context of oil shocks and stagflation, political forces coalesced to fixate reforms not on the concrete relations of production but rather in the realm most visible to Fordist worker-consumers: the sphere of exchange, consumption, and the market. Specifically, the project became to purify this "economic" sphere and use social power to construct the conditions for a free and competitive market. Under the abstract forces of the market, entrepreneurial freedom is only legible through the logics of fair competition. Collective attempts at wealth redistribution, affirmative action, and taxes for social services all are constructed as unfair political (i.e., "playing politics") interventions within a realm that must not be political at all—if by *politics* we mean struggles for justice against the market. Politics itself is framed as a threat to freedom. Even today the discourse of fairness is all around. In response to the Occupy Wall Street movement, President Obama has recently shifted his rhetoric toward making the market fair again. In his 2012 State of the Union address (and many other speeches), his answer to the tyranny of the 1 percent is to "restore an economy where everyone gets a fair shot, and everyone does their fair share, and everyone plays by the same set of rules."[27]

Thus when social and political forces emerge to attack the working classes—as we have seen in the United States for the last four decades—the blame does not focus on the market itself (at least until very recently with the rise of the Occupy movement) but rather the forces impeding the fair operation of the market: Wall Street manipulators, Big Oil, and Big Government bureaucrats. According to this view, the origins of injustice cannot be the subsumption of life to impersonal forces of the market but rather *personalized* interventions into that market, vestiges of feudal unfreedoms and face-to-face domination. If any personalized forms of domination remained, they actively constituted the *privatized* "realm of freedom" through the territorial construction of racially exclusive neighborhood associations, gated communities, and the continuation of gendered domination within the patriarchal "private" sphere of the household.[28] As Corey Robin points out, although neoliberal ideology thrives on a populist celebration of the "free market," it also relies substantially on the maintenance of hierarchy and domination in a quasi-feudal sense in the realms of "the family, the factory, the field. There ordinary men, and sometimes women, get to play the part of little lords and ladies, supervising their underlings, as if they belong to a feudal estate."[29]

Thus oil powered a particular conception of neoliberal freedom composed of atomized individual choosers. It is easy to ridicule neoliberal notion of freedom as *completely* individualistic. This is part of larger critique of bourgeois notions of freedom going back at least to Marx himself. As he stated in the essay "On the Jewish Question," the bourgeois construction of freedom only celebrated the abstract individual "egoistic" man: "But the right of man to freedom is not based on the association of man with man but rather on the separation of man from man. It is the right of this separation, the right of the *restricted* individual, restricted to himself. The practical application of the right of man to freedom is the right of man to *private property*."[30]

This passage from Marx indicates a peculiar form of *antisocial* freedom, or the right to act without interference from others. This corresponds to the quintessential aspect of what Eric Foner labels "conservative freedom" expressed by members of the "silent majority"—the right to "being left alone by others."[31] Yet this antisocial notion of freedom obscures the deeply *social* world view at the core of the outlook of entrepreneurial life. This vision of life is not only rooted in the "social" realm of family values and the church,[32] but also in a more economic logic that lays the social conditions to *make a living for* oneself. The meaning of entrepreneurial life depends on a particular conception of "the social" as a field of competition and equal opportunity, an even playing field wherein work and life choices rightfully produce a clear set of property relations and material products. As Corey Robin again put it, "conservative political economy envisions freedom as something more than a simple 'don't tread on me'; it celebrates the everyman entrepreneur, making his own destiny, imagining a world and then creating it."[33] Again, the real subsumption of life under capital must include a vision of life as ultimately *productive*. This process of entrepreneurial creation depends on the capacities of individuals to shape life outcomes, but this shaping depends on the active intervention of social forces to maintain the rules and rights of a properly competitive economy. The capacity of individuals to both imagine and affect "self-determination" is based on particular social conditions that must not only be in place *a priori* but also be meticulously monitored and enforced by state guarantees of private property, fair markets, and the like. The thrust of popular energy during the neoliberal era looks to the state to *enforce* free and fair markets, not to intervene within them. Foucault recognized that this wider social field is essential to the liberal world view: "Freedom is something which is constantly produced. Liberalism is not the acceptance of freedom; it proposes to manufacture it constantly, to arouse it and produce it, with, of course [the system] . . . of constraints and the problems of cost raised by this production."[34] Much of what passes for "politics" is essentially about laying the conditions for this kind of imagined freedom.

The Forces of the Future

We are left with the question of what kind of energy, for what kind of freedom. The construction of privatized freedom within the realm of social reproduction excludes the things we call work, the economy, and production from the realm of freedom. It is *politicizing* this realm of production that Marx identified as essential to "the social control and regulation of the forces of nature, and the free development of the productive forces of society."[35] Indeed, There is perhaps no industry/sector where the democratization of production is more clearly necessary than that of energy. During the current moment of high prices for fossil fuels, the energy industries are not investing needed amounts toward a non-fossil-fuel-energy transition but are for the most part *doubling down* on the fossil regime through the development of all kinds of unconventional fuels: from shale gas to Tar Sands; from mountaintop removal coal mining to deepwater oil drilling (coming soon to the Arctic!). Private, for-profit energy companies wield tremendous influence over the political process—largely though campaign donations—and thus our "energy policy" (if it can be called this) has largely failed to provoke the large-scale energy transition needed to avoid not only the ongoing climate crisis but also the myriad of local/regional forms of environmental and social destruction bound up with fossil-fuel energy extraction and processing.

It is clear that, for Marx, freedom is premised upon the *capitalist* development of the productive forces along the lines of large-scale industry based on fossil fuel to lay the material conditions for a society beyond capital, a society devoted to relief from labor. Yet efforts to construct a green or ecological Marxism are highly critical of this focus on the productive forces.[36] This critique of Marx's focus on the productive forces is certainly understandable given the historical experience of the Soviet Union, which took this dictum to disastrous environmental ends. Yet simply ignoring the role of the productive forces in a society beyond capital makes it entirely unclear how we can imagine political, democratic social control over the realm of production. It leaves unanswered perhaps the most important political question of our age of anthropogenic climate change: how can we wrestle control over our energy systems from for profit private capital and toward the social direction of energy toward renewable fuels in the *collective* interests of society and the planet as a whole?

Marx believed that there is something inherently emancipatory about large-scale industrialization, and ecosocialists need not be so quick to dismiss this possibility. As this book has attempted to show, the use of oil has engendered millions of American to feel that their everyday lives were based on a certain kind of "freedom." If socialism is about emancipation and freedom we simply cannot deny the role that energy must play in this emancipation. What if the phrase "development of the productive forces" was not simply equated with the expansion of dirty industrial production based on coal, oil, and gas and instead represented the full development of *industrial* energy systems based on cleaner and renewable fuels? For example, David Shwartzman, an ecosocialist biologist/geochemist, suggests that our understanding of a communist future must include solar energy at its core.[37] The amount of solar energy bathing the planet exceeds by any conceivable imagination a sustainable level of human demand for energy.[38] Of course, at the current state of the productive forces, we have not adequately learned how to properly harvest this solar bounty, but this does not mean it is impossible.

This is a vision of ecosocialism quite at odds with many social movements struggling against fossil fuels for a sustainable climate future. Environmental social movements against fossil fuels for good reason focus most of their efforts on critiquing the global and local ecological devastation wrought by fossil-fuel extraction and combustion. Like many aspects of ecological political economy, critiques focus on an external field of "nature" destroyed by a purely social system of capitalism. Yet, as this book has tried to argue, the crux of political and cultural support for specific energy regimes lies in their wider embeddedness within geographies of social reproduction. If environmental critiques of energy extraction have no answer to the populist clamoring for cheap energy for life itself, the opposition is in danger of at best feeling remote or distant from everyday experience and at worst being completely ignored.

Another problem is the impulse to reject all that is global, modern, and industrial about the fossil-fuel regime. For example, a vibrant "transition town" movement has emerged as a response to the impending "peak oil" crisis.[39] This particular vision of transition imagines a world of energy scarcity and *forced* localization. Yet localization is viewed as entirely positive as an antidote to globalization, declining community, and environmental alienation of modern industrial capitalism.[40] Naomi Klein's important article on the need to combine anticapitalist politics with the climate movement makes the case very well. "The cargo ships, jumbo jets and heavy trucks that haul raw resources and finished products across the globe devour fossil fuels and spew greenhouse gases. . . . In an economy organized to respect natural limits, the use of energy-intensive long-haul transport would need to be rationed—reserved for those cases where goods cannot be produced locally or where local production is more carbon-intensive."[41]

The celebration of a return to "localization" as the solution to our energy and climate predicament not only is based on a romantic nostalgia for a preindustrial age of small-scale agriculture but also naïvely downplays the extent to which modern society is fundamentally entangled within fossil-fuel forms of globalized production. To take one example, Vaclav Smil, with his cool, rational calculations, boldly states that 40 percent of humanity would not be alive today were it not for the development of energy-intensive synthetic nitrogen fertilizer made possible by the twentieth century development of the Haber-Bosch process.[42] Apart from the problematic nature of such equations between food and population, it cannot be denied that *automatic machinery* has entirely transformed the nature of work away from human and animal muscles powering the productive forces of society. I am less optimistic about a future that does not include this tremendous energetic relief for the *living bodies* (human and nonhuman) of production.

From a Marxist or historical–materialist standpoint, an emancipatory future will not come from reconstructing old forms of production but rather must emerge out of the conditions set by the current mode of production: "New, higher relations of production never appear before the material conditions of their existence have matured in the womb of the old society itself."[43] Rather than viewing fossil fuels as the ultimate sin of modernity that must be renounced through a reconstruction of prefossil forms of sociality, fossil-fuel energy needs to be viewed as a material condition of an emancipatory future based on cleaner and renewable fuels.

Yet it is a serious question whether or not such a future is *possible* given the finite nature of fossil fuel. The question of when or how imminent peak oil is, of course, a matter of great debate.[44] In the end, the real socioecological problem is the sheer abundance of remaining fossil fuels on the planet that if burned will likely accelerate processes of climate change. But the more fundamental question is what political possibilities exist in a future in which, as Timothy Mitchell suggests, there is "no more counting on oil."[45] Peak oil proponents offer one vision of a postpetroleum world—either a romantic return to agricultural self-sufficiency or a neofeudal world of scarcity, violence, and tribalism. Yet, given that oil has powered such a problematic form of hostile privatism, must a world beyond oil be constructed as so politically bleak? Energy is fundamental to the social production of space. Oil's role in powering a decentralized and privatized transportation system has produced the privatization of space itself. A world with less oil can potentially allow for a total political and social revolution of space.

A new "energy transition" away from oil must also be viewed as a political struggle to produce new spatialities of social life. Rather than spatialities of localized agriculture, it is worth considering whether or not those spatialities might focus on *the urban*, which oil promised an escape from. As Henri Lefebvre recognized, the *urban*—with its diversity and social concentration—contains tremendous revolutionary potential.[46] Oil has allowed for the construction of an *antiurban* geography. What is promised by this antiurban vision is summed up nicely in a flyer my parents were given by their realtor to help sell the suburban St. Louis home I grew up in; it announced "Splendid Seclusion." Our house's backyard and deck were oriented toward a dense forest that lay behind it, and it was this "seclusion"—away from the public sociality common in cities—that was a prime selling point of the property. Completely dependent upon the car, I lived in a subdivision in a valley at least a mile away from any kind of public space. Oil-fired mobility made this kind of privatization possible. Thus lack of oil might promise a renewal of the urban in much more exciting ways than the either the gentrifiers or the bourgeois proponents of "new urbanism" imagine.[47] The urban holds promise not simply because of coffee shops and walkable communities but because of the political energy and the forms of sociality that are made possible within urbanized geographies.

In George W. Bush's 2006 State of the Union address, in which he famously declared, "America is addicted to oil," he also added that "the best way to break this addiction is through technology."[48] Indeed, conventional wisdom often assumes that energy and oil consumption patterns are a purely technical and economic problem and that if only the proper economic incentives are in place, the captains of industry will unveil their latest innovative breakthroughs pushing us onward toward a sustainable energy future. Yet this book has aimed to show that the way in which modes of energy consumption become established is a much more open social and political process. This process responds not only to the imperatives of capital accumulation but also to the culturally specific *meaning of life itself* that underlies any historically specific social formation. During the 1930s, the crisis of capitalism required a total reorganization of the production and reproduction of material life. While much of what happened during the New Deal was not termed—or quarantined—as "energy policy," resurrecting capitalism through the restructuring of everyday patterns of housing, transport, and working-class power over wages necessarily implied dramatic restructurings of the ways people consumed oil and other energy. We need to begin to see our energy problems in these social and political terms: not as a singular "field" of policy intervention but rather as larger social and political process of shaping and reshaping the cultural politics of life itself. In other words, energy should be situated within a broader struggle that aims to place all necessary aspects of life itself (education, health care, food) under social and democratic control against the abstract forces of the market and the privatization of wealth appropriation.

Thus the biggest barrier to energy change is not technical but the cultural and political structures of feeling that have been produced through regimes of energy consumption. Oil has been mobilized through the particular balance of forces shaping our neoliberal age. The mobilization of oil and fossil fuel produced an unprecedented form of individuated power and control over everyday practices, creating the appearance that we are free and on our own. Yet, as Marx suggests, "only when man [sic] has recognized and organized his [own forces] as *social forces* . . . will human emancipation be competed."[49] The cars, homes, roads, and countless petroleum products that make up so much of American life are products not of atomized individuals but broader social relations, public investments, and legacies of social and environmental injustice. The struggle to move "beyond oil" is not only a struggle over a fuel, or a technology, or even simply a struggle against "Big Oil"; it is a struggle to make visible once again the social and collective forces that make any "life" possible.

ACKNOWLEDGMENTS

It has become a cliché to begin like this, but there is no such thing as individual authorship. This book, more than a decade in the making, is the result of numerous conversations, gracious feedback, and networks of family and institutional support. I'd like to take this opportunity to thank all the people who coauthored this book with me. I write this anxiously with fear I will inevitably miss some people. If I do, please know how much I appreciate all the help I've received along the way.

My intellectual journey began with increasing interest in environmental politics alongside a sudden confusion over why I was an economics major. I want to thank Tom Tietenberg for forcing me to refine my constant questions and critiques of environmental economics. My masters work in sociology at Northeastern University was critical in giving me time and space to read and write; thanks to Danny Faber for being an incredible teacher when I had so much to learn.

Once I discovered Geography (and it took awhile), I was hooked. Clark University in Worcester, Massachusetts, was a fantastic place to pursue a PhD, and I accumulated innumerable debts in my time there. Thanks to Mazen Labban for showing me that a dissertation (and book) on oil and Marxism was possible. I'd like to thank all my friends in the CUGS community for providing companionship during the sometimes isolating process of obtaining a PhD. If it weren't for the periodic house parties and impromptu get-togethers at Moynihans, I think I would have gone insane. Special thanks to Marco, Kevin, Steve, Jake, Rebecca, Atlas, Ania, Daniel, Pickles, Rahul, Benoit, Roberta, Maya, Hamil, and Zach for great times. More than anyone else, the ideas on these pages are indebted to conversations with Tim Currie and Diana Ojeda. They both provided critical feedback on the earliest (and crudest) iterations of these arguments. I miss our conversations so much, and Gramsci remains my copilot.

Jody Emel is the adviser that all doctoral students dream about—door always open and ears always ripe for conversation and debate. Most important, her healthy skepticism forced me to more rigorously and clearly communicate the ideas that ended up in this book. I'd like to thank Deb Martin for her invigorating criticism of my writing, especially as a constant check on my verbose and tangential tendencies. Both Jody and Deb were wonderful advisers, but they are even more wonderful people and great friends. Thanks to Dick Peet for his demand for analytical clarity and his sharp sense of what was glaringly missing from my arguments. Thanks to James McCarthy for his support, advice, and incredible insight on my work as it developed. It was his comment in 2005 about a "fossil fuel mode of production" that got me thinking.

The Quadrant Fellowship at the Institute for Advanced Study at the University of Minnesota worked exactly as advertised: it gave me the time and space to completely rethink the dissertation into a book. It was during that fall that the argument I wanted to make in this book (finally) emerged. Thanks to Susannah Smith, Anne Carter, and Ann Waltner for all forms of support during my stay. Thanks to all the IAS fellows for consistently engaging conversations over lunch and in other venues. A special thanks to fellow Quadrant traveler Lisa Uddin; her brilliant work was an inspiration, and I enjoyed our chats over coffee. I spent nearly four months in the Twin Cities, but two hours made the most difference—thanks to Pieter Martin, Anne Carter, Dan Philippon, John Archer, Michael Goldman, George Henderson, and Bruce Braun for all their stunning insights during my Quadrant workshop. Thanks especially to George and Bruce for their friendship and for opening me to the geography community at the University of Minnesota. I express my utmost gratitude to my editor, Pieter Martin, for his support, encouragement, and advice throughout this process.

The meat of this work emerged after my visit to Minnesota, and I want to thank numerous people at Syracuse University who enriched this text. Conversations with Tom Perrault, Bob Wilson, Tod Rutherford, and Jamie Winders strengthened the ideas that appear here. I want to especially thank Don Mitchell, who pored over the entire manuscript with incredible enthusiasm, offering exhaustive comments from major critiques to minor typos. Jenna Loyd and Gretchen Purser provided unbelievable feedback on chapter 5 in our writing group. Thanks to our incredible staff in the Department of Geography: Janet Brieaddy and now Margie Johnson, Jackie Wells, and Chris Chapman. Whether through seminars or conversations, I have benefited from interactions with several graduate students: Mike Dimpfl, Amy

Solar-Doherty, Parvathy Binoy, Anna Davidson, Thor Ritz, Saptarshi Lahri, Alejandro Camargo, Mitul Baruah, Ben Gerlofs, Mike Kantor, Carlo Sica, Renee Huset, Brent Olson, Melinda Gurr, Ben Marley, Keith Lindner, Kate Coddington, and Elvin Delgado. Thank you all!

I have also benefited from several conferences, workshops, and speaking engagements where I was able to test drive some of the arguments in this book. Thanks to everyone (especially Jason Moore and other organizers) at the "Brief Environmental History of Neoliberalism" conference in Lund, Sweden. The encouragement I received in Lund gave me renewed confidence to see the book through. Thanks to Bob Ross for inviting me to give a lecture at Point Park University's Humanities Symposium; it was fantastic to get feedback from such a sharp undergraduate audience. Thanks to Nathan Sayre for organizing my participation in the Environmental Politics Workshop at the University of California at Berkeley and to Arthur Mason for giving such insightful feedback as the discussant on my paper. It was a thrill to get such great feedback from people whose work I respect so much. Thanks to Arthur Mason, Michael Watts, and Hannah Appel for organizing the wonderfully productive "Oil Talk" workshop in New York City. A special thanks to Michael Watts for incisive comments on my paper. It was exciting to see such diverse and inspiring work on the topic of oil.

This book is a work of scholarship that more than anything else relied on documents—primary sources, newspapers, magazines, and academic literature, among other resources. My access to these varied texts was enhanced by numerous gracious and committed staff members at a variety of institutions. Thanks to the many resourceful archivists at the Franklin Delano Roosevelt Museum and Library, the Texas State Archives, the University of Texas–Austin's Dolph Briscoe Center for American History, the East Texas Research Center, the Texas Energy Museum, the Gerald Ford Presidential Library, the Paley Center for Media, the Hagley Museum and Library, the National Archives II–College Park, the Richard Nixon Presidential Library, the Ronald Reagan Presidential Library, the Bancroft Library at UC Berkeley, and the Hoover Institution at Stanford University. The library staffs at Clark and Syracuse Universities were absolutely amazing, fulfilling interlibrary loan requests with utmost efficiency and sometimes even carting boxes of old magazines up to my office!

This book also features several images, and I completely relied on the work of others to make them look as good as they do. Thanks to John Archer for providing a brilliant advertisement from 1917 that basically summed up the book with one image and tagline. Thanks to Joe Stoll for taking my crude images and transforming them into something usable. A very special thanks to David Broda at the Syracuse University's Photo and Imaging Center for taking remarkable photographs of old advertisements from impossibly thick and bound periodicals. Thanks to Matthew Darby at the Dolph Briscoe Center for digging up an old collection of Esso ads from the 1950s. I want to express the utmost appreciation to Nathan Clough, Ivan Bialostosky, and Reecia Orzeck for all going out with a camera on a quest for "Freedom"—gas stations, that is. I ultimately used Reecia's picture, but they were all great!

Words can't express adequately my deepest appreciation and love for my parents, Neil and Meimei Huber. Without them this book would have been impossible. From an early age, I learned from them the value of education, knowledge, and political engagement. Their unwavering support reveals the fallacy of the idea that any life is the product of only individual efforts. Thanks to Jeff for being my best friend and sharing our commitment to a life based in Hubmor. Thanks to Chris for teaching me more about life than I could ever learn in school. I also want to thank my fabulous in-laws, Robert and Rita Nelson. I think it's safe to say that not every spouse would be thrilled to land a job in the town where the in-laws reside, but you two are the absolute best. Angela and I love you both and feel lucky to live so close.

This book was mostly written during the summer months. While I struggled with theoretical debates and the complexities of 1930s politics, or even when I felt like the whole project was impossible, it was always heartening to know that Angela was in the fields producing something tangible and immediate. Angela, you continue to amaze me! You simply radiate love and warmth, and you gave me all the support, patience, and, most important, laughter that I needed to see this project through. I am so thankful for the life and love that we share.

Introduction

1. "Keeping America competitive requires affordable energy. And here we have a serious problem: America is addicted to oil, which is often imported from unstable parts of the world," Bush, "State of the Union Address," January 31, 2006.

2. Stolberg, "Bush's Speech Prod's Middle East Leaders."

3. Bush, "President's Radio Address," June 21, 2008.

4. Stolberg, "News Analysis: Will $4 Gasoline Trump a 27-Year-Old Ban?"

5. Bosman, "Unlikely Allies Campaign for Gas-Tax Holiday."

6. All quotes come from ibid. Of course, oil companies desire higher prices, but not prices that are captured through government taxes.

7. Gingrich, *Drill Here, Drill Now, Pay Less.*

8. Collins, "The Energy Drill."

9. It is no wonder that Europe features smaller cars and more compact cities when most countries tax gasoline at a rate of around $4 to $5 per gallon. In contrast, state and federal gasoline taxes in the United State average around $0.50. See Derek Thompson, "Gas Prices around the World."

10. Hammar, Lofgren, and Sterner, "Political Economy Obstacles to Fuel Taxation"; and Galbraith, "Panel Suggests Gas Tax."

11. Obama, "Remarks of Senator Barack Obama."

12. Associated Press, "Gas Prices Burden Families."

13. Powell, "Obama Says He Would Agree to Some Drilling."

14. The equation of low gas prices with popular support for Obama is evidenced by headlines like this, from the article by Bull: "Signs of Cheaper Gas Could Brighten Obama Campaign."

15. It is often said that we "switched" from coal to oil in the twentieth century, but the discourse of "energy transitions" from the age of coal to the age of oil can lead to problematic ways of thinking about energy. It generalizes a societal shift for

what was a more sectoral shift from coal-steam-powered transportation (e.g., rail-roads and steamships) to oil-powered, internal combustion–powered transporta-tion (e.g., automobiles and airplanes). Moreover, to talk of the present as "the age of oil" leads some to believe that the age of coal is somehow over. Yet coal *remains* a major source of electric power generation that not only underpins everyday usage of lights and appliances but, more important, powers the entire electrified indus-trial production system. In fact, the most dynamic economy on the planet at the moment is a coal-based economy in China (of course, China also consumes a lot of oil for transportation). Timothy Mitchell makes much of the transition from coal to oil because of the different capacities of workers to intervene in their respective production processes (coal workers have much more power). But the way in which he accords the energy source as a crucial determinant of the ability to "advance . . . egalitarian political claims" borders on a form of energy reductionism that appears to be coming back into vogue. See Timothy Mitchell, *Carbon Democracy*, 86. For another perspective that makes too much of the "transition" from coal to oil see Podobnik, *Global Energy Shifts*.

16. Energy Information Administration, "What Are the Major Sources and Us-ers of Energy in the United States," May 18, 2012.

17. Raymond Williams, *Television*, 19.

18. Rutledge, *Addicted to Oil*.

19. See Energy Information Administration, "Energy in Brief: What Are Greenhouse Gases and How Much Are Emitted by the United States?" For a comprehensive look at the social and environmental injustices across the petro-leum commodify chain, see O'Rourke and Connolly, "Just Oil?"

20. This is despite the fact that most of the United States' imports come from places like Canada and Mexico—only 20 percent come from the Persian Gulf, mostly from Saudi Arabia. Energy Information Administration, "U.S. Imports by Country of Origin." Despite the common feeling that our dependence on foreign oil only increases with time, U.S. reliance on foreign oil has recently declined pre-cipitously from 60 percent to 45 percent in the span of five years due to increased U.S. production and slight declines in demand. See Energy Information Adminis-tration, "How Dependent Are We on Foreign Oil?" This discourse of danger and fear of oil dependence not only structures virtually every statement on oil from U.S. politicians and media pundits but also is a commonsense view among a certain left critique of U.S. foreign oil policy. See especially Klare, *Blood and Oil*.

21. See Kunstler, *The Long Emergency*. See also Duany, Plater-Zyberk; and Speck, *Suburban Nation*.

22. Over the last decade, there have been too many "peak oil" publications to count. Some of the most influential include Heinberg, *The Party's Over*; Kunstler, *The Long Emergency*; and Simmons, *Twilight in the Desert*. For some excellent critiques of peak oil discourse, see Retort, *Afflicted Powers*; Labban, "Oil in Paral-lax"; and Bridge, "Past Peak Oil."

23. Linton Weeks, "Pumped Up."

24. There has been a "return" to materiality recently in critical geography and social theory. Some of the most important contributions include Butler, *Bodies that Matter*; Law and Mol, "Notes on Materiality and Sociality"; Bakker and Bridge, "Material Worlds"; and Alaimo and Hekman, *Material Feminisms*. Perhaps the first book to put the materiality of petroleum at the center of the analysis is Timothy Mitchell, *Carbon Democracy*.

25. For variations on this elite-centered, conspiratorial theme see, for example, Yago, *The Decline of Transit*; McShane, *Down the Asphalt Path*; Edwin Black, *Internal Combustion*; Gonzalez, *Urban Sprawl*.

26. Readers might be struck by the total lack of discussion of "Big Oil," geopolitics, and petro-states within this book. This is not only because I want to retain focus on what is obviously an expansive and unwieldy topic but also because there is simply so much work out there on these topics.

27. See Yergin, *The Prize*.

28. See, for example, Kashi and Watts, *Curse of the Black Gold*; and Vitalis, *America's Kingdom*.

29. Timothy Mitchell, *Carbon Democracy*, 5. Although Mitchell offers important interventions in the debates over oil—his account of Middle East oil development as a struggle to *prevent* the production of oil helps us understand the production of scarcity necessary for oil markets (see also chapter 2). He also incorporates an all-too-often-ignored actor in the discussion over energy geopolitics: energy workers. Yet Mitchell remains in the "big" world of strategy between rival companies, foreign policy elites, and grand oil schemes. He also incorporates energy workers through a relatively narrow focus on their *strategic* capacity to interrupt the energy production process. That is, coal and railway workers, and in a different way oil-producing states, have powers of "sabotage" that are explained by "their novel ability to shut down the energy supply" (68) and "paralyse energy systems" (108). As I argue in chapter 1, we need to further understand the social relations that produce the idea that energy is so "strategic" in the first place. Like virtually every other critical approach to energy, Mitchell does not pay much attention to everyday patterns of consumption even if he does pay lip service to the project: "Much more could be said about the role of major oil companies and car manufacturers in helping to produce and popularize ways of living based on very high levels of energy consumption" (42). While I agree that we need to understand these forms of living as "produced," this book's wager is that it is not only big capital doing the producing.

30. Le Billon and El Khatib, "From Free Oil to 'Freedom Oil.'" It is problematic enough that popular ideas of "terrorism" are territorialized to a complex region (the Middle East and the Persian Gulf Oil region in particular), but, as stated, it is also not true that most of U.S. oil imports come from this part of the world.

31. Campbell, "The Biopolitics of Security." David Campbell has brilliantly linked the SUV with "security" discourses of "cultural militarism" and the "consumer's desire to ensure that the family vehicle offers a high level of personal

security" (958) with larger geopolitical imperatives of energy security and American empire.

32. Banerjee, "'Made in America.'"

33. Ibid.

34. Kunstler, "Remarks." Kunstler made these remarks at a 2005 conference called "PetroCollapse," which perhaps explains Vaclav Smil's charge that peak oil believers represent a "catastrophic cult." Vaclav Smil, "Peak Oil."

35. Whether or not U.S. consumers are portrayed as gluttonous zombies or unknowing dupes to the political and economic machinations of "Big Oil" and the auto companies, it appears theories of U.S. oil consumption have not caught up with more nuanced accounts of consumer subjectivity from cultural studies. For example, Peter Jackson examines the role of local culture in shaping consumption practices of supposedly "globalizing" commodities such as Coca-Cola. Jackson, "Local Consumption Cultures."

36. The maintenance of livelihoods is often unproblematically assumed as a moral good. Indeed, study of social movements to protect livelihoods against displacement and destruction is perhaps the central focus of political ecology and development studies. See, for example, Bebbington, "Capitals and Capabilities."

37. For example, James McCarthy problematizes the moral economies of the "Wise Use" movement, which marshals private property rights and defense of livelihood discourses to oppose environmental protection efforts of the centralized federal government. McCarthy, "First World Political Ecology."

38. Foucault, *The Birth of Biopolitics*. See also Barry, Osborne, and Rose, *Foucault and Political Reason; and* Lemke, "The Birth of Bio- Politics."

39. Decker, *Made in America*.

40. See Lizabeth Cohen, *Making a New Deal*; Gordon, *New Deals*; and Jacobs, *Pocketbook Politics*.

41. Cindi Katz, "Vagabond Capitalism," 710.

42. Again, oil's importance here is more about mobility and transportation, whereas electricity largely derives its power from coal, nuclear, natural gas, and hydropower.

43. This concept has emerged out of recent efforts to productively combine Foucault's insights on biopolitical subjectivities and Marx's critique of capital. The most famous of these is, of course, the work of Hardt and Negri, *Empire*. See also Lazzarato, "The Concepts of Life and Living in the Societies of Control"; Terranova, "Another Life"; Ben Anderson, "Affect and Biopower"; and Hannah, "Biopower, Life, and Left Politics." The most sustained philosophical elaboration of these ideas is laid out in Read, *The Micro-Politics of Capital*.

44. Duncan and Lieberson, *Metropolis and Region in Transition*, 119.

45. Marx, *Capital Volume 1*, 932.

46. From a Marxist–Feminist perspective, Kathi Weeks has recently argued for a politics of life against work. Weeks, "Life within and against Work."

47. Marx, *Wage Labour and Capital*, 19.

48. Among the best studies of this phenomena are Davis, *Prisoners of the American Dream*; Edsall and Edsall, *Chain Reaction*; McKenzie, *Privatopia*; McGirr, *Suburban Warriors*; and Lassiter, *The Silent Majority*.

49. Although this history indicates the popular energy for the rise of the right in the United States emerging from the suburbs (particularly in the Sunbelt), I must warn against any strict geographic or spatial determinism. While suburban geographies were certainly *conducive* to ideologies of privatism, suburban areas also contain a wider diversity of political views. See Kruse and Sugrue, *The New Suburban History*.

50. McKenzie, *Privatopia*, 19.

51. See Heynen et al., *Neoliberal Environments*.

52. Similarly, Jason Moore has argued that we need not only to focus on capitalism's effects on the environment but also to theorize the ecology of capital: "Capitalism does not *have* an ecological regime; it *is* an ecological regime." See Jason Moore, "Transcending the Metabolic Rift," 34.

53. After the crash of 2008, there was a breathless impulse to speak of "postneoliberalism." For a skeptical take see Peck, Theodore, and Brenner, "Postneoliberalism and Its Discontents." Writing in 2012, in the age of austerity economics, it is clear that the death of neoliberalism has been exaggerated, but the phenomenon of Occupy Wall Street and mass global protests against economic violence the world over give hope for a more coordinated resistance to neoliberalism.

54. Harvey, *A Brief History of Neoliberalism*; Mirowski and Plehwe, *The Road to Mont Pèlerin*; Peck, *Constructions of Neoliberal Reason*. There is an emerging historical literature around the role of the Sunbelt in the rightward shift of American politics. See Lassiter, *The Silent Majority;* and Nickerson and Dochuk, *Sunbelt Rising*. For a fascinating look at oil and religion in the Southwest, see Dochuk, "Blessed by Oil, Cursed with Crude."

55. This compromise is termed the *capital–labor accord* by the social structures of accumulation school. See Bowles, Gordon, and Weisskopf, "Power and Profits." The "great compromise" is seen as a key institutional basis of what regulationists like Aglietta and Boyer call the Fordist regime of accumulation based on mass production for mass consumption. For a good summation of the regulation approach, see Peck and Tickell, "Accumulation, Regulation, and the Geographies of Post-Fordism."

56. See Edsall and Edsall, *Chain Reaction*.

57. Davis, *Prisoners of the American Dream*, 52–156.

58. Fitzsimmons, "The Matter of Nature."

59. James O'Connor, *Natural Causes*.

60. For a good overview of perspectives on the metabolic rift, see Foster, Clark, and York, *The Ecological Rift: Capitalism's War on the Earth*. Of course, the division between "capitalism" and "the earth" is right there in their subtitle. In the end, the metabolic rift theory—rooted in the soil science of Liebeg that Marx himself studied—constructs a nostalgia of a precapitalist "natural" metabolism

between agricultural producers, the soil, waterways, and so on. While we need to understand the specificities of industrial environmental destruction, precapitalist societies certainly had their own forms of the metabolic rift. See Redman, *Human Impacts on Ancient Environments*. For a different critique of the metabolic rift see Jason Moore, "Transcending the Metabolic Rift."

61. Jason Moore, "Transcending the Metabolic Rift."

62. Braun, "Nature and Culture: On the Career of a False Problem."

63. Locating ecology within the productive forces is different from O'Connor, whose "second contradiction" is *between* the productive forces and social relations of production on the one hand and the *ecological* (as well as labor and infrastructural) *conditions of production* on the other. If energy is understood as fundamental to the productive forces, the "first contradiction" is equally ecological.

64. A useful collection of articles in the tradition of political ecology can be found in Peet and Watts, *Liberation Ecologies*. For a review of "resource geography," see Gavin Bridge, "Material Worlds."

65. It also lends itself to the idea that there are, as Scott Prudham puts it, "nature-centered industries," such as agriculture, timber, and mining. These industries actively confront the biological or biophysical properties of the environment in order to extract value. See Prudham, *Knock on Wood*, 13. It is difficult, however, to draw the line on which industries are and are not "nature centered." All production confronts the biology of living bodies, but a properly dialectical perspective must also acknowledge that any particular moment of manufacturing or informational (or so-called immaterial) production is necessarily linked to moments of extraction and waste—not to mention the fact that these sectors harness the natural forces of heat and chemical transformation (in, for instance, the cement industry) or the electrochemical circuitry of modern computing technology.

66. I am specifically influenced by the regulationist theorization of "mass consumption" central to Fordism. See Aglietta, *A Theory of Capitalist Regulation*, and Boyer, "From Canonical Fordism."

67. Fine, *The World of Consumption*, 82.

68. For example, this approach has proven useful in agro-food studies precisely because it allows a focus on the material and ecological specificities of any particular food commodity (which necessitates particular labor processes and modes of distribution). See Guthman, "Commodified Meanings, Meaningful Commodities."

69. Timothy Mitchell, *Carbon Democracy*, 7.

1. The Power of Oil?

1. Coronil, *The Magical State*.

2. The most famous example of antimonopoly muckraking critiques of "Big Oil" is Tarbell's *The History of the Standard Oil Company*. Yet more anti–"Big

Oil" books are undoubtedly published today—for example, Juhasz, *The Tyranny of Oil*; McElroy, *For the Love of Oil*; or Palast, *Vultures' Picnic*.

3. Bower, *Oil*, 220.

4. See Coronil, *The Magical State*; Karl, *The Paradox of Plenty*; and Watts, "Oil as Money."

5. There is a variety of rich historical scholarship on oil booms and local economic development in the United States. For the earliest case of Pennsylvania, see Brian Black, *Petrolia*, and for the classic case of Texas, see Olien and Hinton, *Wildcatters*. For the case of California see Sabin, *Crude Politics*.

6. In addition to Karl's seminal work, see Michael Ross, *The Oil Curse*; and Dunning, *Crude Democracy*. A good critique of the "resource curse" is found in Watts, "Resource Curse."

7. Karl, *The Paradox of Plenty*

8. Agnew, *Geopolitics*.

9. Again, most of these moments are captured in Yergin's *The Prize*.

10. Cheney's claim that the Middle East "is where the prize ultimately lies" comes from his speech at the London Institute of Petroleum. Cheney, "Full Text of Dick Cheney's Speech."

11. U.S. Senate. "Hearings before the Committee on Armed Services, United States Senate, September 11, 1990." C-SPAN video archives, http://www.c-span video.org/program/13960-1.

12. See Klare, *Rising Powers, Shrinking Planet*.

13. Klare, *Resource Wars*, 27.

14. Harvey, *Cosmopolitanism*, 134.

15. Harvey, *The New Imperialism*, 19.

16. Cole, "Speech to the American Petroleum Institute."

17. Olien and Olien, "Running Out of Oil."

18. See footnote 22 in the introduction to this book.

19. Watts, in "Oil as Money," discusses the equation of oil with money as a particular form of fetishism, but the fetishization of oil as a thing-in-itself is a powerful narrative even apart from its monetary properties.

20. Marx, *Capital Volume 1*, 1005.

21. Ibid., 165.

22. Taussig, *The Devil and Commodity Fetishism*, 35.

23. Marx, *Capital Volume 1*, 164–65.

24. See Ollman, *Alienation*, and Harvey, *Justice, Nature and the Geography of Difference*, especially 46–95.

25. Harvey, "Population, Resources, and the Ideology of Science," 265.

26. David Harvey himself is famous for this approach to commodity fetishism. See Harvey, "Between Space and Time." For a long-overdue critique of commodity chain analysis from the perspective of Marxian value theory see Starosta, "Global Commodity Chains."

27. In an approach he calls "following the carbon," Timothy Mitchell focuses squarely on the material "process through which oil is produced and distributed." Mitchell, *Carbon Democracy*, 7, 5. Mitchell's account takes each stage of the flow of oil—from extraction to pipeline to refining to the flows of money therein—as formative moments in the broader relations between oil, politics, and society. Other accounts focus on one material stage of the oil chain. There are numerous studies that examine the political ecology of oil extraction—for example, Kashi and Watts, *Curse of the Black Gold*, and Sawyer, *Crude Chronicles*. For a detailed look at the environmental injustices of a refinery in Durban, South Africa, see Doyle, *Riding the Dragon*, and on the petrochemical industry in Louisiana see Lerner, *Diamond*. For a comprehensive review of the evidence on social and environmental impacts across the entire petroleum commodity chains see O'Rourke and Connolly, "Just Oil?" A highly readable account of the petroleum commodity chain is Margonelli, *Oil on the Brain*.

28. For a history see Williamson and Daum, *The American Petroleum Industry Volume 1*.

29. A by no means exhaustive list of this work includes Harvey O'Connor, *Empire of Oil* and *World Crisis in Oil*; Nore and Turner, *Oil and Class Struggle*; Bina, *The Economics of the Oil Crisis*; Bromley, *American Hegemony*; Midnight Notes Collective, *Midnight Oil*; Coronil, *The Magical State*; Jhaveri, "Petroimperialism"; Le Billon and El Khatib, "From Free Oil to 'Freedom Oil'"; Caffentzis, "The Petroleum Commons"; Retort, *Afflicted Powers*; Watts, "Empire of Oil"; Labban, *Space, Oil, and Capital*; and Stokes and Raphael, *Global Energy Security*. Although Timothy Mitchell, in *Carbon Democracy*, claims (and does cover) quite new terrain, he is still ultimately concerned with the great struggles of rival companies, imperial powers, and other standard actors in the oil drama.

30. Despite all the talk of "Big Oil" in American politics, it is rarely acknowledged that the history of the oil industry—and the relation of that industry to American politics—has been profoundly shaped by "little" independent oil companies whose sheer number and influence have made them an influential political force. See, for example, Olien and Hinton, *Wildcatters*. On the political influence of the independent oil industry, see Rutledge, "Profitability and Supply Price in the US Domestic Oil Industry."

31. Lefebvre, *The Survival of Capitalism*, 89.

32. The discourse of oil and power stands in stark contrast to the oft-cited critique of power by Michel Foucault: "Power is everywhere . . . Power is not something that is acquired or seized, or shared, something that one holds on to or allows to slip away; power is exercised from innumerable points, in the interplay of nonegalitarian and mobile relations." Foucault, *The History of Sexuality*, 93–94.

33. Marx and Engels, *The German Ideology*, 49.

34. Ibid., 42.

35. Ibid. Emphasis in original.

36. It is well known that Marx's "preface" to the *Contribution to the Critique of Political Economy* contained one of his few clarifying statements on the "guiding thread" of historical materialism: "In the social production of their existence, men inevitably enter into definite relations, which are independent of their will, namely relations of production appropriate to a given stage in the development of their material forces of production. The totality of these relations of production constitutes the economic structure of society, the real foundation, on which arises a legal and political superstructure and to which correspond definite forms of social consciousness" (11). This statement has itself acted as a "base" for a "superstructure" of ill-conceived versions of economic determinism that dominated orthodox Marxism for much of the late nineteenth and early twentieth centuries.

37. Engels, *Origins of the Family*, 71.

38. Marx and Engels, *The German Ideology*, 47.

39. See footnote 43 in the introduction for a list of works in this tradition.

40. "One the one hand, the production of the means of subsistence . . . on the other, the production of human beings themselves, the propagation of the species." Engels, *Origins of the Family*, 71.

41. Increasingly historians and others are (re)reading human history as energy history. See White, *The Organic Machine*; Nye, *Consuming Power*; McNeill, *Something New under the Sun*; Crosby, *Children of the Sun*; Podobnik, *Global Energy Shifts*; Burke, "The Big Story"; Jones, "A Landscape of Energy Abundance"; and Russell et al., "The Nature of Power."

42. The historical–materialist literature on energy—outside of the geopolitical kinds already cited—is surprisingly sparse. The only comprehensive historical–materialist approach to energy is Debeir, Deleage, and Hemery, *In the Servitude of Power*. Recently, several Marxists have begun to think about the relationship between fossil fuels and capitalism. See Burkett and Foster, "Metabolism, Energy, and Entropy in Marx's critique of Political Economy"; Altvater, "The Social and Natural Environment of Fossil Capitalism"; Zalik, "Liquefied Natural Gas and Fossil Capitalism"; Thomas Keefer, "Fossil Fuels, Capitalism, and Class Struggle"; Wendling, *Karl Marx on Technology and Alienation*; and Abramsy, *Sparking a Worldwide Energy Revolution*.

43. Lefebvre, *The Production of Space*.

44. This relationship between materiality and culture is fraught with controversy because of Marx's famous base-superstructure metaphor in the preface to *A Contribution to the Critique of Political Economy* (quoted previously). In what still is one of the most insightful treatments of this problematic, Sayer asserts that Marx was not arguing for an economic determination of culture but, in dialectical fashion, arguing against the imagined separablility of an independent "cultural" sphere. Superstructures are not different levels removed from base but, rather, "ideological forms of appearance of the totality of social relations which make up

the base itself and their ideologicality consists precisely in their appearance of real independence." This is directly relevant to the discussion of fetishism in the introduction. Fetishistic discourses of oil as a powerful "thing" are not simply "false consciousness" but are produced through actual "real" social relations and lived practices. See Sayer, *The Violence of Abstraction*, 91.

45. Gramsci, *Selections from the Prison Notebooks*.

46. Raymond Williams, *Marxism and Literature*, 110, 112.

47. Postone, *Time, Labor, and Social Domination*, 30.

48. See footnote 42.

49. Dukes, "Burning Buried Sunshine."

50. For instance, the energy density of dried wood is 12 to 15 megajoules/kilogram, compared to 28 to 32 for anthracite coal and 40 to 44 for crude oil. Smil, *Energy in World History*, 12.

51. Altvater, "Social and Natural Environment," 41.

52. Clark and York, "Carbon Metabolism,"391.

53. Chakrabarty, "The Climate of History."

54. Steffen, Crutzen, and McNeill, "The Anthropocene."

55. Marx, *Grundrisse*, 524.

56. E. A. Wrigley, *Continuity, Chance, and Change*, 29. See also, more recently, Wrigley, *Energy and the English Industrial Revolution*.

57. For a discussion of coal's role in the removal of "the land constraint" and Europe's rise to global power, see Pomeranz, *The Great Divergence*, and Marks, *The Origins of the Modern World*.

58. David Nye estimates that pretractor American agriculture devoted one quarter of the yield to farm animals. Nye, *Consuming Power*, 113.

59. Remarkably, Wrigley estimates it took 100,000 acres of felled woodlands to produce 10,000 tons of iron (a 10:1 ratio of land to iron), Wrigley, *Continuity, Chance, and Change*, 80. It is difficult to imagine the emergence of our modern steel economy within these land constraints.

60. The prospect of returning to a world wherein substantial geographies of land are devoted to the growing of fuel is no longer hypothetical but has become realized with the global expansion of the agro-fuels industry. Just in the United States, around 40 percent of the corn crop is reportedly devoted to ethanol production. Pear, "After Three Decades, Tax Credit for Ethanol Expires."

61. Findlay and O'Rourke, "Commodity Market Integration, 1500–2000."

62. Harvey, *The Condition of Postmodernity*, 201–326.

63. Burke, "The Big Story"; and Podobnik, *Global Energy Shifts*.

64. Burke, "The Big Story," 35.

65. See Georgescu-Roegen, *The Entropy Law and the Economic Process*. For a historical review see Martinez-Alier, *Ecological Economics*.

66. Many ecological economists have proven the increase of entropy through the concept of "Energy Return on Energy Investment," which shows even if energy's monetary cost might be decreasing its energy cost—that is, the amount of

energy needed to extract it into useable energy—is increasing. See Cleveland et al., "Energy and the U.S. Economy."

67. Martinez-Alier, *Ecological Economics*, 5. Emphasis in original.

68. There has been a resurgence of a new kind of energy reductionism. Take, for instance, this recent astounding claim from prominent environmental historians: "Our thesis is that all power, social as well as physical, derives from energy." Russell et al., "The Nature of Power," 248. At least this article recognized that "energy" is a social and political field, rather than a purely biophysical one.

69. For instance, Heilbroner, "Do Machines Make History?"

70. Harvey, *The Limits to Capital*, 100.

71. Sayer, *The Violence of Abstraction*, 27.

72. Read, *The Micro-Politics of Capital*, 52.

73. "Let us therefore, in the company with the owner of money and the owner of labour-power, leave this noisy sphere, where everything takes place on the surface and in full view of everyone, and follow them into the hidden abode of production, on whose threshold there hangs a notice 'No admittance except on business.'" Marx, *Capital Volume 1*, 279–80. In this section, I rely on Marx's writings on the role of large-scale industry and machinery in establishing specifically capitalist social relations. These include chapter 15 from *Capital Volume 1*, "Machinery and Large-Scale Industry"; the "Fragment on Machines," 690–712, from *Grundrisse*; and the unpublished chapter "The Results of the Immediate Process of Production," in Marx, *Capital Volume 1*, 948–1084. I believe that all these writings speak implicitly to the conceptual transition mapped out in "Results" from the formal to the real subsumption of labor under capital.

74. Marx *Capital Volume 1*, 554, 591.

75. Marx *Capital Volume 1*, 502.

76. Automation has long been a source of interest for Marxian theory, but very few have examined the ecological basis of this automation in terms of fossil-fuel energy. See Marcuse, *One Dimensional Man*, especially 21–58; Noble, *Forces of Production*; Gorz, *Farewell to the Working Class*; and MacKenzie, "Marx and Machine." Lewis Mumford's history of technology and machines actually does take energy seriously in his contrast between the despotism of coal/steam and the liberating properties of electrification. Mumford, *Technics and Civilization*.

77. See Steinberg, *Nature Incorporated*.

78. Marx understood this advantage of steam power: "The flow of water could not be increased at will, it failed at certain seasons of the year, and above all it was essentially local . . . Not till the invention of Watt's second and so-called double-acting steam-engine was a prime mover found which drew its own motive force from the consumption of coal and water, was entirely under man's control, was mobile and a means of locomotion, was urban and not—like the water-wheel—rural, permitted production be concentrated in towns instead of—like the water-wheels—being scattered over the countryside." Marx, *Capital Volume 1*, 499.

79. Marx, *Capital Volume 1*, 775. The fact that he terms these forces "natural" is significant, because it indicates he did not view the productive forces bound up in large-scale machinery as *purely* social. For Marx, the heat of the blast furnace and the power of steam were partly derived from the wealth of nature.

80. See footnote 50.

81. There is increasing evidence that Marx himself was deeply interested in the science of thermodynamics and other "energeticist" debates in the mid-nineteenth century. See Rabinbach, *The Human Motor*, and Wendling, *Karl Marx on Technology and Alienation*.

82. This percentage has actually increased slightly from 79.89 percent in 2000. See World Bank, "Fossil Fuel Energy Consumption (% of Total)."

83. Mostly through Marx's "fragment on machines" from *The Grundrisse*, interest in the role of "machines" in capitalist rule over the working class is also a core interest of autonomist Marxists such as Panzieri, "The Capitalist Use of Machinery," and Virno, "General Intellect."

84. Marx, *Capital Volume 1*, 545.

85. Ibid., 489.

86. Again, this distinction is mapped out in the unpublished chapter "Results of the Immediate Process of Production." Marx, *Capital Volume 1*, 948–1084. Some have attempted to use this distinction to speak of the formal and the real subsumption of nature, but the approach offered here asserts the subsumption of labor is also embedded in nature–society interactions. See Boyd, Prudham, and Schurman, "Industrial Dynamics."

87. Marx, *Capital Volume 1*, 983.

88. Ibid., 695.

89. Marx, *Grundrisse*, 694.

90. Marx, *Capital Volume 1*, 342.

91. Ibid., 617–18.

92. "Labour is the living, form-giving fire." Marx, *Grundrisse*, 361.

93. "Slavery was the most efficient means by which the ambitious and powerful could become richer and more powerful. It was the answer to the energy shortage. Slavery was widespread within the somatic energy regime, notably in those societies short on draft animals. They had no practical options for concentrating energy other than amassing human bodies." McNeill, *Something New under the Sun*, 12.

94. Pomeranz, *The Great Divergence*, 16. Emphasis in original.

95. On subsumption as a constantly ongoing process, see Buck, "The Subsumption of Space and the Spatiality of Subsumption."

96. Before the rise of industrial capitalism, and the spatial concentration of urban factory production, most "production" took place in the same general place as the home. The spatial separation between home and work is specific to the capitalist mode of production. See Harvey, *The Limits to Capital*, 340, and Smith, *Uneven Development*, 74. For a detailed study of the gender dimensions of the

geographies between home and work see Hanson and Pratt, *Gender, Work, and Space.*

97. Marx, *Capital Volume 1,* 718.

98. The focus on social reproduction has emerged out Marxist–feminist approaches to situate reproductive labor at the core of anticapitalist movements. This includes industrialized countries and efforts to value the unpaid labor of the household, such as the "wages for housework" campaign in Italy, but also, the role of woman in subsistence work all over the world. See Dalla Costa and Dalla Costa Women, *Development, and Labor of Reproduction*; Cindi Katz, "Vagabond Capitalism and the Necessity of Social Reproduction;" and Mitchell,. Marston, and Katz, *Life's Work.*

99. Indeed, although there is plenty of treatment of the workplace, *Capital Volume 1* is as much about the horrific conditions of proletariat life, with whole sections in the "miserable" housing of the British working class—for example, Marx, *Capital Volume 1,* 802–70. Of course, the classic study in this respect is Engels, *The Condition of the Working Class in England.*

100. Marx and Engels, "Manifesto of the Communist Party," 500.

101. For a discussion of the importance of property to suburban politics, see Archer, *Architecture and Suburbia.*

102. The classic work on "car culture" is the aptly titled *The Car Culture,* by Flink. More recently, there is an emerging critical literature on automobility. See Featherstone, Thrift, and Urry, *Automobilities.* For a specific cultural history of automobility in the United States, see Selier, *Republic of Drivers.*

103. See Richard Walker, "A Theory of Suburbanization," and Fishman, *Bourgeois Utopias.*

104. Some recent and invaluable broad histories of postwar American suburbanization include Lizabeth Cohen, *A Consumer's Republic*; Beauregard, *When America Became Suburban*; and Knox, *Metrourbia, USA.*

105. The most prominent theorization of "mass consumption" as a functional requirement of capital accumulation is "the regulation approach." See Aglietta, *A Theory of Capitalist Regulation,* and Boyer and Saillard, *Régulation Theory.* For a trenchant critique, see, among others, Brenner and Glick, "The Regulation Approach." Harvey also explicitly theorizes suburban mass consumption as a specific "solution" to the Keynesian problematic of "effective demand." See *The Urban Experience,* 39. The most extensive articulation of this argument was undertaken by Harvey's student, Richard Walker, *The Suburban Solution.*

106. See footnote 43 in the introduction. While others focus on how capital has subsumed subjectivity, affect, and "immaterial labor," I focus on the material transformations of life's reproduction and associated visions of life itself.

107. See Warner, *Streetcar Suburbs.*

108. The relations between suburbanization, automobility, and oil consumption have been analyzed from many perspectives, such as "peak oil" prophecies of the end of oil-fired suburban life (e.g., Kunstler, *The Long Emergency*), critiques

of U.S. foreign policy (e.g., Rutledge, *Addicted to Oil*), and critiques of corporate capital (e.g., Gonzalez, *Urban Sprawl*).

109. Crosby, *Children of the Sun*, 86.

110. Hartshorn, *Oil Trade*, 93.

111. A dialectical perspective refuses the way in which energy forms are particularized as a set of individual energy choices in most technical (and political) debates. Different energy forms are all mutually entangled with one another. Nuclear and hydropower—and indeed solar and wind—are not as much distinct from fossil fuels but have only been realized in the sociohistorical context of fossil-fuel industrial production. It is quite clear—for the time being—that something as complex as a nuclear power plant cannot be constructed without access to fossil-fuel energy. For example, once you break ground you are already deeply reliant on diesel-fired bulldozers and other earth-moving machinery.

112. McKenzie, *Privatopia*, 19.

113. See footnote 48 in introduction.

114. Edsall and Edsall, *Chain Reaction*, 147.

115. For useful combinations of Foucault and Gramsci, see Donald Moore, *Suffering for Territory*, and Ekers and Loftus, "The Power of Water."

116. Foucault, *The Birth of Biopolitics*.

117. Ibid., 148.

118. Ibid., 147. Ordoliberalism is distinguished by its explicit emphasis on the central importance of the state in laying the foundations for a society of property and enterprise. As Foucault says, "government must accompany the market economy from start to finish" (121).

119. Ibid., 148.

120. Ibid., 241.

121. Foucault aims his critique at the Frankfurt school's critique of consumption culture, but many today blame the decline of labor and the left generally on the focus on individuals as "consumers" not "workers." See, for example, Fantasia and Voss, *Hard Work*, 27.

122. Foucault, *The Birth of Biopolitics*, 226.

123. Bush quoted in, "Fact Sheet: America's Ownership Society: Expanding Opportunities."

124. Here is a recent example: "Employment experts have some advice for the many Americans either looking for work or fearing they soon will be: Consider yourself an entrepreneur—of your working life." Flanigan, "Manage Your Career As a Business."

125. Perry Anderson, "The Antinomies of Antonio Gramsci," 30. Emphasis in original.

126. Most famous is Frank, *What's the Matter with Kansas?*

127. Marx, *Capital Volume 1*, 742.

128. Aglietta, *A Theory of Capitalist Regulation*, 81. Emphasis in original.

129. Foucault, *The Birth of Biopolitics*, 248.

130. This is Raymond Williams's term. See Raymond Williams, *Marxism and Literature*, 128–35.

131. Gramsci, *Selections from the Prison Notebooks*, 169–70. I realize I am employing two slightly different meanings of the notion of "force" here. Yet, whether one considers brute physical force (i.e., state military power) or the productive forces of machines, there is a shared materiality in both instances where force produces kinds of "effects."

2. Refueling Capitalism

1. See Yago, *The Decline of Transit*, and Edwin Black, *Internal Combustion*.

2. Tamminen, *Lives per Gallon*, 111.

3. Kain, *Essays on Urban Spatial Structure*, 3.

4. Marx, *Capital Volume 1*, 275.

5. Kaempffert, "Power for the Abundant Life," SM1.

6. Ibid.

7. For a larger critique of oil scarcity discourses, see Huber, "Enforcing Scarcity." Retort, *Afflicted Powers*; Labban, *Space, Oil, and Capital*; and Timothy Mitchell, *Carbon Democracy* also offer powerful critiques of presumed oil scarcity through their investigations into the management of oil abundance.

8. Marx, *Capital, Volume 1*, 614.

9. Nye, *Electrifying America*.

10. Smil, *Energy in World History*, 194.

11. Gramsci, *Selections from the Prison Notebooks*, 286, 302.

12. Taylor quoted by Hoare and Smith in Gramsci, *Selections from the Prison Notebooks*, n. 302. The statement comes from Frederick Taylor, *The Principles of Scientific Management*, 40.

13. Frederick Taylor, *The Principles of Scientific Management*, 38.

14. Ibid., 140.

15. Gramsci, *Selections from the Prison Notebooks*, 302.

16. He claimed this process was in "its initial phase and therefore . . . still idyllic." Ibid., 286.

17. Ibid., 302, 317.

18. Although I'm using the term quite differently, the phrase "bare life" is borrowed from Agamben, *Homo Sacer*.

19. Quoted in Bernstein, *A Caring Society*, 22.

20. Roosevelt, "Inauguration Speech."

21. Bernstein, *A Caring Society*, 19.

22. Terkel, *Hard Times*, 55.

23. See Dickstein, *Dancing in the Dark*, 215–310.

24. Statistics taken from Carter et al., *Historical Statistics of the United States*.

25. Alter, *The Defining Moment*, 2. It is worth pointing out that *today* the mass amount of unemployed bodies is at an average of 12 million or 7.7 percent as of November 2012 (and this is the undercounted number that does not include so-called discouraged and part-time workers. See http://www.bls.gov). Thus the amount of suffering is comparable on a human scale but not a "per-capita" or average scale. For one unemployed individual, does it matter what percentage one is of a population?

26. Wagner quoted in Bernstein, *Turbulent Years*, 15.

27. Dickstein, *Dancing in the Dark*, 16.

28. *New York Times*, "Life in It Yet."

29. *New York Times*, "Capitalism Doomed, Say Fascist and Red."

30. Quoted in Bernstein, *Turbulent Years*, 2.

31. From archival searches of several American newspapers, it appears as if use of the phrase "American way of life" really took off in the 1936 presidential campaign. Republican nominee Alf Landon used the phrase repeatedly to argue that in fact Roosevelt, and his New Deal policies, represented a threat to the democratic values of individualism and free enterprise. His description mirrors what I call "entrepreneurial life": "The American way of life has left men and women free from these restrictions. Our people have been free to develop their own lives as they saw fit and to cooperate with one another on a voluntary basis. They have been encouraged to start any honest enterprise that would enable them to support their families, give the public the goods and services it wanted, and make jobs for themselves and others. Under this encouragement, business has expanded here faster than elsewhere, the public has had more goods; workers have had higher wages and shorter hours; children have had better school facilities; all have had higher standards of living." Landon, *America at the Crossroads*, 32. Illustrating the conjunctural emptiness of such slogans, FDR won in a landslide. A viewing of Google's Ngram Viewer (which allows users to search Google's extensive book/magazine collection and view a historical graph of usages of a certain phrase) also shows a steady rise of use of the phrase "American way of life" in the 1930s, followed by an explosion in World War II and into the postwar era.

32. *New York Times*, "Text of Roosevelt Address," 1.

33. This point is hammered home in Lizabeth Cohen, *Making a New Deal*.

34. Sward, *The Legend of Henry Ford*, 32. This quote was found in Braverman, *Labor and Monopoly Capital*, 102.

35. Quoted in Sward, *The Legend of Henry Ford*, 56. This quote was found in Braverman, *Labor and Monopoly Capital*, 103.

36. Lizabeth Cohen, *Making a New Deal*, 159–212.

37. Marx, *Capital Volume 1*, 381.

38. Bernstein, *Turbulent Years*, 217.

39. Alter, *The Defining Moment*, 2.

40. Teamsters Union, "1934 Minnesota Strike."

41. Lucia, "Bringing Misery out of Hiding."

42. See Bernstein, *Turbulent Years*, 318–51.

43. *New York Times*, "Roosevelt signs the Wagner Bill as 'Just to Labor'."

44. Krock, "5 Cases Decided."

45. *New York Times*, "Wagner Sees Law Ending Labor War."

46. Piven and Cloward, *Poor People's Movements*, 154.

47. Ibid., 147.

48. Matles and Higgins, *Them and Us*, 83. Quoted in Piven and Cloward, *Poor People's Movements*, 156.

49. See footnote 55 in introduction.

50. Aglietta, *A Theory of Capitalist Regulation*, 71.

51. See Alan Brinkley, *The End of Reform*, 65–85, and Jacobs, *Pocketbook Politics*.

52. *New York Times*, "Text of President Roosevelt's Recovery Program Message to Congress."

53. Wagner, "Wagner Defends Bill as Fulfillment of 7a."

54. Bernstein, *Turbulent Years*, 189–90.

55. Ibid., 326.

56. Davis, *Prisoners of the American Dream*, 92. Davis's mention of the "other America" is a reference to Michael Harrington's 1962 book that brought to light horrific poverty amid prosperity during the postwar "boom" of American capitalism. Harrington, *The Other America*.

57. Archer, *Architecture and Suburbia*, 261.

58. On the bourgeois origins of suburbia, see Fishman, *Bourgeois Utopias*. On mass suburbs based on public transit, see Warner, *Streetcar Suburbs*.

59. Quoted in Jackson, *Crabgrass Frontier*, 231.

60. Hoover, "The Home as an Investment," 17.

61. Hoover quoted in Archer, *Architecture and Suburbia*, 264.

62. Coolidge, "A Nation of Homeowners," 17.

63. *The Delineator*, "Better Homes in America," 2.

64. Alyssa Katz, *Our Lot*, 5.

65. *New York Times*, "The President's Message."

66. See, for example, Beauregard, *Voices of Decline*.

67. Quoted in Flink, *Car Culture*, 181.

68. Quoted in Glaab and Brown, *A History of Urban America*, 303.

69. Alyssa Katz, *Our Lot*, 7.

70. For a case study see Cruse, *White Flight*.

71. A striking example is Ross, *The Celebration Chronicles*. See also Davis, *City of Quartz*.

72. Quoted in Lizabeth Cohen, *A Consumer's Republic*, 219.

73. See note 97 in chapter 1.

74. Jackson, *Crabgrass Frontier*, 167.

75. Flink, *Car Culture*, 187.

76. Watkins, *The Hungry Years*, 263. Of course, the WPA was also critical in building up infrastructure in rural spaces.

77. There is a more complex prehistory of the federal interstate system involving struggles over forms of federal and state taxes to support road systems. See Wells, "Fueling the Boom."

78. Watkins, *The Hungry Years*, 213.

79. The entire twenty-three-minute film *To New Horizons* is available at http://www.archive.org.

80. In retrospect, the prospect of safety at 100 mph is laughable.

81. "Space for play" is somewhat inaudible in every version of the film I have seen (including the one on file from General Motors). I am inferring that *play* is the actual word.

82. Continental Oil Company, *Annual Report of the Continental Oil Company (Conoco)* (1950).

83. Roosevelt, "Letter from FDR to John O'Donnell Congrats for Commemoration of Diamond Oil in PA."

84. See note 105 in chapter 1.

85. For an analysis on the role of oil in the imaginary of "the economy," see Timothy Mitchell, *Carbon Democracy*, 109–43.

86. For effective critiques of the economic role of mass consumption in postwar accumulation, see Brenner and Glick, "The Regulation Approach," and Davis, "'Fordism in Crisis." Davis argues instead for the central role of the infusion of state military spending that produced whole regions of economic development centered upon weapons production, aerospace, and other research activities (see 249–56).

87. See Deka "Social and Environmental Justice Issues in Urban Transportation."

88. See Crosby, *Children of the Sun*, 62.

89. Putman and Shipman, *Hot Oil*, 273–74. This sequence is remarkably similar to George Henderson's description of the 1909 film *A Corner of Wheat* in which the main character (a grain speculator) is drowned in wheat. Both can serve as literary examples of the specter of resource gluts that hung over agrarian American culture in the nineteenth and early twentieth centuries. Henderson, *California and the Fictions of Capital*, ix.

90. See Peck and Tickell, "Searching for a New Institutional Fix."

91. Mills, *Martial Law in East Texas*, 3.

92. See footnote 7.

93. See Mommer, *Global Oil and the Nation State*. For a sophisticated Marxist theorization of nature and the "landlord state," see Coronil, *The Magical State*.

94. The confrontation between rural landowners and scheming "land men" (sometimes working on their own, sometime oil prospectors themselves) is part of the historical lore of the American petroleum industry. This confrontation is acquiring renewed salience with the shale gas boom in the United States as the oil

and gas industry scrambles to gobble up "leases" in places like Texas, Oklahoma, and Pennsylvania (the very same iconic states of oil history). For a personal account of this confrontation from a landowner's perspective see McGraw, *The End of Country.*

95. Thornton, *The Law Relating to Oil and Gas,* 43. For a nice discussion of "the rule of capture," see Zimmermann, *Conservation in the Production of Petroleum,* 91–100.

96. This process is described in the 2007 film *There Will Be Blood,* by protagonist Daniel Plainview, as "drinking your milkshake." Mainly for the incredible delivery by actor Daniel Day Lewis, the phrase "I drink your milkshake" has become infused into pop culture vernacular, inspiring Saturday Night Live skits, T-shirts, and websites with Plainview's words playing on a loop. And yet, alas, this pop culture icon has spread without anyone really understanding the incredible importance of the metaphor to understanding the history and legal political economy of the oil industry in the United States.

97. Boatright and Owens, *Tales from the Derrick Floor,* 157. I found this quote on the wall of the Texas Energy Museum in Beaumont, Texas, whose curator had extracted it from the book.

98. For multiple uses of this term, see Lovejoy and Homan, *Economic Aspects of Oil Conservation Regulation,* 130, 132, 136, 163.

99. Penrose, *The Large International Firm in Developing Countries,* 46.

100. Nye, *American Technological Sublime.*

101. See Yergin, *The Prize,* 220–23.

102. Ernest O. Thompson, "Rights of States to Regulate Oil and Gas Production."

103. The term *independent* originally referred to the days of Rockefeller's Standard Oil monopoly and indicated independence from that single company. After the breakup of Standard in 1911, it simply meant independence from the major integrated companies. For a good discussion, see Olien and Hinton, *Wildcatters,* 1–11.

104. Zimmermann, *Conservation in the Production of Petroleum,* 345.

105. See De Janvry, *The Agrarian Question.*

106. Olien and Hinton, *Wildcatters,* 43.

107. For a popular history of the East Texas oil field, see Clark and Halbouty, *The Last Boom.*

108. Mills, *Martial Law in East Texas,* 7.

109. Olien and Hinton, *Wildcatters,* 58.

110. Nordhauser, *The Quest for Stability,* 29.

111. *Flush production* refers to the first tapping of an oil well, at which time oil flows upward at a rapid pace.

112. Mills, *Martial Law in East Texas,* 24.

113. Ibid., 24–25. This is quite similar to the private (and military) security forces now deployed to protect oil infrastructure in multiple regions from Nigeria to Iraq. See James Ferguson, "Seeing Like and Oil Company."

114. Texas State Archives, "Oil—Martial Law in East Texas, August 15–21, 1931."

115. Nash, *United States Oil Policy,* 117.

116. Mills, *Martial Law in East Texas,* 27.

117. Nordhauser, *The Quest for Stability,* 43.

118. Mills, *Martial Law in East Texas,* 37.

119. Ibid., 38.

120. Sterling quoted in ibid., 41.

121. Both quotes from Alan Brinkley, *The End of Reform,* 34.

122. Dallas Morning News, "Editorial: State's Rights."

123. Ickes, "Ickes Hails National Planning."

124. Ickes, "Memo to FDR, 1 May 1933."

125. The classic study is Hawley, *The New Deal and the Problem of Monopoly.*

126. Miriam A. Ferguson, "Telegram to FDR, 23 May 1933."

127. Bridewell, "Letter to FDR, 19 May 1933."

128. These conflicting positions are described with great detail by Nordhauser, *The Quest for Stability,* 116–28. Nash, *United States Oil Policy,* 133–56, also gives an adequate account.

129. Ickes, *The Secret Diary of Harold L. Ickes,* 86.

130. Ibid., 50.

131. Nordhauser, *The Quest for Stability,* 126–28.

132. *New York Times,* "Broad Powers Proposed for Ickes."

133. *Tyler Courier Times Telegraph,* "Editorial," 9.

134. Ernest O. Thompson, "Statement of Thompson on the Thomas Federal Oil Control Bill."

135. Childs, "The Transformation of the Railroad Commission of Texas, 1917–1940," 324–25.

136. *New York Times,* "Ickes Threatens Land Seizures."

137. See Neil Smith, "Remaking Scale."

138. Roosevelt, "Statement on Interstate Oil Compact, 17 May 1935."

139. See Zimmerman, *Conservation in the Production of Petroleum,* 206–8, and Nash, *United States Oil Policy,* 148–51.

140. It should be noted that California—a major oil producer—was not an original member of the IOCC. The politics of oil production in California are marked by an entirely different set of problems and circumstances. Needless to say, however, California was also forced to develop a set of mechanisms through which production could be aligned with the projected "reasonable" demand they serviced in the western United States. For a compelling history, see Sabin, *Crude Politics.*

141. On Texas as the "balance wheel" or "swing producer," see Prindle, *Petroleum Politics and the Texas Railroad Commission.*

142. Libecap, "The Political Economy of Crude Oil Cartelization," 837.

143. See Yergin, *The Prize,* 259.

144. Lovejoy and Homan, *Economic Aspects of Petroleum Conservation*, 282.

145. Although this volatility is disruptive to accumulation as a whole, it is a boon for oil traders and institutional investors wrapped up within the financialization of the oil market. See Labban, "Oil in Parallax."

146. *New York Times*, "Broad Powers Proposed for Ickes."

147. Esso Oilways, "Cartoon on Back of Front Cover," November 1950.

148. Foucault, *Security, Territory, Population*.

149. Timothy Mitchell, *Carbon Democracy*, 109–43.

150. For more information on the methodology of calculating the demand estimates, see National Resources Committee, *Energy Resources and National Policy*, 401–4; U.S. House of Representatives, "Hearings before a Subcommittee of the Committee on Interstate and Foreign Commerce on H.R. 290 and H.R. 7372, 76th Cong., 3rd Sess. (1939)," 167–94; Temporary National Economic Committee, "Hearings before the Temporary National Economic Committee," *Investigation of Concentration of Economic Power*, part 17, Petroleum Industry, 76th Cong., 2nd Sess. (1939), Testimony of Alfred G. White, 9583–603; and U.S. Senate, "Hearings before Special Committee to Study Problems of American Small Business, Part 27, Oil Supply and Distribution Problems, U.S. Senate, 80th Cong., 2nd Sess.," testimony of Alfred G. White, 3138–76.

151. U.S. Senate, "Hearings before Special Committee to Study Problems of American Small Business, Part 27, Oil Supply and Distribution Problems, U.S. Senate, 80th Cong., 2nd Sess.," 3146.

152. Bureau of Mines, *Monthly Petroleum Forecast June 1948*.

153. Zimmerman, *Conservation in the Production of Petroleum*, 46, mentions this in passing at the height of postwar oil profligacy.

154. Quoted in Terkel, *Hard Times*, 339.

155. See the Gulf oil ad in the introduction.

3. Fractionated Lives

1. However, some regions with high levels of crude production and little refining capacity burn crude oil for electricity use. Smil reports that burning oil in its crude state accounts for about 0.5 percent of crude output. See Vaclav Smil, *Oil*, 146.

2. E. J. Williams, "The Impact of Technology," 41–54.

3. Williamson et al., *The American Petroleum Industry, Volume 2*, 844.

4. E. J. Williams, "The Impact of Technology," 52–53.

5. *Business Week*, "Computer Runs Refinery Unit for Texaco," 51.

6. Mallet, *The New Working Class*. Also see Timothy Mitchell, *Carbon Democracy*, 152–53.

7. *Oil and Gas Journal*, "Refinery Strikes Suggest Plants Can Be Run with Still Fewer Men," 106–7.

8. Blundfll, "Oil Union Finds Strikes Are Ineffective."

9. Pomfret, "Shell Strike End Set after a Year."

10. Pomfret, "Shell Strike End Set after a Year," 10.

11. See footnote 55 in introduction.

12. See Harrison and Bluestone, *The Great U-Turn*.

13. Blundfll, "Oil Union Finds Strikes Are Ineffective."

14. Brozen, *Automation*, 38.

15. Hirsch and Macpherson, "Union Membership and Coverage Database."

16. Feagin, *Free Enterprise City*.

17. Perry and Watkins, *The Rise of the Sunbelt Cities*; Schulman, *From Cotton Belt to Sunbelt*. For a city-specific study, see Feagin, *Free Enterprise City*.

18. Markusen et al., *The Rise of the Gunbelt*.

19. Lassiter, *The Silent Majority*, 198.

20. There has been much discussion lately about the rise of neoliberalism as what David Harvey calls "the restoration of class power." See Harvey, *A Brief History of Neoliberalism*. For other work on declining working class power in the United States, see, for example, Bluestone and Harrison, *The Great U-Turn*; Davis, *Prisoners of the American Dream*; and Cowie, *Stayin' Alive*.

21. Smith and Taft, *Foundations of Democracy*, 14.

22. Lizabeth Cohen, *A Consumer's Republic*.

23. Foucault, *The Birth of Biopolitics*, 226.

24. See Downey, *Oil 101*, 1.

25. Yergin, *The Prize*, 4.

26. The heaviness and viscosity of crude oil is generally paralleled by the number of carbon atoms. See Leffler, *Petroleum Refining in Nontechnical Language*, 25–40.

27. Downey, *Oil 101*, 1.

28. Williamson and Daum, *The American Petroleum Industry Volume 1*, 69–72.

29. Ibid., 212.

30. Ibid.

31. Silliman, *Report on the Rock Oil, or Petroleum*, 6, 20. Emphasis in original.

32. Williamson and Daum, *The American Petroleum Industry Vol. 1*, 232–51.

33. Williamson et al., *The American Petroleum Industry Vol. 2*, 435.

34. Ibid., 436.

35. Downey, *Oil 101*, 143.

36. Leffler, *Petroleum Refining in Nontechnical Language*, 76.

37. Williamson et al., *The American Petroleum Industry Vol. 2*, 423; Leffler, *Petroleum Refining in Nontechnical Language*, 53–56.

38. Smil, *Oil*, 156.

39. Allen, "Cradle of a Revolution?"

40. O'Rourke and Connolly, "Just Oil." On refineries, see 603–7.

41. An on-the-ground and visceral account of the precarious explosiveness of refineries is provided by Margonelli, *Oil on the Brain*, 48–65.

42. O'Rourke and Connolly, "Just Oil?," 605.

43. Data from 2010. "TRI Explorer." Accessed 30 July 2012, http://www.epa.gov/triexplorer/industry.htm.

44. For the role of the chemical industry in covering up the cancer risks for workers and communities in the production of polyvinyl chloride, see Markowitz and Rosner, *Deceit and Denial*. For influential accounts of the environmental justice movement in relation to the chemical industry, see Bullard, *Dumping in Dixie*, and Allen, *Uneasy Alchemy*.

45. Smil, *Oil*, 156.

46. Peterson and Mahnovski, *New Forces at Work in Refining*, 48.

47. United Nations, "UNData: Electricity Consumption by Petroleum Refineries." Accessed 30 July 2012, http://data.un.org/Data.aspx?d=EDATA&f=cmID%3AEL%3BtrID%3A0925.

48. Wu et al. *Consumptive Water Use in the Production of Ethanol and Petroleum Gasoline*.

49. Mouawad, "West Adds Strain to Iran's Lifeline."

50. Williamson et al, *The American Petroleum Industry Vol. 2*, 784.

51. Painter, "Oil and the Marshall Plan," 372–75.

52. Crosby, *Children of the Sun*, 62.

53. For one reference, see Cooke, *The American Home Front*, 133.

54. Standard Oil Company of California, *Annual Report, Standard Oil Company of California*, 1943.

55. Tanham, "Memo from James H. Tanham to Paul Ryan, April 30th, 1943."

56. Continental Oil Company, *Annual Report of the Continental Oil Company (Conoco)* (1945), 8.

57. Continental Oil Company, *Annual Report of the Continental Oil Company (Conoco) and its Subsidiary Companies* (1946), 6, 5.

58. Williamson et al., *The American Petroleum Industry Vol. 2*, 790.

59. Ibid., 796.

60. Spitz, *Petrochemicals*, 116–56.

61. Standard Oil of New Jersey, "Standard Oil–New Jersey 75th Anniversary Entertainment Special."

62. "Destination Earth," 1956, American Petroleum Institute, http://www.archive.org/details/Destinat1956.

63. For a nice introduction see Crosby, *Children of the Sun*, 85–100.

64. Marx, *Grundrisse*, 524.

65. Statistics taken from Carter et al., *Historical Statistics of the United States*, Series Aa7 (population) and Df396 (Registrations for Passenger Vehicles and Motorcycles).

66. Lefebvre, *The Production of Space*.

67. See Featherstone, Thrift, and Urry, *Automobilities*.

68. Williams, *Television*, 19.

69. Selier, *Republic of Drivers*, 69–104.

70. Carter et al., *Historical Statistics of the United States*, Series Df334. It's hard to believe that as late as 1947, 65 percent of all passenger vehicles were bought with cash.

71. Jackson, *Crabgrass Frontier*, 181. See also Knox, *Metroburbia, USA*.

72. U.S. Census, *State and Metropolitan Data Book: 2006* (Washington, D.C.: Government Printing Office, 2006), A-340.

73. Statistics taken from Carter et al., *Historical Statistics of the United States*, Series Aa7 (population) and Df389 (Distance Traveled for Passenger Cars and Motorcycles).

74. U.S. Census, "Means of Transportation to Work for the U.S.: 1960–1990," http://www.census.gov/hhes/commuting/data/commuting.html.

75. United States Department of Transportation. *Home to Work Trips and Travel, 1977 Personal Transportation Survey*, 1.

76. As seen in *Saturday Evening Post*, September 20, 1958, 52.

77. See *House Beautiful*, Vol. 98, no. 11 (November 1956).

78. Heard, "The Freedom to be Enterprising."

79. Ibid., 249–50.

80. This is something Foucault discusses a lot in his overview of neoliberal theories of "human capital" personified by the Chicago School economists like Gary Becker. See, Foucault, *The Birth of Biopolitics*, 215–38.

81. Calculated from Carter et al. *Historical Statistics of the United States*, Series Cd153–263.

82. Carter et al., *Historical Statistics of the United States*, Series Df394.

83. Flink, *Car Culture*, 195.

84. Continental Oil Company, *Annual Report of the Continental Oil Company (Conoco)* (1955), 11.

85. Found online at http://users.adam.com.au/gasmaps/esschar.jpg, accessed July 19, 2012. The version online is too low-resolution to print. The only print version (suitable for printing) I could find with the same visuals contained an alternative tagline: "Petroleum Promotes Progress."

86. Downey, *Oil 101*, 230.

87. Leffler, *Petroleum Refining in Nontechnical Language*, 167.

88. Energy Information Administration, "Table 5.11, Petroleum Product Supplied by Type, 1949–2008," http://www.eia.doe.gov/emeu/aer/txt/ptb0511.html, accessed August 14, 2010.

89. I received forty-two ads from this "Esso Works Wonders from Oil" series from The Exxon-Mobil Historical Collection, The Briscoe Center for American History, University of Texas–Austin, Austin, Tex.

90. Kaszynski, *The American Highway*.

91. "Technically, oil is even more indispensable for lubrication between all kinds of moving surfaces." Hartshorn, *Oil Trade*, 94.

92. Marx, *Capital Volume 1*, 927.

93. Ibid., 928.

94. The use of "peasantry" as a figure of premodern backwardness is, of course, hugely problematic. I use it only in line with Marx's admittedly ethnocentric conceptions of "precapitalist" economic formations. See Marx, *Pre-capitalist Economic Formations*. But Marx's construction of "the peasant" actually belies the role of peasant movements in making progressive social change. There is some evidence that late in life Marx began to reconsider his negative views of peasants and communal forms of rural production in Russia. Kevin Anderson, *Marx at the Margins*.

95. Smith, "The People's Capitalism," 317.

96. Barry, "America," 242.

97. House Beautiful, "No Man Need be Common, No Life Need Be Ordinary," 223.

98. Ibid.

99. Wheatland, *The Frankfurt School in Exile*.

100. Carter et al., *Historical Statistics of the United States*, Series, Dc1105.

101. U.S. Census, "Homeownership Rates," http://www.census.gov/hhes/www/housing/census/historic/owner.html.

102. Jackson, *Crabgrass Frontier*, 326.

103. Kunstler, *The Long Emergency*, 233. Kunstler seems completely unwilling to confront the logic of this putative "misallocation" that actually served to save capitalism (which, granted, is an insane system) from depression and restored profitability and prosperity to millions of capitalists and workers in the United States.

104. This literature is too vast to cite, but some of the most influential works include Benson, "The Political Economy of Women's Liberation"; Dalla Costa and James, *The Power of Woman*; Holmstrom, "Women's Work"; Gimenez, "The Dialectics of Waged and Unwaged Work"; Cindi Katz, "Vagabond Capitalism"; and Mitchell, Marston, and Katz, *Life's Work*.

105. There is a vast literature on housework and technology. For example, Cowan, *More Work for Mother*, Hayden, *Redesigning the American Dream*, Wajcman, *Feminism Confronts Technology*

106. As seen in *The Saturday Evening Post*, October 4, 1958, 107. Emphasis in original.

107. As stated in the introduction, petroleum is only a minor contributor to the electric power sector. It represented around 10 percent of electric power generation in the 1950s before peaking around 17 percent in the 1970s. The trauma of the "oil shocks" compelled nearly all electric utilities to switch to coal or gas for their source of power. As of 2010, just under 1 percent of the energy for electric power generation came from petroleum. Energy Information Administration, "Table 2.1f Electric Power Sector Energy Consumption, 1949–2010."

108. As seen in Esso ad collection, ExxonMobil Historical Collection, the Dolph Briscoe Center for American History, University of Texas at Austin.

109. Ibid.

110. A seen in *Life*, 43, 12 (September 16, 1957): 6.

111. Ibid., 6.

112. Ibid., 114.

113. Leffler, *Petroleum Refining in Nontechnical Language*, 187–92.

114. Meikle, *American Plastic*, 177.

115. Ibid., 178–79.

116. Ibid., 179.

117. *Good Housekeeping*, "A New Way of Life in One Word." Emphasis in original.

118. Ibid., 88. On concern with plastics see, Schapiro, "Toxic Inaction."

119. Gladstone, "Home Improvement."

120. Markowitz and Rosner, *Deceit and Denial*, 185. For an excellent look behind the world of vinyl siding see the film *Blue Vinyl*.

121. U.S. Census Bureau, "Characteristics of New Housing," http://www.census.gov/const/www/charindex.html.

122. As seen in, *Life* 43, no. 4 (July 22, 1957): 54.

123. Several chapters in the volume *Life's Work*, edited by Mitchell et al., tackle this issue. George Henderson sums up the body as a particular problem of capitalist wage labor and social reproduction: "Bodies persist. That they are *waged* bodies is a capitalist solution. That they are waged *bodies* is a capitalist problem . . . Of course, within this constraint there is also opportunity for the inability to fully substitute for the bodily reproduction of the worker and labour power has come to occasion a whole realm of capitalist production for consumption and reproduction, the realm of capitalist-produced commodities that are sold and bought *for* reproduction (food, housing, etc.)." Henderson, *California and the Fictions of Capital*, 41. Emphasis in original.

124. Worster, *Dust Bowl*.

125. Carter et al., *Historical Statistics of the United States*, Series Da2.

126. See Marx, *Capital Volume 1*, 873–940.

127. Aglietta, *A Theory of Capitalist Regulation*, 80.

128. Carter et al., *Historical Statistics of the United States*, Series Cd153-263. One might assume that cheap food "freed up" consumers to pursue uncommodified realms, but the opposite is true—cheap food allowed for the deepening of commodity relations into nonfood items like housing, transportation and entertainment.

129. Goodman and Redclift, *Refashioning Food*, 87–132.

130. Bartlett, "Forgotten Fundamentals of the Energy Crisis," 880.

131. Cochrane and Ryan, *American Farm Policy*, 5.

132. Olmstead and Rhode. "Reshaping the Landscape,"666.

133. Downey, *Oil 101*, 205–6.

134. Smil, *Enriching the Earth*.

135. Smith, "Nitrogenase Reveals Its Inner Secrets."

136. Malakoff and Lafitte, "Death by Suffocation in the Gulf of Mexico."

137. See MacIntyre, "Why Pesticides Received Extensive Treatment in America," 534–77.

138. U.S. Department of Agriculture. *Per Capita Food Consumption Data System.*

139. Goodman and Redclift, *Refashioning Food,* 109.

140. Michael Pollan and Eric Schlosser have both in different ways called attention to the conditions of meat production in the United States. See Pollan, *The Omnivore's Dilemma,* and Schlosser, *Fast Food Nation.*

141. The tendency of food movements and debates to ignore production is tackled by Guthman, *Weighing In,* 140–62.

142. For a critique of the biopolitics of "fat" and food choice, see Guthman, *Weighing In,* and Guthman; and DuPuis, "Embodying Neoliberalism."

143. As seen in *Life* 43, no. 7 (August 12, 1957): 73.

144. Slotboom, "Plentitude from Petroleum," 90.

145. As seen in *Life* 42, no. 18 (May 6, 1957): 19.

146. As seen in *Life* 42, no. 20 (May 20, 1957): 6.

147. Ibid., 43, no. 12 (September 16, 1957): 7.

148. *Trade Secrets: A Moyers Report* (Public Broadcasting Service, 2001), accessed June 27, 2012, http://www.pbs.org/tradesecrets/transcript.html.

149. Much of the film is based on the work of Markowitz and Rosner, *Deceit and Denial.*

150. *Trade Secrets: A Moyers Report.*

151. Weber, *The Protestant Work Ethic*; Decker, *Made in America.*

152. Davis, *Prisoners of the American Dream,* viii.

153. Of course, much of it was negotiated through the not-yet-commodified housework of woman. Yet this arrangement emerged out of the masculinist nature of the American labor movement, which struggled to produce the *male* wage as the *family wage* in the 1930s and into the postwar era. The collapse of this arrangement in the 1970s and the entrance of masses of women into the labor force predictably led to the creeping commodification of various aspects of social reproduction, including housework and child care. The commodifiablity of such reproductive practices was always present from the outset.

154. Davis, *Prisoners of the America Dream,* 129–30.

155. McKenzie, *Privatopia,* 19.

156. Davis, *Prisoners of the America Dream,* 171.

157. Foucault, *The Birth of Biopolitics,* 148.

4. Shocked!

1. Levittown, Pennsylvania, was a follow-up from the first (and perhaps more iconic) Levittown planned community on Long Island. The second version actually responded to many critiques of the drabness of the first community: "Determined to avoid the monotony and regimentation of their original Long Island suburb, the Levitts paid particular attention to the communal design of

their Pennsylvania suburb through such features as small, compact neighborhoods with curvilinear streets, irregular-shaped sections, and extensive trees and landscaping that created a 'park-like setting.'" See David Anderson, "Levittown Is Burning," 58. Over a decade before the gas riots discussed later on in this chapter, Herbert Gans's sociological study of the third Levittown, New Jersey, made a huge impact on popular understandings and critiques of suburbia. Gans, *The Levittowners*.

2. See Lizabeth Cohen, *A Consumer's Republic*, 217–18.

3. Fiege, *Republic of Nature*, 388–89.

4. United Press International, "Rigs Tie up Bucks County Highways."

5. David Anderson, "Levittown Is Burning," 47.

6. Tulley, "Police Placed at Corner to Prevent Gasoline Riot."

7. Wandling and Foley, "117 Arrested, 100 Hurt in Bucks Riots."

8. See Kimmel, "No Gas, My Ass!"

9. Gerard Mullin, "Drama at the Crossroads."

10. Quoted in Kimmel, "No Gas, My Ass!," 347.

11. Horowitz, *Jimmy Carter and the Energy Crisis of the 1970s*, 111.

12. Kimmel, "No Gas, My Ass!," 341.

13. A similar argument can be made about the broad attention to the school shootings in so-called normal white Littleton, Colorado. See Kobayashi and Peake, "Racism out of Place."

14. George Will, "Levittown Revisited."

15. Mullin, "Drama at the Crossroads"

16. Schulman, *The Seventies*, xv.

17. Most accounts of the 1970s oil crisis deal with the big forces at work between the oil companies, OPEC, and U.S. foreign policy and do not engage with the complex cultural politics of everyday life. An exception is Nye, *Consuming Power*, 217–48. Even Timothy Mitchell's fascinating account includes sweeping caricatures of U.S. consumers. He claims the public did not make the link between the oil crisis, the U.S. relationship with Israel, and the Palestine Question: "The general public . . . was too busy queuing for petrol, thinking only of the laws of the market." Timothy Mitchell, *Carbon Democracy*, 185. I actually found several letters to Nixon's energy czar that engaged the Israel–Palestine question specifically. For example, one citizen proclaimed, "In fact this crushing and catastrophic situation need not happen at all if this administration would recognize the legitimate rights of the Palestinian people to a just settlement in the Middle East." The letter devolved into quite an anti-Semitic rant, but the engagement with the Palestine question is clear. Box 8, White House Central Files, Staff Member Office Files, Energy Policy Office, John A. Love, Richard Nixon Presidential Library, Yorba Linda, Calif.

18. In an exhaustive study of various polling data, Richman concludes that "the predominant view is that oil shortages have been contrived, particularly by the oil companies, to raise prices and profits" (576). For example, at the height

of the gasoline line crisis in February 1974, one Roper poll revealed that only 18 percent of those polled felt the crisis represented a "real shortage," whereas 73 percent believe it was "not a real shortage," and 9 percent admitted not knowing. Fast forward five years later at the height of the second oil shock in July 1979, and the numbers for each only varied slightly to 24 percent, 58 percent and 8 percent respectively. See Richman, "Public Attitudes toward the Energy Crisis."

19. Reagan, "Op-Ed—Exploring New Energy Sources." Incidentally, Reagan's concept of scarcity sits uncomfortably close to a whole literature in radical geography and beyond that examines the social production of scarcity. See Huber, "Enforcing Scarcity."

20. *Fortune*, "The Market System and the Energy Crisis."

21. Timothy Mitchell's account emphasizes how the oil crisis was often marshaled as a "classic" case of market economics and supply and demand. The usefulness of an example of a sudden decrease of supply notwithstanding, Mitchell ignores the fact that most discussion of the oil crisis in the 1970s was focused on forces *impeding* the free play of the market through supply and demand. See Timothy Mitchell, *Carbon Democracy*, 173–99.

22. Foucault, *The Birth of Biopolitics*, 147–48.

23. Jevons, *The Coal Question*.

24. Olien and Olien, "Running Out of Oil."

25. The classic account is Yergin, *The Prize*, 543–680. Also see Merrill, *The Oil Crisis of 1973–1974*; Horowitz, *Jimmy Carter and the Energy Crisis of the 1970s*; and Fiege, *Republic of Nature*, 358–402.

26.Energy Information Administration, "U.S. Field Production of Crude Oil.

27. Hemmingsen, "At the Base of Hubbert's Peak."

28. See footnote 22 in the introduction.

29. Vietor, *Energy Policy in America since 1945*, 199. The Maximum Efficient Rate of Recovery is a physical conservation tool that basically sets the maximum production rate from a particular well without reducing long-term prospects for recovery—for example, damage to the gas or water pressure needed to push to subterranean oil up to the surface. See Zimmerman, *Conservation in the Production of Petroleum*.

30. *New York Times*, "Texas Oil Rate at 100% for First Time since '48."

31. Prindle, *Petroleum Politics and the Texas Railroad Commission*, 70–94.

32. Keohane, *After Hegemony*, 170–71.

33. Vietor, *Energy Policy in America since 1945*, 199.

34. American Petroleum Institute, *Petroleum Facts and Figures*, 101.

35. Meadows et al., *The Limits to Growth*.

36. *New York Times*, "Editorial: An Age of Scarcity."

37. A wonderful review of a variety of critiques of consumer culture—from Lewis Mumford to Betty Friedan—is Horowitz, *Anxieties of Affluence*.

38. *Sarasota Herald-Tribune*, "Depth of America's Energy Crisis Called Endemic and also Incurable," April 23, 1972, E1.

39. *Simpson's Leader Times*, "Shortages Everywhere."

40. *Lockhart Post-Register*, "Letter: Figures Fuel Shortage Will Be Overcome by Using Heads."

41. *The News*, "Automobilicus Americanus—1893–1973."

42. *The Register*, "Letter: Energy Hubbub? Go Back to Basics."

43. See Harvey, *The Limits to Capital*, especially, 204–445; Brenner, "Between Fixity and Motion."

44. Walker, *Inside/Outside*. See also Agnew, "The Territorial Trap," and Ó Tuathail, *Critical Geopolitics*.

45. In August of 1974, congressional hearings were held in the House on "Oil Imports and Energy Security." U.S. House of Representatives, "Oil Imports and Energy Security," Hearings before the Ad Hoc Committee on the Domestic and International Monetary Effect of Energy and Other Natural Resource Pricing of the Committee on Banking and Currency, House of Representatives, 93rd Cong., Second Sess., August 9 and 12, 1974. The term *energy security* stretches back into the nineteenth century and emerged in relation to mechanized warfare's reliance on fossil fuel. Farrell, Zerriffi, and Dowlatabadi, "Energy Infrastructure and Security."

46. Yergin, *The Prize*, 385–86.

47. See Vitalis, *America's Kingdom*.

48. President's Materials Policy Commission, *Resources for Freedom*.

49. Greenberger, *Caught Unawares*.

50. Nordhauser, *The Quest for Stability*, vii.

51. Bohi and Russell, *Limiting Oil Imports*.

52. Prindle, *Petroleum Politics and the Texas Railroad Commission*, 75.

53. De Chazeau and Khan, *Integration and Competition in the Petroleum Industry*, 210, note 22.

54. Readers familiar with Harvey's famous theory of the "spatial fix" will notice that his double meaning of the term *fix* slightly differs from mine. For Harvey the spatial "fix" is a solution to capitalism's addiction to expansion and growth and a geographical "fix" in space. Mine is a "fix" of the market in addition to a "fix" in space.

55. Recall the quote from chapter 2: "The whole system of conservation regulation is designed to prevent market competition." Lovejoy and Homan, *Economic Aspects of Oil Conservation Regulation*, 282.

56. Bohi and Russell, *Limiting Oil Imports*, 22–23.

57. Ibid., 277.

58. Ibid., 17.

59. Harvey, *The Condition of Postmodernity*, 196.

60. A great summary of this period is found in Libecap, "The Political Economy of Crude Oil Cartelization."

61. This viewpoint became particularly fashionable among conservative "neorealist" international relations theorists like Keohane, *After Hegemony*.

62. Examples include Ross, "OPEC's Challenge to the West," and Levy, "Oil and the Decline of the West."

63. On "popular geopolitics," see Sharp, "Publishing American Identity."

64. Box 15, White House Central Files, Staff Member Office Files, Energy Policy Office, John A. Love, Richard Nixon Presidential Library, Yorba Linda, Calif.

65. Box 8, White House Central Files, Staff Member Office Files, Energy Policy Office, John A. Love, Richard Nixon Presidential Library, Yorba Linda, Calif.

66. *Oakland Tribune*, "More Areas Planning Gas Rationing."

67. Associated Press, "Crisis Produces Incidents."

68. See the section titled "Give Me Gas or I Will Kill You" in Fiege, *Republic of Nature*, 379–84.

69. Box 6, White House Central Files, Staff Member Office Files, Energy Policy Office, John A. Love, Richard Nixon Presidential Library, Yorba Linda, Calif. Emphasis always in original.

70. Box 17, White House Central Files, Staff Member Office Files, Energy Policy Office, John A. Love, Richard Nixon Presidential Library, Yorba Linda, Calif.

71. *High-Point Enterprise*, "Letter: Rationing Would Be Better."

72. Stevens, "Gasoline Shortages Are Forcing Exurbanites to Readjust Their Life-Style."

73. *Time*, "Gas Fever," 35.

74. Stevens, "Gasoline Shortages Are Forcing Exurbanites to Readjust Their Life-Style."

75. Box 7, White House Central Files, Staff Member Office Files, Energy Policy Office, John A. Love, Richard Nixon Presidential Library, Yorba Linda, Calif.

76. Ibid.

77. Stevens, "Gasoline Shortages Are Forcing Exurbanites to Readjust Their Life-Style."

78. For example, Jensen, "Inflation Replaces Energy," and *New York Times*, "Living Costs Are Held Top Problem."

79. See Matusow, *Nixon's Economy*.

80. Polanyi, *The Great Transformation*.

81. Cost of Living Council, *Inflation: On Prices and Wages*.

82. The theories of monetarism, which locate the quantity of the money supply as the sole cause of inflation, are best summed up by Milton Friedman's famous statement: "Inflation is always and everywhere a monetary phenomenon in the sense that it is and can be produced only by a more rapid increase in the quantity of money than in output." Milton Friedman, *The Counter-Revolution in Monetary Theory*, 24.

83. Reagan, "Radio Commentary: Inflation."

84. Greenspan, "The Impact of the 1973–1974 Oil Price Increase on the United States Economy to 1980."

85. Haberler, "Thoughts on Inflation." He goes on to focus on the importance of government regulations—like the Wagner Act—in institutionalizing the monopoly power of unions.

86. Cowie, *Stayin' Alive*, 223–24.

87. Nixon, "The Continuing Fight Against Inflation."

88. Reynolds, "The Case against Wage and Price Controls."

89. Adams, "Profit Sharing," 1298.

90. Box 8, White House Central Files, Staff Member Office Files, Energy Policy Office, John A. Love, Richard Nixon Presidential Library, Yorba Linda, Calif.

91. Klein, *The Shock Doctrine*.

92. Yergin, "How to Break the Cartel," 14.

93. Simon, "Statement of William Simon before the House Interstate and Foreign Commerce Subcommittee on Energy and Power, 2/17/75."

94. *New York Times*, "Editorial: The 'Energy Recession.'"

95. Schultze, "Recovery Now Relapse Ahead," 8.

96. Watts, "Resource Curse?," 53.

97. The mainstream debates over the "resource curse" were capitulated in Humphreys, Sachs, and Stiglitz, *Escaping the Resource Curse*.

98. Harvey, *Spaces of Global Capitalism*, 7–68.

99. Box 7, White House Central Files, Staff Member Office Files, Energy Policy Office, John A. Love, Richard Nixon Presidential Library, Yorba Linda, Calif.

100. Box 15, White House Central Files, Staff Member Office Files, Energy Policy Office, John A. Love, Richard Nixon Presidential Library, Yorba Linda, Calif.

101. The program was transcribed into print and included conservative economist Paul McKracken (moderator), Walter Mondale (liberal senator), Charles Murphy (oil executive), James McKie (oil-friendly economist from the University of Texas), and Stanley Ruttenberg (AFL-CIO). The American Enterprise Institute, *Is the Energy Crisis Contrived?*

102. Golden, "Op-ED: Oil and the Economy."

103. Ryan, "'Oil Weapon' of Arabs Stronger than Armies."

104. Richman, "Public Attitudes toward the Energy Crisis," 580. One poll taken throughout the 1970s shows that the public blamed the oil companies over the OPEC countries by 56 percent to 22 percent in 1974 and 72 percent to 51 percent in 1979.

105. Tarbell, *The History of the Standard Oil Company*.

106. Sampson, *The Seven Sisters*; Engler, *The Brotherhood of Oil*; and Blair, *The Control of Oil*.

107. Box 8, White House Central Files, Staff Member Office Files, Energy Policy Office, John A. Love, Richard Nixon Presidential Library, Yorba Linda, Calif.

108. *Williamson Daily News*, "Editorial: Cooking with Garbage."

109. Knight, "Straight Talk on the Energy Crisis."

110. Both quotes from Buckhorn, "America and the Energy Crisis," 6.

111. Box 9, White House Central Files, Staff Member Office Files, Energy Policy Office, John A. Love, Richard Nixon Presidential Library, Yorba Linda, Calif.

112. *Observer-Reporter*, "Nader Again Charges Energy Crisis 'Phony,'" A-8.

113. Box 17, White House Central Files, Staff Member Office Files, Energy Policy Office, John A. Love, Richard Nixon Presidential Library, Yorba Linda, Calif.

114. Box 6, White House Central Files, Staff Member Office Files, Energy Policy Office, John A. Love, Richard Nixon Presidential Library, Yorba Linda, Calif.

115. *Daily News-Record*, "Letter-to-the-Editor: Corporate Power."

116. *The Register*, "America's Foundation is the Land of Opportunity."

117. Quoted in Jacobs, "The Conservative Struggle and the Energy Crisis," 209.

118. *Los Angeles Times*, "Easing the Jolt at the Pump."

119. Again, in opposition to Timothy Mitchell's claim that the oil crisis represented a classic case for economists of market laws of supply and demand, neoliberal economists used the oil crisis as a prime example of government interference with these laws.

120. Friedman and Friedman, *Free to Choose*, 14. Of course, Friedman and Friedman fail to mention that the decades prior to the 1970s were marked by substantial bureaucratic state-level price controls (albeit indirect) through agencies like the TRC. As discussed in chapter 2, such "conservation" commissions served to stabilize prices against ruinous forces of competition, price volatility, and overproduction that proved anything but smooth.

121. *National Review*, "What's Ahead: Hot War and Cold Hoses," B165.

122. Buckley, "Gas Rationing?," 2-B.

123. Box 17, White House Central Files, Staff Member Office Files, Energy Policy Office, John A. Love, Richard Nixon Presidential Library, Yorba Linda, Calif.

124. Box 8, White House Central Files, Staff Member Office Files, Energy Policy Office, John A. Love, Richard Nixon Presidential Library, Yorba Linda, Calif.

125. Ibid.

126. Box 6, White House Central Files, Staff Member Office Files, Energy Policy Office, John A. Love, Richard Nixon Presidential Library, Yorba Linda, Calif.

127. Box 7, White House Central Files, Staff Member Office Files, Energy Policy Office, John A. Love, Richard Nixon Presidential Library, Yorba Linda, Calif.

128. Hayek, *The Road to Serfdom*, 145.

129. Ibid.

130. Ibid., 21.

131. See Schulman and Zelizer, *Rightward Bound*.

132. Edsall and Edsall, *Chain Reaction*.

133. See footnote 48 in the introduction. Again, this is not to say that *all* suburbanites (from the Sunbelt or anywhere else) espoused these ideologies but rather that suburban lived experience was conducive to these forms of politics, and indeed the popular energy often emerged from suburban geographies.

134. See Frank, *The Conquest of Cool*, 10–14.

135. For the example of Southern California see Pulido, *Black, Brown, Yellow, and Left*. Compare with McGirr, *Suburban Warriors*.

136. Belasco, *Appetite for Change*.

137. Phillips, *The Emerging Republican Majority*.

138. Lassiter, *The Silent Majority*, 3.

139. One example is the following: "Of immediate, pressing urgency in the management of the energy crisis: stop the bussing of children for 'racial balance,' thus saving *millions* of gallons of gasoline and oil . . . Children should go to the nearest school in town—the one they can walk to" (emphasis in original). Box 8, White House Central Files, Staff Member Office Files, Energy Policy Office, John A. Love, Richard Nixon Presidential Library, Yorba Linda, Calif.

140. Edsall and Edsall, *Chain Reaction*, 147.

141. Ibid., 146.

142. Hayek, *The Road to Serfdom*, 17.

143. Quoted in Lassiter, *The Silent Majority*, 1.

144. Silence was also allowable in a context where those who stood silent had representatives, like Nixon, in positions of power! I thank Nancy Peluso for this insight. The metaphor of the "silent majority" also contradicts the actual *vocal* and organized social movements that constituted suburban conservatism. See McGirr, *Suburban Warriors*, and Davis, *City of Quartz*, on the role of homeowners associations in fighting to protect property values against various forms of imagined degradation (be it racial or environmental).

145. McKenzie, *Privatopia*, 19.

146. On the role of the suburbs in the environmental movement, see, Rome, *The Bulldozer in the Countryside*.

147. *The Daily Herald*, "Letter—Taken for a Ride."

148. Shaffer, "'Energy Crisis.'"

149. Box 7, White House Central Files, Staff Member Office Files, Energy Policy Office, John A. Love, Richard Nixon Presidential Library, Yorba Linda, Calif.

150. Box 8, White House Central Files, Staff Member Office Files, Energy Policy Office, John A. Love, Richard Nixon Presidential Library, Yorba Linda, Calif.

151. Box 6, White House Central Files, Staff Member Office Files, Energy Policy Office, John A. Love, Richard Nixon Presidential Library, Yorba Linda, Calif.

152. Box 47, "Ronald Reagan Statements on Energy, Environment, Resources, Preliminary Draft," Ronald Reagan 1980 Presidential Campaign Papers, 1964–1980, Ronald Reagan Presidential Library, Simi Valley, Calif.

153. Foucault, *The Birth of Biopolitics*, 121.

154. Shabecoff, "A Quiet and behind the Scenes Drive," 4.

155. Quoted in Faber, *Capitalizing on Environmental Injustice*, 128.

156. Ibid.

157. See Gowan, *The Global Gamble*; Harvey, *A Brief History of Neoliberalism*; Wade "The First-World Debt Crisis of 2007–2010 in Global Perspective"; and McNally, *Global Slump*.

158. For "insider" expertise on the financialization of the oil market see the work of Phillip Verleger at http://www.pkverlegerllc.com. Also see Yergin, *The Prize*, 697–725, and Juhasz, *The Tyranny of Oil*, 126–68.

159. Timothy Mitchell, *Carbon Democracy*, 197–98.

160. Harvey, *A Brief History of Neoliberalism*, 39–63.

161. See Edsall and Edsall, *Chain Reaction*, 167–68; Juhasz, *The Tyranny of Oil*; and McElroy, *For The Love of Oil*.

162. Edsall and Edsall, *Chain Reaction*, 167–68.

163. Rutledge, "Profitability and Supply Price in the US Domestic Oil Industry," statistics on 4–5. The *New York Times* estimates eight million royalty owners, Urbina, "Learning Too Late of the Perils in Gas Well Leases."

164. Watson, "Oilmen Struggle to Keep High Political Profile,"1110.

165. Ibid., 3.

166. Ibid.

167. Vernon, "The Influence of the U.S. Government upon Multinational Enterprises," 65.

5. Pain at the Pump

1. Cave, "States Get in on Calls for a Gas Tax Holiday."

2. Stranahan, "Running on Empty."

3. I received this e-mail myself and it is accessible at http://toddshammer .wordpress.com/2007/05.

4. Postone, *Time, Labor and Social Domination*, 17.

5. See, for example, Duménil and Lévy, "Neoliberal Income Trends"; Harvey, *A Brief History of Neoliberalism*; and McNally, *Global Slump*.

6. McNally, *Global Slump*, 58.

7. On the biopolitics of the SUV see Campbell, "The Biopolitics of Security." See also Don Mitchell, "The S.U.V. Model of Citizenship." On "edge cities" see the classic text, Garreau, *Edge City*. On the expansion of the America metropolis see Knox, *Metrourbia, USA*.

8. I use this term following David Harvey's conceptualization of neoliberalism as the "restoration of class power." Harvey, *Spaces of Global Capitalism*, 7–68.

9. See Jakle and Sculle, *The Gas Station in America*.

10. Bridge, "Resource Triumphalism."

11. Hartshorn, *Oil Trade*, 93.

12. Penrose, *The Large International Firm in Developing Countries*, 46.

13. Cater et al., *Historical Statistics of the United States: Millennial Online Edition*, Table De183-219—Retail establishments, by type of business: 1939–1997.

14. For a reasonable explanation of this see, Smil, *Oil*, 153.

15. On the international trade politics of California's attempt to regulate MBTE, see McCarthy, "Privatizing the Conditions of Production."

16. Freudenberger, *Alcohol Fuel*, 10.

17. Steve Cohen, *Understanding Environmental Policy,* 62.

18. Ibid., 63.

19. Of course, price, or exchange value, is but the expression of value, which, according to Marx, is based in the socially necessary labor time underlying commodities. Yet price movements are the primary quantitative ways in which ordinary workers *experience* value both in and outside the workplace.

20. Billig actually mentions national flags at petrol station "forecourts" as a quintessential example of this everyday form of national identity. Billig, *Banal Nationalism,* 39.

21. Harvey, *The Limits to Capital,* 48.

22. Mann, *Our Daily Bread,* 26.

23. Ibid., 52.

24. Ranii and Murawski, "$6.55, The Ups, Downs of New Wage," A1. While at a conference in Athens, Ohio, in the fall of 2008 I saw a left-leaning flier on a lamppost that invoked the idea of expressing wages in "gallons per hour."

25. FSU News, "Higher Gas Prices Leave Many Workers Running on Empty."

26. Cowie, *Stayin' Alive.*

27. Evelyn S. Taylor, *P.A.T.C.O. and Reagan.*

28. See, for example, Wolff, *Capitalism Hits the Fan.*

29. McNally, *Global Slump,* 38.

30. See Harvey, *Spaces of Global Capitalism,* 7–68.

31. For a similar argument, see Jason Moore, "The End of the Road."

32. McNally, *Global Slump,* 58.

33. Yergin, *The Prize,* 733.

34. A standard account by the World Bank is Varangis, Akiyama, and Mitchell, *Managing Commodity Booms and Busts.*

35. A classic study of this boom–bust cycle through the case of Venezuela and other petroleum exporting countries is Karl, *The Paradox of Plenty.* The lack of diversification of economies centered on commodities with substantial price volatility has become a standard explanation behind the so-called curse of natural resources. See Auty, *Sustaining Development in Mineral Economies,* 8. This has led to a curious form of what Michael Watts calls "commodity determinism" where poverty and inequality are (a) blamed on "things" rather than social relations and (b) territorialized as a pure problem of national countries severed from global political economic relations through a focus on *national* statistics surrounding resource production and economic growth. See Watts, "Resource Curse?" Gavin Bridge makes this territorial critique of the "resource curse" in Bridge, "Global Production Networks and The Extractive Sector," 393.

36. Peet and Hartwick, *Theories of Development,* 90.

37. See Jaffee, *Brewing Justice,* 44.

38. Pollan, *The Omnivore's Dilemma,* 52.

39. The preceding paragraph relies mainly on the history provided by Yergin, *The Prize,* 726–49.

40. The literature documenting these processes are too numerous to cite fully. On food, see Araghi, "Accumulation by Displacement," and Jason Moore, "The End of the Road." On mining see Bridge, "Mapping the Bonanza."

41. Good overviews of conflicts over land and resources can be found in Peet and Watts, *Liberation Ecologies*.

42. James Ferguson, *Global Shadows*.

43. For a standard left critique of oil price commodity traders, see Juhasz, *The Tyranny of Oil*, 126–68. A much more sophisticated critique of the "financialization" of the oil industry in relation to theories of "peak oil" is Labban, "Oil In Parallax."

44. Citrin and Martin, *After the Tax Revolt*.

45. Schulman, *The Seventies*, 210.

46. Edsall and Edsall, *Chain Reaction*, 214.

47. Ibid., 4.

48. For a fascinating look at radical feminist peace activists in Los Angeles during the 1960s who did focus on war and military spending as the main driver of high taxes, see Loyd, "Peace Is Our Only Shelter."

49. For a fascinating ethnographic look into the "Wednesday meeting" of conservative activists convened by Grover Norquist, see Medvetz, "The Strength of Weekly Ties."

50. See Frank, *What's the Matter with Kansas?* Frank's argument that middle-lower-class voters vote against their "economic interests" because of "cultural issues" ignores (a) most data reveals that lower-income voters overall (if they vote at all) vote Democratic, and the Republican base remains wealthy and highly suburban, and (b) most so-called family-values issues are deeply entangled within the politics of the private sphere and the household, which, as I have argued throughout, is central to a politics of entrepreneurial life that is deeply economic and cultural.

51. The Cato Institute, "Chapter 41: Environmental Protection."

52. A basic view of market-oriented environmental policy is presented in Titenberg and Lewis, *Environmental Economics and Policy*. A critical collection of essays on neoliberal environmentalism is Heynen, et al. *Neoliberal Environments*. The definitive presentation of the utopic view of "green capitalism" is Hawken, Lovins, and Lovins, *Natural Capitalism*. A scathing critique of such optimistic views of the profitability of green business is Rodgers, *Green Gone Wrong*.

53. See, for example, Stern et al., *Environmentally Significant Consumption*. A more critical view is Princen, Maniates, and Conca, *Confronting Consumption*.

54. Thomas Friedman, "The Real Patriot Act."

55. Gore, *Earth in the Balance*, 341.

56. Ibid., 341.

57. Although this system is universally heralded as a "success," not only does it raise disturbing environmental justice questions for those communities living near plants who buy their way to more pollution, but some critics have even raised

questions on the system's role in demonstrated decreases in pollution. Critics bring up important questions regarding already existing patterns of off-shoring dirty industries, pollution control innovations preexisting the 1990 act, and the fact that non-cap-and-trade systems induced even larger pollution decreases in Europe. See Carlson et al. "Sulfur Dioxide Control by Electric Utilities"; Gar Lipow, "Emissions Trading"; and Taylor, Rubin, and Hounshell, "Regulation as the Mother of Invention."

58. Passell, "Cheapest Protection of Nature May Lie In Taxes, Not Laws."

59. Repetto et al., *Green Fees*.

60. Ibid., 4.

61. Ibid., 7.

62. Clinton, "State of the Union, 1993."

63. Erlandson, "The BTU Tax Experience," 175.

64. Salpukas, "Going for the Kill on the Energy Tax Plan"; Wines, "Tax's Demise Illustrates the First Rule of Lobbying."

65. Joel Brinkley, "Cultivating the Grass Roots."

66. Mobil Corporation, "The BTU Tax Is a Bad Idea."

67. *Christian Science Monitor,* "Letter to the Editor (William F. O'Keefe)."

68. Wolf, "Tax Revolt Is Picking up Steam."

69. *Washington Times,* "Letter to the Editor (Kent Jeffreys)."

70. *Houston Chronicle,* "Letter to the Editor: BTU Tax Is a Bad Idea."

71. *St. Petersburg Times,* "Letter to the Editor," *St. Petersburg Times,* June 4, 1993, A13.

72. Crow, "U.S. Industry Girding for Battle Against Clinton Energy Tax Plan," 19.

73. *New York Times,* "How the Energy Tax Would Affect Three Families."

74. Krauss, "Some Senate Democrats Push More Spending Cuts."

75. Boren, "US Economic Policy."

76. *St. Petersburg Times,* "Letter to the Editor," *St. Petersburg Times,* February 19, 1993, A15.

77. Pianin and Hilzenrath, "Hill Agrees to Raise Gas Tax 4.3 Cents."

78. Crow, "U.S. Senate Deficit Bill Shifts Focus to Transport Fuels Taxes.

79. For a comparison see Derek Thompson, "Gas Prices around the World"

80. Lafsky, "How Often Is the Gas Tax Raised?"

81. "Wacky, 2004." The Museum of the Moving Image. Accessed July 30, 2012, http://www.livingroomcandidate.org/commercials/2004/wacky.

82. *Wall Street Journal,* "OP-ED: The Cap and Tax Fiction."

83. Loris and Lieberman, "The 2009 Energy Bill."

84. Ibid.

85. *Seattle Times,* "Letter to the Editor: Life with Cap-and-Trade Means Economy Will Sink."

86. The fact that this statement is a direct quote is somewhat astounding. Not only can one find this phrase among several hateful blog and comment postings

throughout the netherworlds of the Internet, but more disturbingly, the short-lived presidential hopeful, Donald Trump, uttered this very phrase on the record in an interview with *New York Magazine:* "I always heard that when we went into Iraq, we went in for the oil. I said, 'Eh, that sounds smart.' That sounds smart. Yes, blood for oil! Yes, blood for oil!," http://nymag.com/daily/intel/2011/04/you_really_have_to_listen_to_d.html.

87. Uchitelle and Thee, "Americans Are Cautiously Open to Gas Tax Rise, Poll Shows."

88. See Timothy Mitchell, *Carbon Democracy.*

89. There are too many books and articles making this connection to count. Two straightforward accounts that situate the war in the proper historical context of long-standing U.S. "petro-imperialism" are Jhaveri, "US Oil Interests and the Iraq War," and Le Billon and El Khatib, "From Free Oil to 'Freedom Oil?" The most nuanced account of the relation between oil and the War in Iraq is Retort, *Afflicted Powers,* especially chapter 2, "Blood for Oil?," 38–77. The Retort collective takes much of its analysis of oil from Jonathan Nitzan and Simon Bichler (too much according to Nitzan and Bichler themselves!) and their analysis of the "weapondollar-petrodollar coalition." Nitzan and Bichler, *The Global Political Economy of Israel,* especially chapter 5, "The Weapondollar-Petrodollar Coalition," 198–273.

90. Mazen Labban suggests this connection in a footnote. See Labban, *Space, Oil, and Capital,* 163.

91. See footnote 86.

92. *The Economist,* "A Greener Bush."

93. See Klare, *Blood and Oil,* 3–4.

94. Babcock, "Iraq Isn't about Oil."

95. Ibid.

96. Stokes and Raphael, *Global Energy Security.*

97. Kaufman, "Americans Still Split on Global Warming, Poll Shows."

98. Gingrich, *Drill Here, Drill Now, Pay Less.*

99. Ibid., 1–2.

100. Ibid., 3.

101. A celebratory account is found in Yergin, *The Quest.*

102. Stolberg, "Will $4 Gasoline Trump a 27-Year-Old Ban?"

Conclusion

1. Byron, "Terror Free Oil Makes Its US Debut."

2. Ibid.

3. Ibid.

4. Friedman and Friedman, *Free to Choose.*

5. See Steinberg, "Can Capitalism Save the Planet?"

6. Marx, *Capital Volume 3,* 958–59.

7. "[The capitalist] is fanatically intent on the valorization of value; consequently, he ruthlessly forces the human race to produce for production's sake. In this way he spurs on the development of society's productive forces, and the creation of those material conditions of production which alone can form the real basis of a higher form of society, a society in which the full and free development of every individual forms the ruling principle." Marx, *Capital Volume 1*, 739.

8. Wendling, *Karl Marx on Technology and Alienation*, 13.

9. See, for example, Klein, "Capitalism vs. the Climate"; and McKibben, *Eaarth*.

10. Of course, it is not as if fossil capitalism has relieved the world of hard manual labor. It still remains in those forms of the labor process that cannot (as of yet) be mechanized, or the places and communities throughout the world that capital (in its finicky ways) has decided are not worth its investment.

11. Marx, *Capital Volume 1*, 742. David Harvey often uses this phrase as "accumulation for accumulation's sake" in reference to the driving force of capital. See Harvey, *The Limits to Capital*, 29.

12. Harvey, *Spaces of Global Capitalism*, 7–68.

13. Gramsci, *Selections from the Prison Notebooks*, 193.

14. Nye, *Consuming Power*, 187–216.

15. Marx, *Grundrisse*, 694.

16. For a concise global history see Blum, *Killing Hope*.

17. For a country-specific study of American empire and postwar oil production, see Vitalis, *America's Kingdom*.

18. See Blum, *Killing Hope*, 64–71.

19. See Agence France-Presse, "Saudi Arabia," and the article from just over two weeks later, Landler and Myers, "With $30 Billion Arms Deal, U.S. Bolsters Saudi Ties."

20. Kashi and Watts, *Curse of the Black Gold*.

21. Nikiforuk, *Tar Sands*.

22. See footnote 55 in introduction. The "capital–labor accord" has always been seen as the "limited capital–labor accord," not only because it excluded massive segments of the population, but also because it maintained capitalist control over the production process. "Under this accord, newly organized unions and workers—primarily those in manufacturing—guaranteed labor peace in exchange for job security and a share in the growing economic pie." Albeda and Tilly, "Toward a Broader Vision," 213.

23. Harris, *The Right to Manage*, 99.

24. Foner, *The Story of American Freedom*, 264.

25. Kerr, *Industrialism and Industrial Man*, 295.

26. Harvey, *Spaces of Global Capitalism*, 98.

27. Obama, "State of the Union Address, 2012." It must be admitted that the incredible mobilizing discourses of the 1 percent versus the 99 percent is at least partly rooted in the neoliberal conviction that a free and fair market cannot be

dominated by an elite group of monopolists. Of course, much of the Occupy movement is not simply calling for the restoration of what has never existed—a free and fair market—but is fundamentally questioning the nature of capitalism itself.

28. See Low, *Behind the Gates.*

29. Robin, *The Reactionary Mind,* 99.

30. Marx, "On the Jewish Question," 229. Emphasis in original.

31. Foner, *The Story of American Freedom,* 328.

32. Made much of by the flawed "culturalist" explanation of Conservative hegemony in the United States by Frank, *What's the Matter with Kansas?*

33. Robin, "Reclaiming the Politics of Freedom."

34. Foucault, *The Birth of Biopolitics,* 65.

35. Marx, *Capital Volume 1,* 928.

36. For example, writing in the midst of the emergence of the modern environmental movement in the 1970s, Hans Magnus Enzenberger asserts a typical "green" critique of Marx: "the development of the productive forces is not a linear process to which political hopes can be attached . . . The industrial process, insofar as it depends on these deformed productive forces, threatens its very existence and the existence of human society." Enzenberger, "A Critique of Political Ecology," 22–23. In another classic take, Ted Benton suggests that the ecological crisis forces new meanings of socialism: "Socialists can no longer hold out the promise of a future society of abundance. The future too belongs to the realm of necessity, and humankind is now faced with the problem of survival, not the hope of abundance." Benton, "Introduction to Part I," 10.

37. See Shwartzman, "Ecosocialism or Ecocatastrophe?"

38. See Smil, "21st Century Energy."

39. For a summary see North, "Eco-Localisation."

40. For a nice critique of "the local," see Albo, "The Limits of Eco-Localism."

41. Klein, "Capitalism vs. the Climate."

42. This leaves unanswered whether or not the planet's population could subsist without synthetic nitrogen, but Smil's point is only that the 40 percent of the population, *as it exists today,* is dependent upon this industrial form of fertilized farming. Smil, *Enriching the Earth,* 159.

43. Marx, "Critique of the Gotha Program," 321.

44. See Bridge, "Past Peak Oil."

45. Timothy Mitchell, *Carbon Democracy,* 231–54.

46. Lefebvre, *The Urban Revolution.* David Harvey has paraphrased Lefebvre as saying, "The revolution has to be urban, in the broadest sense of that term, or nothing at all" (40). Harvey, "The Right to the City."

47. Harvey, "New Urbanism and the Communitarian Trap."

48. Bush, "State of the Union Address, January 31, 2006."

49. Marx, "On the Jewish Question," 234.

Abramsy, Kolya, ed. *Sparking a Worldwide Energy Revolution: Social Struggles in the Transition to a Post-Petrol World.* Oakland, Calif.: AK Press, 2010.

Adams, Mildred. "Profit Sharing: A Proposal to Halt Inflation." *National Review* 23 (November 1973): 1298.

Agamben, Giorgio. *Homo Sacer: Sovereign Power and Bare Life.* Princeton, N.J.: Princeton University Press, 1998.

Agence France-Presse. "Saudi Arabia: Woman Is Beheaded after Being Convicted of Witchcraft." *New York Times,* December 13, 2011, A14.

Aglietta, Michel. *A Theory of Capitalist Regulation: The US Experience.* London: Verso, 1979.

Agnew, John. *Geopolitics: Re-Visioning World Politics.* London: Routledge, 2003.
———. "The Territorial Trap: The Geographical Assumptions of International Relations Theory." *Review of International Political Economy* 1, no. 1 (1994): 53–80.

Alaimo, Stacy, and Susan Hekman, eds. *Material Feminisms.* Bloomington: Indiana University Press, 2008.

Albeda, Randy, and Chris Tilly. "Toward a Broader Vision: Race, Gender, and Labor Market Segmentation in the Social Structure of Accumulation Framework." In *Social Structures of Accumulation: The Political Economy of Growth and Crisis,* edited by David M. Kotz, Terrence McDonough, and Michael Reich, 212–30. Cambridge, UK: Cambridge University Press, 1994.

Albo, Greg. "The Limits of Eco-Localism: Scale, Strategy, Socialism." In *Coming to Terms with Nature,* edited by Leo Panitch and Colin Leys, 337–63. London: Merlin, 2007.

Allen, Barbara. "Cradle of a Revolution? The Industrial Transformation of Louisiana's Lower Mississippi River." *Technology and Culture* 47, no. 1 (2006): 112–19.

———. *Uneasy Alchemy: Citizens and Experts in Louisiana's Chemical Corridor Disputes*. Cambridge, Mass.: MIT Press, 2003.

Alter, Jonathan. *The Defining Moment: FDR'S Hundred Days and the Triumph of Hope*. New York: Simon and Schuster, 2006.

Altvater, Elmar. "The Social and Natural Environment of Fossil Capitalism." In *Coming to Terms with Nature*, edited by Leo Panitch and Colin Leys, 37–60. London: Merlin, 2006.

American Enterprise Institute. *Is the Energy Crisis Contrived? An AEI Round Table Held on 22 July 1974 at the American Enterprise Institute for Public Policy Research, Washington, D.C.* Washington, D.C.: American Enterprise Institute for Public Policy Research, 1974.

American Petroleum Institute. *Petroleum Facts and Figures*. New York: API, 1971.

Anderson, Ben. "Affect and Biopower: Towards a Politics of Life." *Transactions of the Institute of British Geographers* 37, no. 1 (2011): 28–43.

Anderson, David. "Levittown Is Burning! The 1979 Levittown, Pennsylvania, Gas Line Riot and the Decline of the Blue-Collar American Dream." *Labor* 2, no. 3 (2005): 47–66.

Anderson, Kevin. *Marx at the Margins: On Nationalism, Ethnicity, and Non-Western Societies*. Chicago, Ill.: University of Chicago Press, 2010.

Anderson, Perry. "The Antinomies of Antonio Gramsci." *New Left Review* 1, no. 100 (November–December 1976): 5–78.

Araghi, Farshad. "Accumulation by Displacement: Global Enclosures, Food Crisis, and the Ecological Contradictions of Capitalism." *Review: A Journal of Fernand Braudel Center* 32, no. 1 (2009): 113–46.

Archer, John. *Architecture and Suburbia: From English Villa to American Dream House*. Minneapolis: University of Minnesota Press, 2005.

Associated Press. "Gas Prices Burden Families, Obama Says at Food Pantry." July 2, 2008.

———. "Crisis Produces Incidents." *The Progress*, February 25, 1974, 6.

"Automobilicus Americanus—1893–1973." *The News, Port-Arthur, Texas*, November 25, 1973, 4.

Auty, Richard. *Sustaining Development in Mineral Economies: The Resource Curse Thesis*. London: Routledge, 1993.

Babcock, Michael A. "Iraq Isn't about Oil—But at Some Point We Have to Fight for Oil." *The Free Lance-Star*, September 2, 2005, A9.

Bakker, Karen, and Gavin Bridge. "Material Worlds? Resource Geographies and 'the Matter of Nature.'" *Progress in Human Geography* 30, no. 1 (2006): 5–27.

Banerjee, Neela. "'Made in America,' and Never Mind the Gas Mileage." *New York Times*, November 23, 2001.

Barry, Andrew, Thomas Osborne, and Nikolas Rose, eds. *Foucault and Political Reason: Liberalism, Neo-Liberalism, and Rationalities of Government*. Chicago, Ill.: University of Chicago Press, 1996.

Barry, Joeseph A. "America—Body and Soul." *House Beautiful* 98, no. 11 (November 1956): 238–42.

Bartlett, A. "Forgotten Fundamentals of the Energy Crisis." *American Journal of Physics* 46, no. 9 (1978): 876–88.

Beauregard, Robert A. *Voices of Decline: The Postwar Fate of US Cities.* London: Routledge, 2002.

———. *When America Became Suburban.* Minneapolis: University of Minnesota Press, 2006.

Bebbington, Anthony. "Capitals and Capabilities: A Framework for Analyzing Peasant Viability, Rural Livelihoods and Poverty." *World Development* 27, no. 12 (1999): 2021–44.

Belasco, Warren J. *Appetite for Change: How Counterculture Took on the Food Industry.* New York: Pantheon, 1989.

Benson, Margaret. "The Political Economy of Women's Liberation." *Monthly Review* 21, no. 4 (1969): 13–27.

Benton, Ted. "Introduction to Part I." In *The Greening of Marxism,* edited by Ted Benton, 7–15. New York: Guilford, 1996.

Bernstein, Irving. *A Caring Society: The New Deal, the Worker, and the Great Depression.* Boston, Mass.: Houghton Mifflin Co., 1985.

———. *Turbulent Years: A History of the American Worker, 1933–1941.* Boston, Mass.: Houghton Mifflin Co., 1971.

Billig, Michael. *Banal Nationalism.* London: Sage, 1995.

Bina, Cyrus. *The Economics of the Oil Crisis: Theories of Oil Crisis, Oil Rent, and the Internationalization of Capital in the Oil Industry.* New York: St. Martin's Press, 1985.

Black, Brian. *Petrolia: The Landscape of America's First Oil Boom.* Baltimore, Md.: Johns Hopkins University Press, 2000.

Black, Edwin. *Internal Combustion: How Corporations and Governments Addicted the World to Oil and Derailed the Alternatives.* New York: St. Martin's Press, 2006.

Blair, John. *The Control of Oil.* London: Macmillan, 1976.

Blum, William. *Killing Hope: U.S. Military and CIA Interventions since World War II.* London: Zed, 2003.

Blundfll, William E. "Oil Union Finds Strikes Are Ineffective at Automated Plants." *Wall Street Journal,* January 19, 1962, 1.

Boatright, Mody Coggin, and William A. Owens. *Tales from the Derrick Floor: A People's History of the Oil Industry.* New York: Doubleday, 1970.

Bohi, Douglas R., and Milton Russell. *Limiting Oil Imports: An Economic History and Analysis.* Baltimore, Md.: Johns Hopkins University Press, 1978.

Boren, David. "US Economic Policy." June 9, 1993, Speech at the American Council for Capital Formation, Washington, D.C. http://www.c-spanvideo.org/program/42644-1.

Bosman, Julie. "Unlikely Allies Campaign for Gas-Tax Holiday." *New York Times*, May 2, 2008.

Bower, Tom. *Oil: Money, Politics and Power in the 21st Century*. New York: Grand Central Publishing, 2009.

Bowles, Samuel, David Gordon, and Thomas Weisskopf. "Power and Profits: The Social Structure of Accumulation and the Profitability of the Postwar US Economy." *Review of Radical Political Economics* 18, no. 1–2 (1986): 132–67.

Boyd, William, Scott Prudham, and Rachel Schurman. "Industrial Dynamics and the Problem of Nature." *Society and Natural Resources* 14, no. 7 (2001): 555–70.

Boyer, Robert. "From Canonical Fordism to Different Modes of Development." In *Régulation Theory: State of the Art*, edited by Robert Boyer and Yves Saillard, 231–37. New York and London: Routledge, 2002.

Boyer, Robert, and Yves Saillard, eds. *Régulation Theory: The State of the Art*. London: Routledge, 2002.

Braun, Bruce. "Nature and Culture: On the Career of a False Problem." In *A Companion to Cultural Geography*, edited by James Duncan, Nuala Johnson, and Richard Schein, 151–79. Oxford: Blackwell, 2004.

Braverman, Harry. *Labor and Monopoly Capital*. New York: Monthly Review Press, 1974.

Brenner, Neil. "Between Fixity and Motion: Accumulation, Territorial Organization and the Historical Geography of Spatial Scales." *Environment and Planning D: Society and Space* 16, no. 4 (1998): 459–81.

Brenner, Robert, and Mark Glick. "The Regulation Approach: Theory and History." *New Left Review* 188 (1991): 45–119.

Bridewell, W. F. "Letter to FDR, 19 May 1933." FDR Official File 56, Box 1, Franklin D. Roosevelt Library and Museum, Hyde Park, N.Y.

Bridge, Gavin. "Global Production Networks and the Extractive Sector: Governing Resource-Based Development." *Journal of Economic Geography* 8, no. 3 (2008): 389–419.

———. "Mapping the Bonanza: Geographies of Mining Investment in the Era of Neoliberal Reform." *The Professional Geographer* 56, no. 3 (2004): 406–21.

———. "Material Worlds: Natural Resources, Resource Geography and the Material Economy." *Geography Compass* 3, no. 3 (2009): 1217–44.

———. "Past Peak Oil: Political Economy of Energy Crises." In *Global Political Ecology*, edited by Richard Peet, Paul Robbins, and Michael Watts, 307–24. London and New York: Routledge, 2011.

———. "Resource Triumphalism: Postindustrial Narratives of Primary Commodity Production." *Environment and Planning A* 33 (2001): 2149–73.

Brinkley, Alan. *The End of Reform: New Deal Liberalism in Recession and War*. New York: Vintage, 1996.

Brinkley, Joel. "Cultivating the Grass Roots to Reap Legislative Benefits." *New York Times*, November 1, 1993, A1.

Bromley, Simon. *American Hegemony and World Oil*. Philadelphia: University of Pennsylvania Press, 1991.

Brozen, Yale. *Automation: The Impact of Technological Change*. Washington, D.C.: The American Enterprise Institute, 1963.

Buck, Daniel. "The Subsumption of Space and the Spatiality of Subsumption: Primitive Accumulation and the Transition to Capitalism in Shanghai, China." *Antipode* 39, no. 4 (2007): 757–44.

Buckhorn, Robert F. "America and the Energy Crisis: How Did It Happen, Where Will It Lead?" *Uklah Daily Journal*, March 6, 1974, 6.

Buckley, William F. "Gas Rationing?" *The Big Spring Herald*, November 15, 1973, 2-B.

Bull, Alister. "Signs of Cheaper Gas Could Brighten Obama Campaign." Reuters, April 23, 2012.

Bullard, Robert D. *Dumping in Dixie: Race, Class and Environmental Quality*. 3rd ed. Boulder, Colo.: Westview Press, 2000.

Bureau of Mines. *Monthly Petroleum Forecast June 1948*. Washington, D.C.: Bureau of Mines, 1948.

Burke, Edmund, III. "The Big Story: Human History, Energy Regimes, and the Environment." In *The Environment and World History*, edited by Edmund Burke III and Kenneth Pomeranz, 33–53. Berkeley: University of California Press, 2009.

Burkett, Paul, and John Bellamy Foster. "Metabolism, Energy, and Entropy in Marx's critique of Political Economy: Beyond the Podolinsky Myth." *Theory and Society* 35, no. 1 (2006): 109–56.

Bush, George W. "President's Radio Address." June 21, 2008. http://georgewbush-whitehouse.archives.gov.

———. "State of the Union Address," January 31, 2006. Washington, D.C., http://georgewbush-whitehouse.archives.gov.

——— "Fact Sheet: America's Ownership Society: Expanding Opportunities." http://georgewbush-whitehouse.archives.gov/news/releases/2004/08/20040809-9.html

Business Week. "Computer Runs Refinery Unit for Texaco." *Business Week*, April 4, 1959.

Butler, Judith. *Bodies That Matter: On the Discursive Limits of Sex*. New York and London: Routledge, 1993.

Byron, Kate. "Terror Free Oil Makes Its US Debut." *CNN Money*, February 1, 2007. Accessed January 10, 2012. http://money.cnn.com/2007/02/01/news/economy/oil_terror/index.htm.

Caffentzis, George. "The Petroleum Commons: Local, Islamic, and Global." *Alternatives: Turkish Journal of International Relations* 4, no. 1–2 (2005): 108–23.

Calvino, Italo. "The Petrol Pump." In *Numbers in the Dark and Other Stories*, translated by Tim Parks, 170–75. New York: Pantheon, 1995.

Campbell, David. "The Biopolitics of Security: Oil, Empire, and the Sports Utility Vehicle." *American Quarterly* 57, no. 3 (2005): 943–72.

Carlson, Curtis, Dallas Burtraw, Maureen Cropper, and Karen L. Palmer. "Sulfur Dioxide Control by Electric Utilities: What Are the Gains from Trade?" *Journal of Political Economy* 108 (2000): 1292–326.

Carter, Susan B., Scott Sigmund Gartner, Michael R. Hainesh, Alan L. Olmstead, Richard Sutch, and Gavin Wright. *Historical Statistics of the United States, Earliest Times to the Present*. New York: Cambridge University Press, 2006.

Cato Institute. "Chapter 41: Environmental Protection." In *(Washington, D.C.: Cato Institute, 1997)*. http://www.cato.org/pubs/handbook/hb105/105-41.pdf.

Cave, Damien. "States Get in on Calls for a Gas Tax Holiday." *New York Times*, May 6, 2008.

Chakrabarty, Dipesh. "The Climate of History: Four Theses." *Critical Inquiry* 35 (2009): 197–222.

Cheney, Richard. "Full Text of Dick Cheney's Speech at the IP Autumn Lunch." Speech Given at the London Institute of Petroleum Autumn Lunch, November 15, 1999. http://web.archive.org/web/20000414054656/http://www.petroleum.co.uk/speeches.htm.

Childs, William R. "The Transformation of the Railroad Commission of Texas, 1917–1940: Business-Government Relations and the Importance of Personality, Agency Culture, and Regional Differences." *Business History Review* 65, no. 2 (1991): 285–344.

Citrin, Jack, and Isaac Martin, eds. *After the Tax Revolt: California's Proposition 13 Turns 30*. Berkeley, Calif.: Berkeley Public Policy Press, 2009.

Clark, Brett, and Richard York. "Carbon Metabolism: Global Capitalism, Climate Change and the Biospheric Rift." *Theory and Society* 34, no. 4 (2005): 391–428.

Clark, James A., and Michael T. Halbouty. *The Last Boom*. New York: Random House, 1972.

Cleveland, Cutler J., Robert Costanza, Charles Hall, and Robert Kaufmann. "Energy and the U.S. Economy: A Biophysical Perspective." *Science* 225, no. 4665 (1984): 890–97.

Clinton, W. J. "State of the Union, February 17, 1993." Washington, D.C., http://www.washingtonpost.com/wp-srv/politics/special/states/docs/sou93.htm.

Cochrane, W. W., and M. E. Ryan. *American Farm Policy, 1948–1973*. Minneapolis: University of Minnesota Press, 1976.

Cohen, Lizabeth. *A Consumer's Republic: The Politics of Mass Consumption in Postwar America*. New York: Vintage, 2004.

———. *Making a New Deal: Industrial Workers in Chicago*. New York: Cambridge University Press, 1991.

Cohen, Steve. *Understanding Environmental Policy*. New York: Columbia University Press, 2005.

Cole, William P. "Speech to the American Petroleum Institute." November 5, 1941, FDR Official File #1585, Interstate Oil Compact Commission, The Franklin D. Roosevelt Presidential Library, Hyde Park, N.Y.

Collins, Gail. "The Energy Drill." *New York Times*, August 7, 2008, A25.

Continental Oil Company. *Annual Report of the Continental Oil Company (Conoco) and its Subsidiary Companies.* Ponca City, Okla.: Conoco, Inc., 1945. Hagley Museum and Library, Wilmington, Del.

―――. *Annual Report of the Continental Oil Company (Conoco) and its Subsidiary Companies.* Ponca City, Okla.: Conoco, Inc., 1946. Hagley Museum and Library, Wilmington, Del.

―――. *Annual Report of the Continental Oil Company (Conoco) and its Subsidiary Companies.* Ponca City, Okla.: Conoco, Inc., 1950. Hagley Museum and Library, Wilmington, Del.

Coolidge, Calvin. "A Nation of Homeowners." *The Delineator*, October 1922, 16–17.

Cooke, Alistair. *The American Home Front: 1941–1942*. New York: Grove, 2006.

Coronil, Fernando. *The Magical State: Nature, Money and Modernity in Venezuela.* Chicago, Ill.: University of Chicago Press, 1997.

Cost of Living Council. *Inflation: On Prices and Wages and Running Amok.* Washington, D.C.: Government Printing Office, 1973.

Cowan, Ruth Schwartz. *More Work for Mother: The Ironies of Household Technology from the Open Hearth to the Microwave.* New York: Basic Books, 1983.

Cowie, Jefferson. *Stayin' Alive: The 1970s and the Last Days of the Working Class.* New York: New Press, 2010.

Crosby, Alfred. *Children of the Sun: A History of Humanity's Unappeasable Appetite for Energy.* New York: W. W. Norton, 2006.

Crow, Patrick. "U.S. Industry Girding for Battle against Clinton Energy Tax Plan." *Oil and Gas Journal*, March 1, 1993.

―――. "U.S. Senate Deficit Bill Shifts Focus to Transport Fuels Taxes, Spending Cuts." *Oil and Gas Journal*, June 21, 1993.

Cruse, Kevin M. *White Flight: Atlanta and the Making of Modern Conservatism.* Princeton, N.J.: Princeton University Press, 2005.

Daily Herald. "Letter—Taken for a Ride." *The Daily Herald*, July 4, 1979, 10.

Daily News-Record. "Letter to the Editor: Corporate Power." *Daily News-Record*, May 3, 1979, 6.

Dalla Costa, Mariarosa, and F. Giocanna, eds. *Women, Development, and Labor of Reproduction: Struggles and Movements.* Trenton, N.J.: Africa World Press, 1999.

Dalla Costa, Mariarosa, and Selma James, eds. *The Power of Woman and the Subversion of Community.* Bristol: Falling Wall Press, 1972.

Dallas Morning News. "Editorial: State's Rights." *Dallas Morning News,* November 24, 1939.

Davis, Mike. *City of Quartz: Excavating the Future in Los Angeles.* London: Verso, 1990.

———. "'Fordism' in Crisis: A Review of Michel Aglietta's *Regulation et Crises: L'Expérience des États Unis.*" *Review* 2, no. 2 (1978): 207–69.

———. *Prisoners of the American Dream: Politics and Economy in the History of the American Working Class.* London: Verso, 1986.

Debeir, Jean-Claude, Jean-Paul Deleage, and Daniel Hemery. *In the Servitude of Power: Energy and Civilization through the Ages.* London: Zed, 1991.

Decker, Jeffrey Louis. *Made In America: Self-Styled Success from Horatio Alger to Oprah Winfrey.* Minneapolis: University of Minnesota Press, 1997.

De Chazeau, Melvin G., and Alfred E. Khan. *Integration and Competition in the Petroleum Industry.* New Haven, Conn.: Yale University Press, 1959.

De Janvry, Alain. *The Agrarian Question and Reformism in Latin America.* Baltimore, Md.: Johns Hopkins University Press, 1981.

Deka, Devajyoti. "Social and Environmental Justice Issues in Urban Transportation." In *Urban Transportation Geography,* edited by Susan Hanson and Genevieve Giuliano, 332–55. 3rd ed. New York: Guilford, 2004.

The Delineator. "Better Homes in America" *The Delineator,* June 1923, 2.

Dickstein, Morris. *Dancing in the Dark: A Cultural History of the Great Depression.* New York: W. W. Norton, 2009.

Dochuk, Darren. "Blessed by Oil, Cursed with Crude: God and Black Gold in the American Southwest." *The Journal of American History* 99, no. 1 (2012): 51–62.

Downey, Morgan. *Oil 101.* LaVergne, Tenn.: Wooden Table Press, 2009.

Doyle, Jack. *Riding the Dragon: Royal Dutch Shell and Fossil Fire.* Boston, Mass.: Environmental Health Fund, 2002.

Duany, Andres, Elizabeth Plater-Zyberk, and Jeff Speck. *Suburban Nation: The Rise of Sprawl and the Decline of the American Dream.* New York: North Point Press, 2000.

Dukes, Jeffrey S. "Burning Buried Sunshine: Human Consumption of Ancient Solar Energy." *Climatic Change* 61 (2003): 31–44.

Duménil, Gérard, and Dominique Lévy. "Neoliberal Income Trends," *New Left Review* 30 (November–December 2004): 105–33.

Duncan, Beverly, and Stanley Lieberson. *Metropolis and Region in Transition.* Beverly Hills, Calif.: Sage, 1970.

Dunning, Thad. *Crude Democracy: Natural Resource Wealth and Political Regimes.* New York: Cambridge University Press, 2008.

The Economist. "A Greener Bush." *The Economist,* February 13, 2003.

Edsall, Thomas, and Mary Edsall. *Chain Reaction: The Impact of Race, Rights and Taxes on American Politics.* New York: W. W. Norton, 1991.

Ekers, Michael, and Alex Loftus. "The Power of Water: Developing Dialogues between Foucault and Gramsci." *Environment and Planning D: Society and Space* 26, no. 4 (2008): 698–718.

Energy Information Administration. "Energy in Brief: What Are Greenhouse Gases and How Much Are Emitted by the United States?" June 21, 2012. http://www.eia.gov/cfapps/energy_in_brief/greenhouse_gas.cfm.

———. "Table 2.1f Electric Power Sector Energy Consumption, 1949–2010." http://www.eia.gov/totalenergy/data/annual/showtext.cfm?t=ptb0201f.

———. "How Dependent Are We on Foreign Oil?" July 13, 2012. http://www.eia.gov/energy_in_brief/article/foreign_oil_dependence.cfm.

———."U.S. Field Production of Crude Oil (Thousands of Barrels per Day) 1859–2011," http://www.eia.gov/dnav/pet/hist/LeafHandler.ashx?n=pet&s=mcrfpus2&f=m

———. "U.S. Imports by Country of Origin." http://www.eia.gov/dnav/pet/pet_move_impcus_a2_nus_ep00_im0_mbbl_m.htm.

———. "What Are the Major Sources and Users of Energy in the United States." May 18, 2012. http://www.eia.gov/energy_in_brief/article/major_energy_sources_and_users.cfm.

Engels, Freidrich. *The Condition of the Working Class in England.* London: Penguin, 2009.

———. *The Origins of the Family, Private Property and the State.* New York: International, 1972.

Engler, John. *The Brotherhood of Oil: Energy Policy and the Public Interest.* Chicago, Ill.: University of Chicago Press, 1977.

Enzenberger, Hans Magnus. "A Critique of Political Ecology." *New Left Review* 84 (1974): 3–32.

Erlandson, Dawn. "The BTU Tax Experience: What Happened and Why It Happened." *Pace Environmental Law Review* 12, no. 1 (1994): 173–84.

Esso Oilways. "Cartoon on Back of Front Cover." *Esso Oilways,* November 1950.

Faber, Daniel. *Capitalizing on Environmental Injustice: The Polluter-Industrial Complex in the Age of Globalization.* Lanham, Md.: Rowman and Littlefield, 2008.

Fantasia, Rick, and Kim Voss. *Hard Work: Remaking the American Labor Movement.* Berkeley: University of California Press, 2004.

Farrell, Alexander E., Hisham Zerriffi, and Hadi Dowlatabadi. "Energy Infrastructure and Security." *Annual Review of Environment and Resources* 29 (2004): 421–69.

Feagin, Joe R. *The Free Enterprise City: Houston in Political-Economic Perspective.* New Brunswick, N.J.: Rutgers University Press, 1988.

Featherstone, Mike, Nigel J. Thrift, and John Urry, eds. *Automobilities.* Thousand Oaks, Calif.: Sage, 2005.

Ferguson, James. *Global Shadows: Africa in the Neoliberal World Order.* Durham, N.C.: Duke University Press, 2006.

———. "Seeing Like and Oil Company: Space, Security, and Global Capital in Neoliberal Africa." *American Anthropologist* 107, no. 3 (2005): 377–82.

Ferguson, Miriam A. "Telegram to FDR, 23 May 1933." FDR Official File 56, Box 1, Franklin D. Roosevelt Library and Museum, Hyde Park, N.Y.

Fiege, Mark. *Republic of Nature: An Environmental History of the United States.* Seattle: University of Washington Press, 2012.

Findlay, R., and K. H. O'Rourke. "Commodity Market Integration, 1500–2000." In *Globalization in Historical Perspective*, edited by M. D. Bordo, A. M. Taylor, and J. G. Williamson, 13–64. Chicago: Chicago University Press, 2003.

Fine, Ben. *The World of Consumption: The Material and Cultural Revisited.* London: Routledge, 2002.

Fishman, Robert. *Bourgeois Utopias: The Rise and Fall of Suburbia.* New York: Basic Books, 1987.

Fitzsimmons, Margaret. "The Matter of Nature." *Antipode* 21, no. 2 (1989): 106–20.

Flanigan, James. "Manage Your Career As a Business." *New York Times*, October 14, 2009, B4.

Flink, James J. *The Car Culture.* Cambridge, Mass.: MIT Press, 1976.

Foner, Eric. *The Story of American Freedom.* New York: W. W. Norton, 1998.

Fortune. "The Market System and the Energy Crisis." *Fortune*, December 1973, 72.

Foster, John Bellamy, Brett Clark, and Richard York. *The Ecological Rift: Capitalism's War on the Earth.* New York: Monthly Review Press, 2010.

Foucault, Michel. *The Birth of Biopolitics: Lectures at the Collège de France, 1978–1979*, translated by Graham Burcell. New York: Palgrave Macmillan, 2008.

———. *The History of Sexuality, Vol. I: An Introduction.* New York: Pantheon, 1978.

———. *Security, Territory, Population, Lectures at the Collège De France, 1977–1978.* New York: Palgrave Macmillan, 2007.

Frank, Thomas. *The Conquest of Cool: Business Culture, Counterculture, and the Rise of Hip Consumerism.* Chicago: University of Chicago Press, 1997.

———. *What's the Matter with Kansas?: How Conservatives Won the Heart of America.* New York: Metropolitan Books, 2004.

Freudenberger, Richard. *Alcohol Fuel: A Guide to Making and Using Ethanol as a Renewable Fuel.* Gabriola Island, Canada: New Society, 2009.

Friedman, Milton. *The Counter-Revolution in Monetary Theory.* London: Institute of Economic Affairs, 1970.

Friedman, Milton, and Rose Friedman. *Free to Choose: A Personal Statement.* New York: Harcourt Brace Jovanovich, 1980.

Friedman, Thomas. "The Real Patriot Act." *New York Times*, October 5, 2003.

FSU News. "Higher Gas Prices Leave Many Workers Running on Empty." May 11, 2007. Accessed July 30, 2012, http://www.fsu.edu/news/2007/05/11/gas.prices.

Galbraith, Kate. "Panel Suggests Gas Tax." *New York Times*, February 26, 2009, B5.

Gans, Herbert. *The Levittowners: Ways of Life and Politics in a New Suburban Community.* New York: Knopf, 1967.

Garreau, Joel. *Edge City: Life on the New Frontier.* New York: Anchor Books, 1991.

Georgescu-Roegen, Nicholas. *The Entropy Law and the Economic Process.* Cambridge, Mass.: Harvard University Press, 1971.

Gimenez, Martha. "The Dialectics of Waged and Unwaged Work." In *Work Without Wages: Comparative Studies of Domestic Work and Self-Employment Within Capitalism,* edited by Jane L. Collins and Martha Gimenez, 25–46. Albany, N.Y.: SUNY Press, 1990.

Gingrich, Newt. *Drill Here, Drill Now, Pay Less: A Handbook for Slashing Gas Prices and Solving our Energy Crisis.* Washington, D.C.: Regnery, 2008.

Glaab, Charles Nelson, and A. Theodore Brown. *A History of Urban America.* New York: Macmillan, 1967.

Gladstone, Bernard. "Home Improvement: New Vinyl Sidings." *New York Times,* April 23, 1967.

Golden, S. "Op-Ed: Oil and the Economy: No Great Spur Seen in Arab Action, but Output and Prices are Factors." *New York Times,* March 15, 1974.

Gonzalez, George. A. *Urban Sprawl, Global Warming, and the Empire of Capital.* Albany, N.Y.: SUNY Press, 2009.

Good Housekeeping. "A New Way of Life in One Word: Plastics." *Good Housekeeping* 150 (April 1960): 84–94, 237–38.

Goodman, David, and Michael Redclift. *Refashioning Food: Food, Ecology, and Culture.* London: Routledge, 1991.

Gordon, Colin. *New Deals: Business, Labor and Politics in America, 1920–1935.* New York: Cambridge University Press, 1994.

Gore, Al. *Earth in the Balance: Ecology and the Human Spirit.* New York: Plume, 1993.

Gorz, André. *Farewell to the Working Class.* London: Pluto Press, 1982.

Gowan, Peter. *The Global Gamble: Washington's Faustian Bid for Global Dominance.* London: Verso, 1999.

Gramsci, Antonio. *Selections from the Prison Notebooks.* New York: International, 1971.

Greenberger, Martin. *Caught Unawares: The Energy Decade in Retrospect.* Cambridge, Mass.: Ballinger, 1983.

Greenspan, Alan. "The Impact of the 1973–1974 Oil Price Increase on the United States Economy to 1980." U.S. Council of Economic Advisors, Alan Greenspan, Box 48, Folder 1, Gerald Ford Presidential Library, Ann Arbor, Mich.

Guthman, Julie. "Commodified Meanings, Meaningful Commodities: Re-Thinking Production—Consumption Links through the Organic System of Provision." *Sociologia Ruralis* 42, no. 4 (2002): 295–311.

———. *Weighing In: Obesity, Food Justice, and the Limits of Capitalism.* Berkeley: University of California Press, 2011.

Guthman, Julie, and Melanie DuPuis. "Embodying Neoliberalism: Economy, Culture, and the Politics of Fat." *Environment and Planning D: Society and Space* 24, no. 3 (2006): 427–48.

Haberler, Gottfied. "Thoughts on Inflation: The Basic Forces, 23 September, 1974," Gottfried Haberler Papers, Box 45, The Hoover Institution, Stanford University, Palo Alto, Calif.

Hammar, Henrik, Asa Lofgren, and Thomas Sterner. "Political Economy Obstacles to Fuel Taxation." *The Energy Journal* 25, no. 3 (2004): 1–17.

Hannah, Matthew. "Biopower, Life, and Left Politics." *Antipode* 43, no. 4 (2011): 1034–55.

Hanson, Susan and Geraldine Pratt. *Gender, Work, and Space.* London: Routledge, 1995.

Hardt, Michael, and Antonio Negri. *Empire.* Cambridge, Mass.: Harvard University Press, 2000.

Harrington, Michael. *The Other America: Poverty in the United States.* New York: Touchstone, 1962.

Harris, Howell John. *The Right to Manage: Industrial Relations Policies of American Business in the 1940s.* Madison: University of Wisconsin Press, 1982.

Harrison, Bennett, and Barry Bluestone. *The Great U-Turn: Corporate Restructuring and the Polarizing of America.* New York: Basic Books, 1988.

Hartshorn, J. E. *Oil Trade: Prospects and Politics.* New York: Cambridge University Press, 1993.

Harvey, David. "Between Space and Time: Reflections on the Geographical Imagination." *Annals of the Association of American Geographers* 80, no. 3 (1990): 418–34.

———. *A Brief History of Neoliberalism.* Oxford: Oxford University Press, 2005.

———. *The Condition of Postmodernity: An Enquiry into the Origins of Cultural Change.* Oxford: Blackwell, 1989.

———. *Cosmopolitanism and the Geographies of Freedom.* New York: Columbia University Press, 2009.

———. *Justice, Nature and the Geography of Difference.* Oxford: Blackwell, 1996.

———. *The Limits to Capital.* Oxford: Blackwell, 1982.

———. *The New Imperialism.* New York: Oxford University Press, 2003.

———. "New Urbanism and the Communitarian Trap." *Harvard Design Magazine* 1 (Winter–Spring 1997): 1–3.

———. "Population, Resources, and the Ideology of Science." *Economic Geography* 50, no. 3 (1974): 256–77.

———. "The Right to the City." *New Left Review* 53 (September–October 2008): 23–40.

———. *Spaces of Global Capitalism: A Theory of Uneven Geographical Development.* London: Verso, 2006.

———. *The Urban Experience*. Oxford: Blackwell, 1989.

Hawken, Paul, Amory Lovins, and Hunter Lovins. *Natural Capitalism: Creating the Next Industrial Revolution*. Boston, Mass.: Little, Brown and Co., 1999.

Hawley, E. W. *The New Deal and the Problem of Monopoly: A Study in Economic Ambivalence*. Princeton, N.J.: Princeton University Press, 1966.

Hayden, Delores. *Redesigning the American Dream: The Future of Housing, Work and Family Life*. New York: W. W. Norton, 1984.

Hayek, Friedrich. *The Road to Serfdom*. Chicago, Ill.: University of Chicago Press, 1944.

Heard, Frances. "The Freedom to be Enterprising." *House Beautiful* 98, no. 11 (November 1956): 246–53.

Heilbroner, Robert. "Do Machines Make History?" *Technology and Culture* 8, no. 3 (1967): 335–45.

Heinberg, Richard. *The Party's Over: Oil, War, and the Fate of Industrial Societies*. Gabriola Island, Canada: New Society, 2003.

Hemmingsen, Emma. "At the Base of Hubbert's Peak: Grounding the Debate on Petroleum Scarcity." *Geoforum* 41, no. 4 (2010): 531–40.

Henderson, George. *California and the Fictions of Capital*. Philadelphia, Pa.: Temple University Press, 1999.

Heynen, Nik, James McCarthy, Scott Prudham, and Paul Robbins, eds. *Neoliberal Environments: False Promises and Unnatural Consequences*. London: Routledge, 2007.

High-Point Enterprise. "Letter: Rationing Would Be Better." *The High-Point Enterprise*, March 5, 1974, 4A.

Hirsch, Barry T., and David A. Macpherson. "Union Membership and Coverage Database from the Current Population Survey." http://unionstats.gsu.edu.

Holmstrom, Nancy. "Women's Work, the Family and Capitalism." *Science and Society* 45 (Summer 1981): 186–211.

Hoover, Herbert. "The Home as an Investment." *The Delineator*, October 1922, 17, 91.

Horowitz, Daniel. *Anxieties of Affluence: Critiques of Consumer Culture, 1939–1979*. Amherst: University of Massachusetts Press, 2004.

———. *Jimmy Carter and the Energy Crisis of the 1970s: The "Crisis of Confidence" Speech of July 15, 1979*. New York: Bedford/St. Martin's Press, 2005.

House Beautiful. "No Man Need Be Common, No Life Need Be Ordinary." *House Beautiful* 98, no. 11 (November 1956): 220–25.

Houston Chronicle. "Letter to the Editor: BTU Tax Is a Bad Idea." *Houston Chronicle*, May 27, 1993, A29.

Huber, Matthew T. "Enforcing Scarcity: Oil, Violence, and the Making of the Market." *Annals of the Association of American Geographers* 101, no. 4 (2011): 816–26.

Humphreys, Macartan, Jeffrey Sachs, and Joseph E Stiglitz, eds. *Escaping the Resource Curse*. New York: Columbia University Press, 2007.

Ickes, Harold. "Memo to FDR, 1 May 1933." FDR Official File 56, Box 1, Franklin D. Roosevelt Library and Museum, Hyde Park, N.Y.

———. *The Secret Diary of Harold L. Ickes: The First Thousand Days, 1933–1936*. New York: Simon and Schuster, 1953.

Jackson, Kenneth T. *Crabgrass Frontier: The Suburbanization of the United States*. New York: Oxford, 1985.

Jackson, Peter. "Local Consumption Cultures in a Globalizing World." *Transactions of the Institute of British Geographers* 29, no. 2 (2004): 165–78.

Jacobs, Meg. "The Conservative Struggle and the Energy Crisis." In *Rightward Bound: Making America Conservative in the 1970s*, edited by Bruce J. Schulman and Julian E. Zelizer, 193–209. Cambridge, Mass.: Harvard University Press, 2009.

———. *Pocketbook Politics: Economic Citizenship in 20th Century America*. Princeton, N.J.: Princeton University Press, 2005.

Jaffee, Daniel. *Brewing Justice: Fair Trade Coffee, Sustainability, and Survival*. Berkeley, Calif.: University of California Press, 2007.

Jakle, John A., and Keith A. Sculle. *The Gas Station in America*. Baltimore, Md.: Johns Hopkins University Press, 1994.

Jeffereys, Kent. "Letter to the Editor." *The Washington Times*, May 24, 1993, E2.

Jensen, Michael. "Inflation Replaces Energy as Nation's Main Concern." *New York Times*, July 14, 1974, 1.

Jevons, William Stanley. *The Coal Question: An Enquiry Concerning the Progress of the Nation and the Probable Exhaustion of our Coal Mines*. London: Macmillan, 1866.

Jhaveri, Nayna. "Petroimperialism: US Interests and the Iraq War." *Antipode* 36, no. 1 (2004): 2–11.

Jones, Christopher. "A Landscape of Energy Abundance: Anthracite Coal Canals and the Roots of American Fossil Fuel Dependence, 1820–1860." *Environmental History* 15, no. 3 (2010): 449–84.

Juhasz, Antonia. *The Tyranny of Oil: The World's Most Powerful Industry—and What We Must Do to Stop It*. New York: William Morrow, 2008.

Kaempffert, Waldemar. "Power for the Abundant Life." *New York Times*, August 23, 1936.

Kain, J. F. *Essays on Urban Spatial Structure*. Cambridge, Mass.: Ballinger, 1975.

Karl, Terry Lynn. *The Paradox of Plenty: Oil Booms and Petro-States*. Berkeley, Calif.: University of California Press, 1997.

Kashi, Ed, and Michael Watts. *The Curse of the Black Gold: 50 Years of Oil in the Niger Delta*. New York: Powerhouse Books, 2008.

Kaszynski, William. *The American Highway: The History and Culture of Roads in the United States*. Jefferson, N.C.: McFarland and Co., 2000.

Katz, Alyssa. *Our Lot: How Real Estate Came to Own Us*. New York: Bloomsbury, 2009.

Katz, Cindi. "Vagabond Capitalism and the Necessity of Social Reproduction." *Antipode* 33, no. 4 (2001): 709–28.

Kaufman, Leslie. "Americans Still Split on Global Warming, Poll Shows." June 9, 2011. *Green* (blog). http://green.blogs.nytimes.com.

Keefer, Thomas. "Fossil Fuels, Capitalism, and Class Struggle." *The Commoner* 13 (2009): 15–21.

Kerr, Clark. *Industrialism and Industrial Man.* Cambridge, Mass.: Harvard University Press, 1960.

Keohane, Robert O. *After Hegemony: Cooperation and Discord in the World Political Economy.* Princeton, N.J.: Princeton University Press, 1984.

Kimmel, Chad M. "'No Gas, My Ass!' Marking the End of the Postwar Period in Levittown." In *Second Suburb: Levittown, PA,* edited by Dianne Harris, 340–53. Pittsburgh, Pa.: University of Pittsburgh Press, 2010.

Klare, Michael. *Rising Powers, Shrinking Planet: The New Geopolitics of Energy.* New York: Holt, 2008.

———. *Blood and Oil: The Dangers and Consequences of America's Growing Dependency on Imported Petroleum.* New York: Metropolitan Books, 2004.

———. *Resource Wars: The New Landscape of Global Conflict.* New York: Henry Holt, 2001.

Klein, Naomi. "Capitalism vs. the Climate." *The Nation,* November 28, 2011.

———. *The Shock Doctrine: The Rise of Disaster Capitalism.* New York: Metropolitan, 2007.

Knight, John S. "Straight Talk on the Energy Crisis." *Lakeland Ledger,* November 13, 1973, 6A.

Knox, Paul L. *Metrourbia, USA.* New Brunswick, N.J.: Rutgers University Press, 2008.

Kobayashi, Audrey, and Linda Peake. "Racism out of Place: Thoughts on Whiteness and an Antiracist Geography in the New Millennium." *Annals of the Association of American Geographers* 90, no. 2 (2000): 392–403.

Krauss, Clifford. "Some Senate Democrats Push More Spending Cuts." *New York Times,* March 6, 1993, A1.

Krock, Arthur. "5 Cases Decided." *New York Times,* April 13, 1937, 1.

Kruse, Kevin M., and Thomas J. Sugrue, eds. *The New Suburban History.* Chicago, Ill.: University of Chicago Press, 2006.

Kunstler, James Howard. *The Long Emergency: Surviving the End of Oil, Climate Change, and Other Converging Catastrophes of the Twenty-First Century.* New York: Atlantic Monthly Press, 2005.

———. "Remarks." PetroCollapse Conference, New York, N.Y., October 5, 2005. http://www.kunstler.com.

Labban, Mazen. "Oil in Parallax: Scarcity, Markets, and the Financialization of Accumulation." *Geoforum* 41, no. 4 (2010): 541–52.

———. *Space, Oil, and Capital*. London: Routledge, 2008.

Lafsky, Melissa. "How Often Is the Gas Tax Raised? Most Americans Have No Clue." *The Infrastructurist*, January 21, 2010. Accessed July 30, 2012. http://www.infrastructurist.com/2010/01/21/how-often-is-the-gas-tax-raised-most-americans-have-noclue.

Landler, Mark, and Steven Lee Myers. "With $30 Billion Arms Deal, U.S. Bolsters Saudi Ties." *New York Times*, December 30, 2011, A10.

Landon, Alfred M. *America at the Crossroads*. Port Washington, N.Y.: Kennikat Press, 1971.

Lassiter, Matthew. *The Silent Majority: Suburban Politics in the Sunbelt South*. Princeton, N.J.: Princeton University Press, 2006.

Law, John, and Anne Marie Mol. "Notes on Materiality and Sociality." *The Sociological Review* 43, no. 2 (1995): 274–94.

Lazzarato, Mauruzio. "The Concepts of Life and Living in the Societies of Control." In *Deluze and the Social*, edited by Martin Fuglsang and Bent Meier Sorensen, 171–90. Edinburgh, U.K.: Edinburgh University Press, 2006.

Le Billon, Philippe, and Fouad El Khatib. "From Free Oil to 'Freedom Oil': Terrorism, War and US Geopolitics in the Persian Gulf." *Geopolitics* 9, no. 1 (2004): 109–37.

Lefebvre, Henri. *The Production of Space*. Translated by Donald Nicholson-Smith. Oxford: Blackwell, 1991.

———. *The Survival of Capitalism: Reproduction of the Relations of Production*. New York: St. Martins, 1973.

———. *The Urban Revolution*. Translated by Robert Bononno. Minneapolis: University of Minnesota Press, 2003.

Leffler, William L. *Petroleum Refining in Nontechnical Language*. 4th ed. Tulsa, Okla.: PennWell Books, 2008.

Lemke, Thomas. "'The Birth of Bio-Politics': Michel Foucault's Lecture at the Collège de France on Neo-Liberal Governmentality." *Economy and Society* 30, no. 2 (2001): 190–207.

Lerner, Steve. *Diamond: A Struggle for Environmental Justice in Louisiana's Chemical Corridor*. Cambridge, Mass.: MIT Press, 2005.

Levy, Walter. "Oil and the Decline of the West." *Foreign Affairs* 58, no. 5 (1980): 999–1015.

Libecap, Gary D. "The Political Economy of Crude Oil Cartelization in the United States, 1933–1972." *The Journal of Economic History* 49, no. 4 (1989): 833–55.

Lipow, Gar. "Emissions Trading: A Mixed Record with Plenty of Failures." February 20, 2007. http://www.grist.org.

Lockhart Post-Register. "Letter: Figures Fuel Shortage Will Be Overcome by Using Heads." *Lockhart Post-Register*, December 6, 1973, 2.

Loris, Nicolas, and Ben Lieberman. "The 2009 Energy Bill: Anti-Market and Anti-Consumer." http://www.heritage.org.

Los Angeles Times. "Easing the Jolt at the Pump." *Los Angeles Times,* August 15, 1975.

Lovejoy, Wallace F., and Paul T. Homan. *Economic Aspects of Oil Conservation Regulation.* Baltimore, Md.: Johns Hopkins University Press, 1967.

Low, Setha. *Behind the Gates: Life, Security, and the Pursuit of Happiness in Fortress America.* New York: Routledge, 2003.

Loyd, Jenna. "'Peace Is Our Only Shelter': Questioning Domesticities of Militarization and White Privilege." *Antipode* 43, no. 3 (2011): 845–73.

Lucia, Danny. "Bringing Misery out of Hiding: The Unemployed Movement of the 1930s." *International Socialist Review* 71 (May–June 2010). http://www.isreview.org/issues/71/feat-unemployed.shtml.

Maass, Peter. *Crude World: The Violent Twilight of Oil.* New York: Knopf, 2009.

MacIntyre, August A. "Why Pesticides Received Extensive Treatment in America: A Political Economy of Agricultural Pest Management to 1970." *Natural Resources Journal* 27 (Summer 1987): 534–77.

MacKenzie, Donald. "Marx and Machine." *Technology and Culture* 25, no. 3. (1984): 473–502.

Malakoff, D., and L. Lafitte. "Death by Suffocation in the Gulf of Mexico." *Science* 281, no. 5374 (1998): 190–92.

Mallet, Serge. *The New Working Class.* Translated by Andrée Shepard and Bob Shepard. Nottingham: Bertrand Russell Peace Foundation for Spokesman Books, 1975.

Mann, Geoff. *Our Daily Bread: Wages, Workers, and the Political Economy of the American West.* Chapel Hill: University of North Carolina Press, 2007.

Marcuse, Herbert. *One Dimensional Man: Studies in the Ideology of Advanced Industrial Society.* London and New York: Routledge, 1964.

Margonelli, Lisa. *Oil on the Brain: Petroleum's Long Strange Trip to Your Tank.* New York: Broadway Books, 2008.

Markowitz, Gerald, and David Rosner. *Deceit and Denial: The Deadly Politics of Industrial Pollution.* Berkeley and Los Angeles: University of California Press, 2002.

Marks, Robert. *The Origins of the Modern World: A Global and Ecological Narrative from the Fifteenth to Twenty-first Century.* Lanham, Md.: Rowman and Littlefield, 2002.

Markusen, Ann, Peter Hall, Scott Campbell, and Sabina Deitrick. *The Rise of the Gunbelt: The Military Remapping of Industrial America.* New York: Oxford University Press, 1991.

Martinez-Alier, Joan. *Ecological Economics: Energy, Environment and Society.* Oxford: Blackwell, 1987.

Marx, Karl. *Capital Volume 1.* Translated by Ben Fowkes. London: Penguin, [1867] 1976.

———. *Capital Volume 3.* Translated by David Fernbach. London: Penguin, [1894] 1981.

———. *Contribution to the Critique of Political Economy*. New York: International, [1859] 1979.

———. "Critique of the Gotha Program." In *Karl Marx: Selected Writings*, edited by Lawrence H. Simon, 315–32. Indianapolis, Ind.: Hackett, [1875] 1994.

———. *Grundrisse*. Translated by Martin Nicolaus. London: Penguin, [1857–58] 1973.

———. "On the Jewish Question." In *Early Writings*. Translated by Rodney Livingstone and Gregor Benton, 211–42. New York: Vintage, [1843] 1975.

———. *Pre-Capitalist Economic Formations*. Edited by E. Hobsbawm. Translated by J. Cohen. London: Lawrence and Wishart, [1857–58] 1964.

———. "Theses on Feuerbach." In *The Marx-Engels Reader*, edited by Robert C. Tucker, 143–45. New York: W. W. Norton, [1845] 1978.

———. *Wage Labour and Capital*. New York: International, [1847] 1933.

Marx, Karl, and Frederick Engels. *The German Ideology*. London: Lawrence and Wishart, [1845] 1970.

———. "Manifesto of the Communist Party." In *The Marx-Engels Reader*, edited by Robert Tucker, 469–500. New York: W. W. Norton, [1848] 1978.

Matles, James J., and James J. Higgins. *Them and Us: Struggles of a Rank-and-File Union*. Engelwood Cliffs, N.J.: Prentice-Hall, 1974.

Matusow, Allen J. *Nixon's Economy: Booms, Busts, Dollars, and Votes*. Lawrence: University of Kansas Press, 1998.

McCarthy, James. "First World Political Ecology: Lessons from the Wise Use Movement." *Environment and Planning A* 34, no. 7 (2002): 1281–302.

———. "Privatizing the Conditions of Production: Trade Agreements as Neoliberal Environmental Governance." *Geoforum* 35, no. 3 (2004): 327–41.

McElroy, John C. *For The Love of Oil: The Fleecing of the American Consumer by Big Oil Companies, Politicians, and Wallstreet Commodity Traders*. Bloomington, Ind.: Authorhouse, 2006.

McGirr, Lisa. *Suburban Warriors: The Origins of the New American Right*. Princeton, N.J.: Princeton University Press, 2001.

McGraw, Seamus. *The End of Country: Dispatches from the Frack Zone*. New York: Random House, 2011.

McKenzie, Evan. *Privatopia: Homeowners Associations and the Rise of the Rise of Residential Private Government*. New Haven, Conn.: Yale University Press, 1994.

McKibben, Bill. *Eaarth: Making a Life on a Tough New Planet*. New York: Henry Holt and Co., 2010.

McNally, David. *Global Slump: The Economics and Politics of Crisis and Resistance*. Oakland, Calif.: PM Press, 2011.

McNeill, J. R. *Something New under the Sun: An Environmental History of the 20th Century*. New York: W. W. Norton, 2000.

McShane, Clay. *Down the Asphalt Path: The Automobile and the American City.* New York: Columbia University Press, 1994.

Meadows, Donella H., Jorgen Randers, Dennis L. Meadows, and William W. Behrens. *The Limits to Growth: A Report for the Club of Rome's Project on the Predicament of Mankind.* New York: Universe, 1972.

Medvetz, Thomas. "The Strength of Weekly Ties: Relations of Material and Symbolic Exchange in the Conservative Movement." *Politics and Society* 34, no. 3 (2006): 343–68.

Meikle, Jeffrey L. *American Plastic: A Cultural History.* New Brunswick, N.J.: Rutgers University Press, 1995.

Merrill, Karen R. *The Oil Crisis of 1973–1974: A Brief History with Documents.* New York: Bedford/St. Martins, 2007.

Midnight Notes Collective, *Midnight Oil: Energy, Work and War, 1973–1992.* Brooklyn, N.Y.: Autonomedia, 1992.

Mills, Warner E. *Martial Law in East Texas.* Tuscaloosa: University of Alabama, 1960.

Mirowski, Phillip, and Dieter Plehwe, eds. *The Road to Mont Pèlerin: The Making of the Neoliberal Thought Collective.* Cambridge, Mass.: Harvard University Press, 2009.

Mitchell, D. "The S.U.V. Model of Citizenship: Floating Bubbles, Buffer Zones, and the Rise of the 'Purely Atomic' Individual." *Political Geography* 24, no. 1 (2005): 77–100.

Mitchell, Katharyne, Sallie A. Marston, and Cindi Katz, eds. *Life's Work: Geographies of Social Reproduction.* Oxford: Blackwell, 2004.

Mitchell, Timothy. *Carbon Democracy: Political Power in the Age of Oil.* London: Verso, 2011.

Mobil Corporation. "The BTU Tax Is a Bad Idea (advertisement)." *New York Times,* May 6, 1993, A27.

Mommer, Bernard. *Global Oil and the Nation State.* New York: Oxford University Press, 2002.

Moore, Donald. *Suffering for Territory: Race, Place, and Power in Zimbabwe.* Durham, N.C.: Duke University Press, 2005.

Moore, Jason. "The End of the Road? Agricultural Revolutions in the Capitalist World-Ecology." *Journal of Agrarian Change* 10, no. 3 (2010): 389–413.

———. "Transcending the Metabolic Rift: A Theory of Crisis in the Capitalist World Ecology." *Journal of Peasant Studies* 38, no. 1 (2011): 1–46.

Mouawad, Jad. "West Adds Strain to Iran's Lifeline." *New York Times,* February 13, 2007.

Mullin, Gerard. "Drama at the Crossroads: The Levittown Gas Riots." *Levittown Leader.* July 14, 2011. Accessed July 30, 2012. http://www.levittown leader.com/Articles-Hometown-Local-History-c-2011-07-14-188244.114126 -Drama-at-the-Crossroads.html.

Mumford, Lewis. *Technics and Civilization.* Chicago, Ill.: University of Chicago Press, 1934.

Nash, Gerald D. *United States Oil Policy: 1890–1964, Business and Government in Twentieth Century America.* Pittsburgh, Pa.: University of Pittsburgh Press, 1968.

National Resources Committee. *Energy Resources and National Policy.* Washington, D.C.: U.S. Government Printing Office, 1939.

National Review. "What's Ahead: Hot War and Cold Hoses." *National Review Bulletin,* November 2, 1973, B165.

New York Times. "Broad Powers Proposed for Ickes" *New York Times,* May 1, 1934, 19.

———. "Capitalism Doomed, Say Fascist and Red." *New York Times,* March 5, 1934, 18.

———. "Editorial: An Age of Scarcity." *New York Times,* April 7, 1974.

———. "Editorial: The 'Energy Recession.'" *New York Times,* December 1, 1975.

———. "How the Energy Tax Would Affect Three Families." *New York Times,* February 27, 1993, L33.

———. "Ickes Hails National Planning." *New York Times,* October 14, 1934, SM1.

———. "Ickes Threatens Land Seizures." *New York Times,* November 15, 1934.

———. "Life in It Yet." *New York Times,* December 16, 1934, E4.

———. "Living Costs Are Held Top Problem in U.S. a Gallup Poll Reports." *New York Times,* July 30, 1978.

———. "The President's Message." *New York Times,* April 14, 1933, 2.

———. "Roosevelt Signs the Wagner Bill as 'Just to Labor.'" *New York Times,* July 6, 1935, 1.

———. "Texas Oil Rate at 100% for First Time since '48." *New York Times,* March 17, 1972.

———. "Text of President Roosevelt's Recovery Program Message to Congress." *New York Times,* April 15, 1938, 12.

———. "Text of Roosevelt Address." *New York Times,* June 28, 1936.

———. "Wagner Sees Law Ending Labor War." *New York Times,* May 9, 1937, 12.

Nickerson, Michelle, and Darren Dochuk, eds. *Sunbelt Rising: The Politics of Space, Place, and Region.* Philadelphia: Pennsylvania University Press, 2011.

Nikiforuk, Andrew. *Tar Sands: Dirty Oil and the Future of a Continent.* Vancouver, Canada: Greystone Books, 2010.

Nitzan, Jonathan, and Simon Bichler. *The Global Political Economy of Israel.* London: Pluto Press, 2002.

Nixon, Richard. "The Continuing Fight against Inflation." Address to the Nation, October 7, 1971. http://www.presidency.ucsb.edu/ws/index.php?pid=3183.

Noble, David. *Forces of Production: A Social History Automation.* New York: Knopf, 1984.

Nordhauser, Norman E. *The Quest for Stability: Domestic Oil Regulation, 1917–1935.* New York: Garland, 1979.

Nore, Peter, and Terisa Turner, eds., *Oil and Class Struggle.* London: Zed, 1980.

North, Peter. "Eco-Localisation as a Progressive Response to Peak Oil and Climate Change—A Sympathetic Critique." *Geoforum* 41, no. 4 (2010): 585–94.

Nye, David. *American Technological Sublime.* Cambridge, Mass.: MIT Press, 1996.

———. *Consuming Power: A Social History of American Energies.* Cambridge, Mass.: MIT Press, 1998.

———. *Electrifying America: Social Meanings of a New Technology, 1880–1940.* Cambridge, Mass.: MIT Press, 1992.

Oakland Tribune. "More Areas Planning Gas Rationing." *The Oakland Tribune,* February 10, 1974, 1.

Obama, Barack. "Remarks of Senator Barack Obama: Town Hall on Energy, Cedar Rapids, IA, 31 July 2008." http://2008election.procon.org.

———. "State of the Union Address, January 24, 2012." http://www.whitehouse.gov/state-of-the-union-2012.

Observer-Reporter. "Nader Again Charges Energy Crisis 'Phony.'" *Observer-Reporter,* March 22, 1974, A-8.

O'Connor, Harvey. *Empire of Oil.* New York: Monthly Review, 1955.

———. *World Crisis in Oil.* New York: Monthly Review, 1962.

O'Connor, James. *Natural Causes: Essays in Ecological Marxism.* New York: Guilford, 1998.

Oil and Gas Journal. "Refinery Strikes Suggest Plants Can Be Run with Still Fewer Men." *Oil and Gas Journal,* November 12, 1962.

O'Keefe, William. "Letter to the Editor." *Christian Science Monitor* 20, March 19, 1993, 20.

Olien, Roger M., and Diana Davids Hinton. *Wildcatters: Texas Independent Oil Men.* College Station: Texas A&M University Press, 2007.

Olien, Diana, and Roger Olien. "Running Out of Oil: Discourse and Public Policy, 1909–1929." *Business and Economic History* 22, no. 2 (1993): 36–66.

Ollman, Bertell. *Alienation: Marx's Conception of Man in Capitalist Society.* New York: Cambridge University Press, 1976.

Olmstead, A. L., and P. W. Rhode. "Reshaping the Landscape: The Impact and Diffusion of the Tractor in American Agriculture, 1910–1960." *Journal of Economic History* 61 (2001): 663–98.

O'Rourke, Dara, and Sarah Connolly. "Just Oil? The Distribution of Environmental and Social Impacts of Oil Production and Consumption." *Annual Review of Environment and Resources* 28 (2003): 587–617.

Ó Tuathail, Gearóid. *Critical Geopolitics: The Politics of Writing Global Space.* Minneapolis: University of Minnesota Press, 1996.

Painter, David S. "Oil and the Marshall Plan." *Business History Review* 58, no. 3 (1984): 359–83.

Palast, Greg. *Vultures' Picnic: In Pursuit of Petroleum Pigs, Power Pirates, and High-Finance Carnivores.* New York: Dutton Adult, 2011.

Panzieri, Raniero. "The Capitalist Use of Machinery: Marx versus the 'Objectivists.'" In *Outlines of a Critique of Technology,* edited by Phil Slater, 44–68. London: Humanities, 1980.

Passell, Peter. "Cheapest Protection of Nature May Lie in Taxes, Not Laws." *New York Times,* November 24, 1992, C1.

Pear, Robert. "After Three Decades, Tax Credit for Ethanol Expires." *New York Times,* January 1, 2012, A11.

Peck, Jamie. *Constructions of Neoliberal Reason.* New York: Oxford University Press, 2010.

Peck, Jamie, and Adam Tickell. "Accumulation, Regulation, and the Geographies of Post-Fordism." *Progress in Human Geography* 16, no. 2 (1992): 190–218.

———. "Searching for a New Institutional Fix: The After-Fordist Crisis and the Global-Local Disorder." In *Post-Fordism: A Reader,* edited by Ash Amin 280–315. Oxford: Blackwell, 1994.

Peck, Jamie, Nik Theodore, and Neil Brenner. "Postneoliberalism and its Discontents." *Antipode* 41, no. s1 (2010): 94–116.

Peet, Richard, and Elaine Hartwick. *Theories of Development: Contentions, Arguments, Alternatives.* New York: Guilford, 2009.

Peet, Richard, and Michael Watts, eds. *Liberation Ecologies: Environment, Development, Social Movements.* 2nd ed. London: Routledge, 2004.

Penrose, Edith T. *The Large International Firm in Developing Countries: The International Petroleum Industry.* Cambridge, Mass.: MIT Press, 1968.

Perry, David C., and Alfred J. Watkins, eds. *The Rise of the Sunbelt Cities.* Thousand Oaks, Calif.: Sage, 1977.

Peterson, D. J., and Sergej Mahnovski. *New Forces at Work in Refining: Industry Views of Critical Business and Operations Trends.* Santa Monica, Calif.: Rand, 2003.

Phillips, Kevin. *The Emerging Republican Majority.* New Rochelle, N.Y.: Arlington House, 1969.

Pianin, Eric, and David S. Hilzenrath. "Hill Agrees to Raise Gas Tax 4.3 Cents: Accord Clears Big Hurdle for Budget." *Washington Post,* July 30, 1993, A1.

Piven, Francis Fox, and Richard A. Cloward. *Poor People's Movements: Why They Succeed, How They Fail.* New York: Pantheon, 1977.

Podobnik, Bruce. *Global Energy Shifts: Fostering Sustainability in a Turbulent Age.* Philadelphia, Pa.: Temple University Press, 2006.

Polanyi, Karl. *The Great Transformation: The Political and Economic Origins of Our Time.* Boston, Mass.: Beacon Press, 1944.

Pollan, Michael. *The Omnivore's Dilemma: A Natural History of Four Meals.* London: Penguin, 2006.

Pomeranz, Kenneth. *The Great Divergence: China, Europe and the Making of the Modern World Economy.* Princeton, N.J.: Princeton University Press, 2000.

Pomfret, John P. "Shell Strike End Set after a Year." *New York Times,* August 5, 1963, 10.

Postone, Moishe. *Time, Labor, and Social Domination: A Reinterpretation of Marx's Critical Theory.* New York: Cambridge University Press, 1993.

Powell, Michael. "Obama Says He Would Agree to Some Drilling." *New York Times,* August 3, 2008.

President's Materials Policy Commission. *Resources for Freedom: A Report to the President.* Washington, D.C.: Government Printing Office, 1952.

Princen, Thomas, Michael Maniates, and Ken Conca, eds. *Confronting Consumption.* Cambridge, Mass.: MIT Press, 2002.

Prindle, David F. *Petroleum Politics and the Texas Railroad Commission.* Austin: University of Texas Press, 1981.

Prudham, Scott. *Knock on Wood: Nature as Commodity in Douglas-Fir Country.* London: Routledge, 2005.

Pulido, Laura. *Black, Brown, Yellow, and Left: Radical Activism in Los Angeles.* Berkeley: University of California Press, 2006.

Putman, George Palmer, and Nell Shipman. *Hot Oil.* New York: Greenberg, 1935.

Rabinbach, Anson. *The Human Motor: Energy, Fatigue, and the Origins of Modernity.* New York: Basic Books, 1990.

Ranii, David, and John Murawski. "$6.55, The Ups, Downs of New Wage: For N.C. Workers, It's 40 Cents More Per Hour. For Employers, It's a Tough Time to Raise Costs." *Charlotte Observer,* A1.

Read, Jason. *The Micro-Politics of Capital: Marx and a Pre-History of the Present.* Albany, N.Y.: SUNY Press, 2003.

Reagan, Ronald. "Op-Ed—Exploring New Energy Sources." *Long Beach Press-Telegram,* November 7, 1975, 22.

———. "Radio Commentary: Inflation." August 15, 1977, Box 13, Pre-Presidential Papers, Ronald Reagan Presidential Library, Simi Valley, Calif.

Redman, James. *Human Impacts on Ancient Environments.* Tucson: University of Arizona Press, 1999.

Register. "America's Foundation Is the Land of Opportunity." *The Register* 27 (August 1980): C12.

———. "Letter: Energy Hubbub? Go Back to Basics." *The Register,* October 4, 1981, K11.

Repetto, Robert, Roger Dower, Robin Jenkins, and Jacqueline Geoghegan. *Green Fees: How a Tax Shift Can Work for the Environment and the Economy.* Washington, D.C.: World Resources Institute, 1992.

Retort. *Afflicted Powers: Capital and Spectacle in a New Age of War.* London: Verso, 2005.

Reynolds, Alan. "The Case against Wage and Price Controls." *National Review,* September 24, 1971, 1051–55.

Richman, Al. "Public Attitudes toward the Energy Crisis." *The Public Opinion Quarterly* 43, no. 4 (1979): 576–85.

Robin, Corey. *The Reactionary Mind: Conservatism from Edmund Burke to Sarah Palin.* Oxford: Oxford University Press, 2011.

———. "Reclaiming the Politics of Freedom." *The Nation* 25 (April 2011).

Rodgers, Heather. *Green Gone Wrong: How Our Economy Is Undermining the Environmental Revolution.* New York: Scribner, 2010.

Rome, Adam. *The Bulldozer in the Countryside: Suburban Sprawl and the Rise of American Environmentalism.* Cambridge, UK: Cambridge University Press, 2001.

Roosevelt, Franklin Delano. "Inauguration Speech, 20 January, 1937." Accessed July 5, 2010. http://historymatters.gmu.edu/d/5105.

———. "Letter from FDR to John O'Donnell Congrats for Commemoration of Diamond Oil in PA, 20 August 1934," FDR Personal File 1719, Franklin D. Roosevelt Presidential Library and Museum, Hyde Park, N.Y.

———. "Statement on Interstate Oil Compact, 17 May 1935," FDR Official File 1585, FDR Official File—Interstate Oil Compact Commission. Franklin D. Roosevelt Presidential Library and Museum, Hyde Park, N.Y.

Ross, Andrew. *The Celebration Chronicles: Life, Liberty, and the Pursuit of Property Value in Disney's New Town.* New York: Ballantine, 1999.

Ross, Arthur. "OPEC's Challenge to the West." *Washington Quarterly* 3, no. 1 (1980): 50–57.

Ross, Michael. *The Oil Curse: How Petroleum Wealth Shapes the Development of Nations.* Princeton, N.J.: Princeton University Press, 2012.

Russell, Edmund, James Allison, Thomas Finger, John K. Brown, Brian Balogh, and W. Bernard Carlson. "The Nature of Power: Synthesizing the History of Technology and Environmental History." *Technology and Culture* 52 (2011): 246–59.

Rutledge, Ian. *Addicted to Oil: America's Relentless Drive for Energy Security.* New York: I. B. Tauris, 2005.

———. "Profitability and Supply Price in the US Domestic Oil Industry: Implications for the Political Economy of Oil in the Twenty-First Century." *Cambridge Journal of Economics* 27 (2003): 1–23.

Ryan, William J. "'Oil Weapon' of Arabs Stronger than Armies." *Abilene Reporter News*, November 23, 1973, 10.

Sabin, Paul. *Crude Politics: The California Oil Market, 1900–1940.* Berkeley: University of California Press, 2005.

Salpukas, Agis. "Going for the Kill on the Energy Tax Plan." *New York Times*, June 5, 1993, 37.

Sampson, Anthony. *The Seven Sisters: The Great Oil Companies and the World They Made.* London: Hodder and Stoughton, 1975.

Sarasota Herald-Tribune. "Depth of America's Energy Crisis Called Endemic and Also Incurable." *Sarasota Herald-Tribune*, April 23, 1972, E1.

Sawyer, Suzana. *Crude Chronicles: Indigenous Politics, Multinational Oil, and Neoliberalism in Ecuador.* Durham, N.C.: Duke University Press, 2004.

Sayer, Derek. *The Violence of Abstraction.* Oxford: Blackwell, 1987.

Schapiro, Mark. "Toxic Inaction: Why Poisonous, Unregulated Chemicals End Up in Our Blood." *Harpers*, October 2007, 78–83.

Schlosser, Eric. *Fast Food Nation: The Dark Side of the All-American Meal.* New York: Houghton Mifflin, 2001.

Schulman, Bruce J. *From Cotton Belt to Sunbelt: Federal Policy, Economic Development, and the Transformation of the South 1938–1980.* Durham, N.C.: Duke University Press, 1994.

———. *The Seventies: The Great Shift in American Culture, Society and Politics.* New York: Free Press, 2001.

Schulman, Bruce, and Julian Zelizer, eds. *Rightward Bound: Making America Conservative in the 1970s.* Cambridge, Mass.: Harvard University Press, 2009.

Schultze, Charles A. "Recovery Now, Relapse Ahead: Another Oil Recession." *The New Republic*, June 5 and 12, 1975, 8–10.

Seattle Times. "Letter to the Editor: Life with Cap-and-Trade Means Economy Will Sink." *Seattle Times*, July 1, 2009.

Selier, Cotton. *Republic of Drivers: A Cultural History of Automobility.* Chicago, Ill.: University of Chicago Press, 2008.

Shabecoff, Phillip. "A Quiet and behind the Scenes Drive." *The Times-News*, January 29, 1983, 4.

Sharp, Joanne. "Publishing American Identity: Popular Geopolitics, Myth and *The Reader's Digest.*" *Political Geography* 12, no. 6 (1993): 491–503.

Shaffer, Butler D. "'Energy Crisis': The Highway to Government Omnipotence." *The Register*, April 14, 1977, D8.

Shwartzman, David. "Ecosocialism or Ecocatastrophe?" *Capitalism, Nature, Socialism* 20, no. 1 (2009): 6–33.

Silliman, Benjamin, Jr. *Report on the Rock Oil, or Petroleum.* New Haven, Conn.: J. H. Benham's Steam Power Press, 1855.

Simmons, Matthew. *Twilight in the Desert: The Coming Saudi Oil Shock and the World Economy.* Hoboken, N.J.: Wiley, 2005.

Simon, William. "Statement of William Simon before the House Interstate and Foreign Commerce Subcommittee on Energy and Power, 2/17/75." Box 2, Policy Subject Files of Sidney Jones, National Archives, College Park, Md.

Simpson's Leader Times. "Shortages Everywhere." *Simpson's Leader Times*, January 10, 1974, 6.

Slotboom, H. W. "Plentitude from Petroleum." *New Scientist* 399 (July 9, 1964): 89–90.

Smil, Vaclav. *Energy in World History.* Boulder, Colo.: Westview, 1994.

———. *Enriching the Earth: Fritz Haber, Carl Bosch and the Transformation of World Food Production.* Cambridge, Mass.: MIT Press, 2001.

———. *Oil: A Beginner's Guide.* Oxford: Oneworld, 2008.

———."Peak Oil: A Catastrophic Cult and Complex Realities." *WorldWatch* 19 (January–February 2006): 22–24.

———. "21st Century Energy: Some Sobering Thoughts." *OCED Observer* 258–59 (December 2006): 22–23.

Smith, Barry E. "Nitrogenase Reveals Its Inner Secrets." *Science* 297 (September 6, 2002): 1654–55.

Smith, Neil. "Remaking Scale: Competition, Cooperation in Prenational and Post-national Europe." In *Competitive European Peripheries*, edited by H. Eskelinen and F. Snickars, 123–56. Berlin: Springer, 1995.

———. *Uneven Development: Nature, Capital and the Production of Space*. Athens: University of Georgia Press, 2009.

Smith, Thomas V., and Robert A. Taft. *Foundations of Democracy: A Series of Debates*. New York: Knopf, 1939.

Smith, T. V. "The People's Capitalism." *House Beautiful* 98, no. 11 (November 1956): 226, 317.

Spitz, Peter H. *Petrochemicals: The Rise of an Industry*. New York: Wiley, 1991.

Standard Oil Company of California. *Annual Report, Standard Oil Company of California, 1943*. Hagley Museum and Library, Wilmington, Del.

Standard Oil of New Jersey. "Standard Oil–New Jersey 75th Anniversary Entertainment Special." The Paley Center for Media, New York.

Starosta, Guido. "Global Commodity Chains and the Marxian Law of Value." *Antipode* 42, no. 2 (2010): 433–65.

Steffen, Will, Paul J. Crutzen, John R. McNeill. "The Anthropocene: Are Humans Now Overwhelming the Great Forces of Nature?" *AMBIO: A Journal of the Human Environment* 36, no. 8 (2007): 614–21.

Steinberg, Ted. *Nature Incorporated: Industrialization and the Waters of New England*. Amherst: University of Massachusetts Press, 1991.

———. "Can Capitalism Save the Planet? On the Origins of Green Liberalism." *Radical History Review* 107 (2010): 7–24.

Stern, Paul C., Thomas Dietz, Vernon W. Ruttan, Robert H. Socolow, and James L. Sweeney, eds. *Environmentally Significant Consumption: New Research Directions*. Washington, D.C.: National Academy Press, 1997.

Stevens, William K. "Gasoline Shortages Are Forcing Exurbanites to Readjust Their Life-Style." *New York Times*, February 7, 1974.

Stokes, Doug, and Sam Raphael. *Global Energy Security and American Hegemony*. Baltimore, Md.: Johns Hopkins University Press, 2010.

Stolberg, Sheryl Gay. "Bush's Speech Prod's Middle East Leaders." *New York Times*, May 19, 2008.

———. "News Analysis: Will $4 Gasoline Trump a 27-Year-Old Ban?" *New York Times*, June 19, 2008.

St. Petersburg Times. "Letter to the Editor." *St. Petersburg Times*, February 19, 1993, A15.

———. "Letter to the Editor." *St. Petersburg Times,* June 4, 1993, A13.

Stranahan, Susan Q. "Running on Empty." *AARP Bulletin* 46, no. 9 (2005): 10–12.

Sward, Keith. *The Legend of Henry Ford.* New York: Rinehart, 1948.

Tamminen, Terry. *Lives per Gallon: The True Cost of Our Oil Addiction.* Washington, D.C.: Island Press, 2006.

Tanham, James H. "Memo from James H. Tanham to Paul Ryan, April 30th, 1943." Alexander Sachs Papers, Box 132, Post-War Readjustments, Franklin D. Roosevelt Library, Hyde Park, N.Y.

Tarbell, Ida. *The History of the Standard Oil Company.* New York: McClure, Phillips & Co., 1904.

Taussig, Michael T. *The Devil and Commodity Fetishism in South America.* Chapel Hill: University of North Carolina Press, 1980.

Taylor, Evelyn S. *P.A.T.C.O. and Reagan: An American Tragedy: The Air Traffic Controllers' Strike of 1981.* Bloomington, Ind.: Authorhouse, 2011.

Taylor, Frederick. *The Principles of Scientific Management.* New York: Harper and Brothers, 1911.

Taylor, Margaret, Edward S. Rubin, and David A. Hounshell. "Regulation as the Mother of Invention: The Case of SO2 Control." *Law and Policy,* 27, no. 2 (2005): 348–78.

Teamsters Union. "1934 Minnesota Strike." http://www.teamster.org/history/teamster-history/1934.

Terkel, Studs. *Hard Times: An Oral History of the Great Depression.* New York: Pantheon, 1970.

Terranova, Tiziana. "Another Life: The Nature and Political Economy of Foucault's Genealogy of Biopolitics." *Theory, Culture, & Society* 26, no. 6: 234–62.

Texas State Archives. "Oil—Martial Law in East Texas, August 15–21, 1931." Ross Sterling, Governor Records, Box 301-457, Folder 1, Texas State Archives, Austin, Tex.

Thompson, Ernest O. "Op-Ed: Rights of States to Regulate Oil and Gas Production: Status as Local Industry Not Subject to Interstate Control by Federal Government Is Urged by Texas Railroad Commissioner." *The United States Daily,* December 20, 1932.

———. "Statement of Thompson on the Thomas Federal Oil Control Bill." Texas Railroad Commission, Commissioner's Records, E. O. Thompson, Box 4/3/330, Texas State Archives, Austin, Tex.

Thompson, Derek. "Gas Prices around the World: Cheaper Than Water and $10 a Gallon." *The Atlantic.* May 3, 2011, http://www.theatlantic.com/business/archive/2011/05/gas-prices-around-the-world-cheaper-than-water-i-and-i-10-a-gallon/238226/

Thornton, W. W. *The Law Relating to Oil and Gas.* Cincinnati, Ohio: W. H. Anderson, 1918.

Time. "Gas Fever: Happiness Is a Full Tank." *Time,* February 18, 1974, 35.

Titenberg, Tom, and Lynne Lewis. *Environmental Economics and Policy*. 6th ed. Boston, Mass.: Pearson, 2010.

Tulley, Andew, III. "Police Placed at Corner to Prevent Gasoline Riot." *Frederick Daily Leader*, June, 26, 1979, 3.

Tyler Courier Times Telegraph. "Editorial." *Tyler Courier Times Telegraph*, December 2, 1934, 9.

Uchitelle, Louis, and Megan Thee. "Americans Are Cautiously Open to Gas Tax Rise, Poll Shows." *New York Times*, February 28, 2006.

United Press International. "Rigs Tie up Bucks County Highways." *Tyrone Daily Herald*, June 28, 1979, 4.

United States Department of Agriculture. *Per Capita Food Consumption Data System*. Washington, D.C.: Economic Research Service, 2002.

United States Department of Transportation. *Home to Work Trips and Travel, 1977 Personal Transportation Survey*. Washington, D.C.: Federal Highway Administration, 1980.

Urbina, Ian. "Learning Too Late of the Perils in Gas Well Leases." *New York Times*, December 2, 2011, A1.

Varangis, Panayotis N., Takamasa Akiyama, and Donald Mitchell. *Managing Commodity Booms and Busts*. Washington, D.C.: World Bank, 1995.

Vernon, Raymond. "The Influence of the U.S. Government upon Multinational Enterprises: The Case of Oil." In *The New Petroleum Order: From the Transnational Company to Relations between Governments*, edited by A. Ayoub, 44–79. Quebec, Canada: Presses de l'Université Laval, 1975.

Vietor, Richard H. K. *Energy Policy in America since 1945: A Study of Business-Government Relations*. New York: Cambridge University Press, 1984.

Virno, Paolo. "General Intellect." *Historical Materialism* 15, no. 3 (2007): 3–8.

Vitalis, Robert. *America's Kingdom: Mythmaking on the Saudi Oil Frontier*. Stanford, Calif.: Stanford University Press, 2007.

Wade, Robert. "The First-World Debt Crisis of 2007–2010 in Global Perspective." *Challenge* 51, no. 4 (2008): 23–54.

Wagner, Robert. "Wagner Defends Bill as Fulfillment of 7a." *New York Times*, May 26, 1935, E10.

Wajcman, Judy. *Feminism Confronts Technology*. Philadelphia, Pa.: Penn University Press, 1991.

Walker, R. B. J. *Inside/Outside: International Relations as Political Theory*. New York: Cambridge University Press, 1993.

Walker, Richard. "The Suburban Solution." PhD diss., Johns Hopkins University, 1977.

———. "A Theory of Suburbanization: Capitalism and the Construction of Urban Space in the United States." In *Urbanization and Urban Planning under Advanced Capitalist Societies*, edited by Michael Dear and Allen Scott, 383–430. New York: Methuen, 1981.

Wall Street Journal. "OP-ED: The Cap and Tax Fiction." *Wall Street Journal,* June 26, 2009, A12.

Wandling, Patricia, and Denise Foley. "117 Arrested, 100 Hurt in Bucks Riots." *The Daily Intelligencer,* June 25, 1979, 1, 2.

Warner, Sam B. *Streetcar Suburbs: The Process of Growth in Boston.* Cambridge, Mass.: Harvard University Press, 1978.

Watkins, T. H. *The Hungry Years: A Narrative History of the Great Depression.* New York: Henry Holt, 1999.

Watson, Thomas. "Oilmen Struggle to Keep High Political Profile." *Congressional Quarterly,* 1109–12.

Watts, Michael. "Empire of Oil: Capitalist Dispossession and the Scramble for Africa." *Monthly Review* 58, no. 4 (2006): 1–17.

———. "Oil as Money: The Devil's Excrement and the Spectacle of Black Gold." In *Reading Economic Geography,* edited by Trevor J. Barnes, Jamie Peck, Eric Sheppard, and Adam Tickell, 205–19. Oxford: Blackwell, 2004.

———. "Resource Curse? Governmentality, Oil and Power in the Niger Delta, Nigeria." *Geopolitics* 9, no. 1 (2004): 50–80.

Weber, Max. *The Protestant Work Ethic and the Spirit of Capitalism.* Mineola, N.Y.: Dover, 2003.

Weeks, Kathi. "Life within and against Work: Affective Labor, Feminist Critique, and Post-Fordist Politics." *Ephemera: Theory & Politics in Organization* 7, no. 1 (2007): 233–49.

Weeks, Linton. "Pumped Up: Are Americans Addicted to Oil?" *National Public Radio,* May 20, 2011. http://www.npr.org.

Wells, Christopher. "Fueling the Boom: Gasoline Taxes, Invisibility, and the Growth of the American Highway Infrastructure, 1919–1956." *Journal of American History* 99, no. 1 (2012): 72–81.

Wendling, Amy. *Karl Marx on Technology and Alienation.* New York: Palgrave Macmillan, 2009.

Wheatland, Thomas. *The Frankfurt School in Exile.* Minneapolis: University of Minnesota Press, 2009.

White, Richard. *The Organic Machine: Remaking the Columbia River.* New York: Hill and Wang, 1996.

Will, George. "Levittown Revisited." *Newsweek,* July 9, 1979, 84.

Williams, E. J. "The Impact of Technology on Employment in the Petroleum Refining Industry in Texas, 1947–1966." PhD diss. University of Texas at Austin, 1971.

Williams, Raymond. *Marxism and Literature.* New York: Oxford University Press, 1978.

———. *Television: Technology and Cultural Form.* London: Routledge, 1974.

Williamson Daily News. "Editorial: Cooking with Garbage." *Williamson Daily News,* January 25, 1974, 4.

Williamson, Harold F., and Arnold Daum. *The American Petroleum Industry Volume 1: The Age of Illumination, 1859–1899*. Evanston, Ill.: Northwestern University Press, 1959.

Williamson, Harold F., Ralph L. Andreano, Arnold R. Daum, and Gilbert C. Klose. *The American Petroleum Industry, Volume 2: The Age of Energy 1899–1959*. Evanston, Ill.: Northwestern University Press, 1963.

Wines, Michael. "Tax's Demise Illustrates the First Rule of Lobbying: Work, Work, Work." *New York Times,* June 14, 1993, A1.

Wolf, Richard. "Tax Revolt Is Picking up Steam." *USA Today,* June 4, 1993, A4.

Wolff, Richard D. *Capitalism Hits the Fan: The Global Economic Meltdown and What to Do about It.* Northampton, Mass.: Olive Branch Press, 2009.

World Bank. "Fossil Fuel Energy Consumption (% of total)." http://data.worldbank.org/indicator/EG.USE.COMM.FO.ZS.

Worster, Donald. *Dust Bowl: The Southern Plains in the 1930s.* New York: Oxford University Press, 1979.

Wrigley, E. A. *Continuity, Chance, and Change: The Character of the Industrial Revolution in Britain.* New York: Cambridge University Press, 1988.

———. *Energy and the English Industrial Revolution.* New York: Cambridge, 2010.

Wu, M., M. Mintz, M. Wang, and S. Arora. *Consumptive Water Use in the Production of Ethanol and Petroleum Gasoline.* Center for Transportation Research, Energy Systems Division, Argonne National Laboratory. Last modified January 2009. http://www.transportation.anl.gov/pdfs/AF/557.pdf.

Yago, Glenn. *The Decline of Transit: Urban Transportation in German and US Cities, 1900–1970.* New York: Cambridge University Press, 1984.

Yergin, Daniel. "How to Break the Cartel: Calling OPEC's Bluff." *The New Republic.* June 5 and 12, 1975, 13–16.

———. *The Prize: The Epic Quest for Oil, Money and Power.* New York: Free Press, 1991.

———. *The Quest: Energy, Security, and the Remaking of the Modern World.* New York: Penguin, 2011.

Zalik, Anna. "Liquefied Natural Gas and Fossil Capitalism." *Monthly Review* 60, no. 6, (2008): 41–53.

Zimmermann, Erich W. *Conservation in the Production of Petroleum: A Study in Industrial Control.* New Haven, Conn.: Yale University Press, 1957.

addiction to oil, ix–xii, 27, 41–42, 168–69
Aglietta, Michel, 23, 36, 86, 179n55
agro-fuels, 134, 184n60
All in the Family, 110–12
American Petroleum Institute (API), 72, 102, 144, 146, 155
"American way of life," 17; and commodities, 58, 131; and conservation, 51; and depression-era politics, 32–34; and entrepreneurial life, xiii–xv, 19–25, 64; and exclusion, 37, 39, 160–61; and gasoline stations, 135, 155–56; history of phrase, 33, 190n31; and home ownership, 38–40; and labor rights, 35; scarcity and limits to, 102; and social reproduction, xv, 82, 157–58; and war, 149–51
apolitical economy, 100, 120–22
asphalt. *See* bitumen
automation, 185n76; and Fordism, 30–32; and fossil fuels, 9, 12–16; and refineries, 62–63
automobile(s): and entrepreneurial life, xiv, 23–25, 73–77; and General Motors conspiracy, 27–28; and infrastructure, 40–43; and oil consumption, xi–x; and petroleum products, 73–77; and privatism, 94; and social reproduction, 17–18, 73–77. *See also* machines: internal-combustion engine; sport-utility vehicles; transportation
automobility. *See* automobile(s)

base-superstructure, 7, 160, 183n36, 183n44
"Big Government," 23, 99, 118–20, 122–27, 163
"Big Oil," 1, 5–6, 117–18, 127, 178n35, 182n30
biofuels. *See* agro-fuels
biopolitics: and the Bureau of Mines, 55–57; entrepreneurial life, 19–25; and food choices, 88–91; and Marxism, 7, 178n43
bitumen, 66, 77
Bureau of Mines (BOM), 54–57
Bush, George H. W., 141, 150
Bush, George W., 1, 21, 142, 148, 152
Canada, viii, 70, 155–56, 160–61, 176n20
cap and trade legislation, 145, 148–49, 212n57

capital: cultural politics of, xv, 14–16, 19; despotism of, xvii, 161; as distinct from capitalism, xv; forces of, 12–19; life as, 19–25, 73–74, 81

"capital-labor accord," xvii, 42, 62, 97, 179n55

Carter, Jimmy, 2, 98, 150

chemicals. See petrochemicals

Cheney, Dick, 2

China, viii, 70, 176n15

climate change, xvii–xviii, 9–10, 76, 132, 151–52, 158, 162, 165–67

coal: benefits over water power, 13, 185n78; and electricity, 178n42, 199n107; energy density of, 18, 184n50; and relief from the "land constraint," 10, 184n59; and steam engines, 12, 30, 73; transition from, 175–76n15. See also fossil fuels

Cold War, 72, 75

commodity chain analysis, 4

commodity futures. See oil futures

competition: and inflation, 113; and neoliberalism, 20, 99–100, 119, 125, 163–64; and the oil industry, 72–73, 117, 161; and overproduction, 49–50; and prorationing, 54–55, 58; and "the second contradiction," xvii

Conoco Oil Company, 42, 71

conservation: and market demand, 46–48, 54–57; and martial law, 49; and state versus federal control, 50–55

consumption deflator, 132, 139. See also ecological deflator

consumption of oil: as basis for conservation policy, 46–48, 54–57; and "cheap ecologies," 137–42; compared to rest of world, viii; and dependence on foreign oil, x, 103–8, 155–56, 176n20; and

entrepreneurial life, 23–25; and food, 86–90; and the gasoline station, 133–37; and General Motors conspiracy, 27–29; and the home, 77–86; and medical supplies, 89–92; and mobility, 73–77; and New Deal policies, 27–43; during oil crisis, 108–10; outstripping domestic supply, 101–3; and social reproduction, 16–19, 74, 85, 109–10; and transportation, xi, 10, 82

cost of living. See inflation

Cowie, Jefferson, 114, 137

Davis, Mike, 37, 94, 191n56, 192n86

dead ecologies, 13–14

dead labor, 13–15

debt, 23, 74, 81, 138

demand for oil: as basis for conservation policy, 46–48, 54–57. See also consumption of oil

depression. See Great Depression

"Drill, Baby, Drill," vii, ix, 151–52

East Texas oil field, 48–50, 59, 104

ecological deflator, 132, 139. See also consumption deflator

ecological economics, 11

Edsall, Thomas and Mary, 19, 121, 142–43

electricity, x, 19, 29–31, 82, 178n42, 199n107

embargo. See oil embargo

energy: and automation, 9, 12–16; difference from oil, ix; policy, 26, 29–30, 58, 125, 142–49, 153, 165, 168; and space, 7–9

"energy independence," 107

energy security, 103, 204n45

entrepreneurial life, xiv, 19–25; and American politics, xiv, 92; the body and, 86–92; and competition, 99–100, 119, 125; debt and, 23, 74,

81; home ownership and, 77–86; inflation and, 112; space and, 73–77; taxation and, 142

environmental impact: and chemicals, 69, 87, 89–92, 197n44; climate change, xvii–xviii, 9–10, 76, 132, 151–52, 158, 162, 165–67; and extraction, xi, 160–61, 182n27; and gas stations, 134; and refineries, 68–69

environmental justice, xi, 69, 160–61, 197n44, 212n57

everyday life: and food, 86–90; and the gasoline station, 133–37; and hegemony, 7–9; and the home, 77–86; and machines, 16–19; and medical supplies, 89–92; and mobility, 73–77; and New Deal policies, 27–43; power, 5–6, 182n32; social reproduction, 16–19

externalities, 144–45

Exxon (Esso), 52, 76–77, 79–80, 83, 85, 88, 90, 93

financialization, 126, 142

Fine, Ben, xix

food: and biopolitics, 86–90; prices, 137–40

Fordism: and standards of consumption, 88; and Taylorism, 30–32; and U.S. oil autarchy, 104–7

foreign oil, 103–8, 155–56, 176n20

formal subsumption: of labor under capital, 14–16, 186n86; of life under capital, 18–20

fossil fuels: and automation, 9, 12–16; and climate change, 9–10; and knowledge, 14; and land use, 10, 184n59; natural gas, 87, 152, 165, 192–93n94; oil, xix, 23, 73–74, 133; and the productive forces, 9–12, 186n79; and space, 10–12; and time, 9–10; versus water

power, 13, 185n78; and wage-labor, 13–16. See also coal

Foster, John Bellamy, xvii

Foucault, Michel, xiv, 19–25, 56, 64, 81, 95, 100, 125, 164, 178n43, 182n32, 188n118, 188n121, 198n80

fracking. See hydrofracking

Frank, Thomas, 22, 143, 215n32

freedom, xv, 18, 22, 33, 47, 74, 77, 79, 86, 109, 123–25, 131, 155–69

Friedman, Milton, 118–19, 205n82, 207n120

Friedman, Thomas, 144

fuel efficiency: and horsepower, 76–78; standards, ix, 131–32

gasoline: 19, 25, 43, 56, 71, 73, 76, 122, 133–37; and 1970s oil crisis, 97–98, 108–10; prices and politics, vii–ix, 129–31, 134–37; and refining, 66–67; taxes, vii–ix, 148–49

gasoline station, 133–37

General Motors: conspiracy, 27–28; "Futurama" exhibit, 41

geopolitics, 1–3, 5, 26, 103–8, 177n26, 177n29, 182n29

Gingrich, Newt, vii, 151–52

Gore, Al, ix, 144

Gramsci, Antonio, 8, 20, 23, 31–32, 158

Great Depression, 32–34; and oil crisis, 43–57

green consumption, 156, 162

Greenspan, Alan, 113

green taxes, 145–49

Gulf Oil, xii–xiii

Harvey, David, 2–5, 11, 103, 106, 116, 135, 138, 158, 162, 181n26, 187n105, 196n20, 204n54, 209n8, 214n11, 215n46

Hayek, Friedrich, 120–21, 125
health: and MBTE, 134; petroleum
    products, 86–91; and polyvinyl chlo-
    ride, 84, 197n44; and refineries, 69
highways, 40–43
historical materialism, 6–9
"hot oil," 43, 48, 52
housing: and entrepreneurial life,
    20; and New Deal, 38–40; and
    petroleum products, 77–86; and
    suburban politics, 120–22
Hubbert, M. King, 101. See also peak
    oil
Hussein, Saddam, 2, 150
hydrocarbons, xx, 65–73
hydrofracking, 152, 165, 192–93n94

Ickes, Harold, 50–53, 55–56
import quota program, 105–6
independent oil producers, 47–55,
    58–59; and foreign oil, 104–7; and
    Republican Party, 126–27
inflation, 110–14; caused by oil prices,
    114–16
internal combustion engine, 18, 43,
    73–74, 134, 175–76n15. See also
    automobile(s)
Interstate Oil Compact Commission
    (IOCC), 54–55, 104, 194n140
Iran, 69, 160
Iraq, 2, 131, 149–51

Jevons, William Stanley, 101

Keynesianism, xiv, xvi, 19, 42, 59,
    113, 187n105. See also New Deal;
    suburbanization: and "effective
    demand"
Klare, Michael, 2, 176n20
Klein, Naomi, 114–15, 166
Kunstler, James Howard, xiii, 81–82,
    178n34, 199n103

labor: and New Deal, 34–37; and
    refineries, 61–64; reproduction of,
    16–19, 82; unions and inflation,
    110, 113–14; value of, 38, 135, 137.
    See also "capital-labor accord";
    social reproduction; Wagner Act
Lefebvre, Henri, 5, 8, 168, 215n46
Levitt, William, 38, 97
Levittown gas riots, 97–99
livelihood, xiii, 178n36
localization, 166–67

machines: electricity and, 30–31;
    Fordism and, 30–32; fossil fuels
    and, 9–20; household and, 16–19,
    82–83; internal-combustion engine,
    18, 43, 73–74, 134, 175–76n15;
    real subsumption and, 12–19
Mann, Geoff, 135
Marx, Karl, xv, xvii, xxi, 3–4, 6, 9–20,
    22, 29, 34, 64, 73, 77–79, 157–59,
    161–69
McNally, David, 132, 138–39
medicine, 65, 88–92
metabolic rift, 179–80n60, xvii
Middle East oil, x, 2–3, 59, 70, 105,
    150–51, 155, 177n29, 177n30,
    202n17
Mitchell, Timothy, xii, xx, 56, 126,
    149, 167, 175–76n15, 177n24,
    177n29, 182n27, 182n29, 192n85,
    202n17, 203n21, 207n119

Nader, Ralph, 117
neoliberalism: cheap ecologies and,
    137–42; decentralization and,
    120–25; ecology of, xv–xvi; entre-
    preneurial life and, 19–25; inflation
    and, 110–14; 1970s shift to, 98–
    100, 110–27; ordoliberalism, 20,
    188n118; suburbanization and, 19–
    25, 120–25; taxation and, 142–43;

wage compression and, 137–42.
See also Friedman, Milton; Hayek,
Friedrich

New Deal: and housing reform, 38–
40; and ideas of competition, 50;
and infrastructure, 40–42; and
labor reform, 34–37; and oil market reform, 44–57; as response to
depression, 32–34

Nigeria, 160

Nixon, Richard, 100, 107–10, 112,
114–15, 121–22

"No Blood for Oil," 2, 26, 149–51

Nye, David, 159, 184n58, 202n17

Obama, Barack, vii–viii, ix, 148, 152,
163, 214–15n27

Occupy Wall Street, 163, 179n53

O'Connor, James, xvii, 180n63

oil embargo, x, 101; and xenophobia,
107–8

oil futures, 126

oil shocks, 114–16

oil spills: gas stations and, 134; Gulf
of Mexico 2010, viii, 132, 152;
refineries and, 68

Organization of Petroleum Exporting Countries, The (OPEC), 54–55,
100, 107, 116, 141–42

overproduction, 43–48. *See also*
conservation

peak oil, x, xiii, 3, 44, 101, 129, 166–
68, 178n34

Penrose, Edith, 46, 133

petrochemicals: and food, 88–90; and
medicine, 89–92; and plastics, 84–
85; and refineries, 68–69, 84

petrol. *See* gasoline

petroleum products: bitumen, 66, 77;
chemicals, 68–69, 88–92; gasoline,
19, 25, 43, 56, 71, 73, 76, 133–37;

kerosene, 66–67; lubricants, 77,
80, 83. *See also* gasoline

petro-state, 5–6

plastics, 84–85

political ecology, xiii, xviii, 178n36,
180n64, 182n27

pollution. *See* environmental impact

Postone, Moishe, 9, 131

price of oil: and bureau of mines,
55–57; and commodity volatility,
55, 141–42; and East Texas crisis, 48–55; and economic "shock,"
114–16; and Fordism, 55; and
Organization of Petroleum Exporting Countries (OPEC), 142; and
politics, vii–ix, 129–31, 134–37;
and the Texas Railroad Commission, 54–55

"primitive accumulation," 16, 77–79

private property: and entrepreneurial
life, 20, 164; and suburbanization,
39–40, 81–82; and U.S. oil production, 44–48

production of oil: in East Texas, 48–
50, 59, 104; and environmental
injustice, xi, 69, 160–61, 197n44,
212n57; and geopolitics, 1–3,
5, 26, 103–8, 177n26, 177n29,
182n29; and overproduction, 43–
48; and price volatility, 141–42;
prorationing, 54–59, 105–6, 161;
and the rule of capture, 44–48

proletariat, 16–18, 22, 38, 88, 132,
138, 187n99

prorationing, 54–59, 105–6, 161

Reagan, Ronald, 98–99, 113, 118,
125–27, 137

real subsumption: of labor under capital, 12–16, 30–32; of life under
capital, xiv–xv, 16–19, 36, 39, 41,
73, 79, 86, 159, 164, 178n43

refineries: and automation, 61–64; and chemistry, 65–70; and cracking technologies, 66–67; and environmental impact, 68–69; and labor, 61–64; and postwar consumption culture, 70–73; and refining capacity, 70. *See also* petroleum products

resource(s): capitalism and, 4–5; curse, 1–2, 5, 116, 141–42, 181n6, 206n97, 210n35; geography, xviii, 180n64; price volatility and, 141–42

Robin, Corey, 163–64

Roosevelt, Franklin Delano: and depression politics, 32–33; and energy, 29–30; and housing policy, 39; and labor policy, 34–37; and oil policy, 42, 50–55; rule of capture, 44–48; and Saudi Arabia, 2, 104

Saudi Arabia, vii–viii, xi, 70, 104, 141, 144, 160, 176n20

Sayer, Derek, 11–12, 183–84n44

scale: and definition of metropolitan areas, 74–75; and 1930s oil reform, 47, 52–55

scarcity, x, 2, 30, 43, 59, 99, 189n7; and abundance, 30, 43, 102, 141, 215n36; 1970s and, 101–3; 1930s lack of, 43–50; social production of, 44, 47, 49–50, 177n29, 203n19. *See also* peak oil

second contradiction of capitalism, xvii, 180n63

shale gas/oil. *See* hydrofracking

Shell, 62, 83–85, 88–89, 98

silent majority, 120–25

Smil, Vaclav, 31, 87, 167, 178n34

social reproduction: xv, 7, 16–19, 21, 31–32, 36, 64, 79, 85, 94, 187n98, 200n123, 201n153; and cheap ecologies, 137–40; entrepreneurial life and, xiv, 19–25; and feminism, 16, 82, 187n98, 199n104, 199n105;

food, 86–90; and freedom, 18, 22, 58, 162, 165; housing, 77–86; mobility, 73–77; and 1970s oil crisis, 109–10; and real subsumption of life, 16–19, 36, 39, 31, 73, 79, 86, 159, 164, 178n43

space: and automobility, 40–43, 73–77; between home and work, 16, 18, 40, 109, 186–87n96; energy and production of, 7–9; and entrepreneurial life, 19–25; fossil fuels and, 10–11; and geopolitical imagination, 2–3

sport-utility vehicles (SUVs), xiii, 23–24, 132, 177–78n31

Standard Oil, 5, 72, 117, 180n2, 193n103

Sterling, Ross, 48–49

suburbanization: and "effective demand," 18, 42, 82, 187n105; and entrepreneurial life, 19–25; 73–86; and gasoline, 73–76, 133–37; and home ownership, 38–40, 77–86; and infrastructure, 40–43; and Levittown, 97–99; and mobility, 73–75; and the New Deal, 34–43; and the 1970s oil crisis, 108–10; and peak oil, x, 81–82; and rightward shift, xv–xvi, 18–19, 63, 94, 179n48; and the silent majority, 120–25

Suez Canal crisis, 102

Sunbelt, xvi, 63–64, 94, 121, 126, 158, 179n49, 179n54

swing producer, 54, 102, 194n141

Tarbell, Ida, 5, 117, 180–81n2

taxation: and gasoline, vii–ix, 148–49; market-based energy/environmental policy, 142–49; and neoliberal ideology, 142–43

Taylor, Frederick, 31

terrorism, x, xiii, 144, 155, 177n30

Texas, 48–55, 59, 102, 104

Texas Railroad Commission, 48–55, 101, 207n120

Thompson, Ernest O., 47, 52–53

tractors, 10, 87

transition towns, 166–67

transportation, 40–42; 73–77; and fossil fuels, 10–11; oil as primary fuel for, ix–x, 175–76n15, 178n42; public, 27–28. *See also* automobile(s)

Tugwell, Rexford, 39, 50

"unitization," 47

value, 4; exchange value, 135–37, 210n19; and gasoline stations, 134–37; of labor power, 38, 135, 137; use value, xix, 5, 38, 61, 65, 70, 135, 137, 150

wage relation, 14–18, 22, 29, 42, 59, 79, 81, 86, 92, 94, 162; "compression," 132, 138; and inflation, 110–14; and New Deal, 34–38. *See also* "capital-labor accord"; labor; Wagner Act

Wagner Act, 34–37. *See also* labor; wage relation

Watts, Michael, 116, 181n19, 210n35

Williams, Raymond, x, 8, 74, 189n130

World Bank, 139, 141

Yergin, Daniel, 115, 139, 141, 181n9, 203n25, 210n39

Zimmermann, Erich, 47, 193n95, 195n153

Matthew T. Huber is assistant professor in the Department of Geography at the Maxwell School of Syracuse University.

Made in the USA
Monee, IL
08 November 2020

47011018R00154